ESSAYS OF TO-DAY

ESSAYS OF TO-DAY

AN ANTHOLOGY

SELECTED BY

F. H. PRITCHARD

AUTHOR OF "ENGLISH EXTRACTS AND EXERCISES"
"INTERMEDIATE ENGLISH EXTRACTS AND EXERCISES"
"JUNIOR ENGLISH EXTRACTS AND EXERCISES"
"TRAINING IN LITERARY APPRECIATION"
"STUDIES IN LITERATURE" ETC

GEORGE G. HARRAP & COMPANY LTD.
LONDON   CALCUTTA   SYDNEY

First published March 1923
by GEORGE G. HARRAP & CO. LTD.
39-41 *Parker Street, Kingsway, London, W.C.*2

Reprinted : June 1923 ; *September* 1923 ;
September 1924 ; *August* 1925 ; *January* 1926 ;
June 1926 ; *November* 1926

PRINTED IN GREAT BRITAIN AT THE PITMAN PRESS, BATH

PREFACE

THE essays in this collection are a very little portion of the wealth of good work that has been produced during the last twenty years or so, yet they may, it is hoped, be claimed not unfairly to represent the main tendencies which expression in that form has taken during that time. It is thought that the presentation of modern questions in a modern way will be of particular interest and value to pupils nearing the time when they must exchange the seclusion of the classroom, where aims are clear-cut and definite, for the hurly-burly of affairs, where so much is conflicting and undecided. They should not go out in ignorance of what is before them or lacking the best guidance that our generation can offer.

Something analogous to the "poetically-effective" order of Palgrave's inimitable anthology has been attempted here, so that each essay may serve as a commentary upon its fellows, and be enriched by reason of its setting. The reading of such a volume as this should set the student browsing for himself in the extensive pastures to which he has been directed ; and it should also give him a desire to set down after some similar fashion the thoughts awakened by the work of these skilled craftsmen. Exercises on each essay are appended so as to draw attention to basic principles, salient points in style, and all those devices for grace and felicity of expression that come only after a long and laborious apprenticeship to the art of letters. Having observed so much, the reader will note that certain topics arising from the essay have

5

been suggested, and on these he may try his own hand. This is an exercise that will have at least three very salutary effects : it will keep him humble ; it will give him a greater respect for his author ; and all the while it will be widening his own range of expression.

It remains for the compiler gratefully to record his indebtedness to the authors and publishers of the volumes from which the essays are taken for granting the necessary permissions to reprint. Sincere thanks are hereby tendered to Messrs T. Fisher Unwin, Ltd., for " On Pirates," from *The Day before Yesterday* ; the author and Messrs John Lane, The Bodley Head, Ltd., for " The Secret Drawer," from *The Golden Age* ; the author and Messrs Methuen and Co., Ltd., for " Landfall and Departure," from *The Mirror of the Sea* ; the author and Messrs Chapman and Hall, Ltd., for " Going Away and Arriving," from *Letters from Solitude* ; the author and Messrs G. Bell and Sons, Ltd., for " A Hermitage in Sight," from *In a Green Shade* ; the author and Messrs Methuen and Co., Ltd., for " A Brother of St Francis," from *About Many Things* ; the author and Messrs Methuen and Co., Ltd., for " Golden Fruit," from *Not That It Matters* ; Mr and Mrs John Scott for " The Doodle Doo," from *A Number of Things* (Foulis); the author and Messrs Methuen and Co., Ltd., for " The Town Week," from *Fireside and Sunshine* ; the author and Messrs Mills and Boon, Ltd., for " On Christmas," from *The Book of This and That* ; the author and Messrs John Lane, The Bodley Head, Ltd., for " Losing One's Train," from *Hortus Vitæ* ; the author for " Autumn " ; the author for " Some London Memories " from *Modern Grub Street* ; the author and Messrs Macmillan and Co., Ltd., for " The Last Gleeman," from *The Celtic Twilight* ; the author and Messrs Methuen and Co., Ltd., for " Delft,"

PREFACE

from *Hills and the Sea* ; the author's literary executor and Messrs Sidgwick and Jackson, Ltd., for " Niagara Falls," from *Letters from America* ; the author and Mr John Murray for " The Soul of a Cathedral," from *The Wander Years* ; the author and Messrs J. M. Dent and Sons, Ltd., for " On a Map of the Oberland," from *Leaves in the Wind* ; the author and Messrs Methuen and Co., Ltd., for " On the Actual Spot," from *Dramatic Values* ; the author and Messrs Duckworth and Co. for " Castles in the Air," from *Success* ; Messrs Duckworth and Co. for " Rain," from *Rosacre Papers* ; Messrs Chatto and Windus for " An Autumn Stroll," from *Enjoying Life, and Other Literary Remains* ; the author and Messrs Chapman and Hall, Ltd., for " Ship's Logs," from *The Patchwork Papers* ; Mr Wilfrid Meynell for " Charmian," from *Hearts of Controversy* (Burns, Oates, and Washbourne); the author and Mr John Murray for " The Pleasures of Work," from *The Thread of Gold* ; the author and Messrs William Heinemann, Ltd., for " Audiences," from *Pastiche and Prejudice* ; the author and Messrs Constable and Co., Ltd., for " War," from *Little Essays* ; Mr Elliot Stock, publisher, 7 Paternoster Row, London, E.C.4, for " Confirmed Readers," from *In the Name of the Bodleian* ; the author and Messrs Grant Richards, Ltd., for " Masters of Nonsense," from *All Manner of Folk* ; the author and Messrs J. M. Dent and Sons, Ltd., for " A Defence of Detective Stories," from *The Defendant* ; the author's literary executor for " My Books," from *The Private Papers of Henry Ryecroft* (Constable) ; the author and Messrs William Heinemann, Ltd., for " The Essays of Mr Lucas," from *Books on the Table* ; the author and Messrs Wm. Collins, Sons and Co., Ltd., for " A Critical Credo," from *Countries of the Mind*.   F. H. P.

CONTENTS

ESSAYS OF TO-DAY

THE SPIRIT OF PLACE

OF LIFE AND LETTERS

INTRODUCTION

THAT divine discontent which has been called " the secret spur of all our enterprises " is certainly the mainspring of our literature. And the milder form of it which gently laments instead of shrieking, shrugging its shoulders good-humouredly rather than trying to smash the furniture, finds its most natural means of expression in the essay. The man who is violently discontented with things as he finds them may preach stirring sermons, write exquisite sonnets, deliver inflammatory harangues, or turn pamphleteer ; he will assuredly not write good essays.

Addison and his friends were dissatisfied with the state of society in their day, cleft as it was by reason of conflicting aims and lack of understanding, but with them dissatisfaction, however deep-rooted, never overcame good-humour. The result is seen in those suave and genial essays that, more effectually than sermon or pamphlet, moulded opinion, mended manners, and brought about a peaceful revolution. Charles Lamb, irked by the drudgery of ledger-entries and invoices, lamented that the noble fir-trees of the forest should, as he put it, " die into desks " similar to the one at which he sat daily expediting mercantile transactions. So his soul in gentle rebellion was moved to express itself in terms of " Old China " and " Roast Pig." The essay, then, perhaps more than any other literary form, is the outcome of a nice equipoise A mild discontent ; a wistful longing for that which is not, but which has been or might be ; an attempt, brief and fragmentary but always sincere, to express a problem in terms of one's personality—these are the essentials of the true essay.

The limitations of length and scope that condition all essay-writing are obvious enough. Brevity and informality are characteristics that all may behold. The essay is modest in its range, and it makes no pretensions. Just a little plot of ground is cultivated, and that after no set fashion. But more important than these obvious limitations is the fact that the essay is primarily an expression of personality. It must be, as Montaigne says, " consubstantial " with its author. By means of it one is placed on terms of close intimacy with the writer ; not hectored from a platform, nor exhorted from a pulpit, but admitted to the familiarity of the fireside. And the style of a good essay reflects this. As Mr Gosse says, that style must be " confidential," as well as " a model of current cultivated ease of expression and a mirror of the best conversation." It is in this personal trait that the essay corresponds most nearly to the lyric. They are both the most intimate revelations of personality that we have in literature. They are both valuable because by means of them we are able to get into close touch with some of the finest and noblest spirits of all time. And unlike as essay and lyric are superficially, there is in this fundamental respect no difference between them.

A man, calmly observant and with a sense of humour withal, muses on things as they are. The most trivial occurrences will serve to set him a-dreaming—the crowing of a cock, the books on his shelves gleaming in the firelight, a scent wafted in through the open window, the patter of raindrops on the leaves—and as gently and equably as he muses, so he writes. Thoughts, irresponsible and unbidden, come straying into his

12

consciousness, and he dreams, perhaps, of what has been in some Golden Age of the past, or, in a glowing vision of the future, of what may be. With a sure but light touch he sets down these fancies in gentle prose, to soothe, to charm, and to encourage his fellows. And as they read, the gentle poignancy and subtle humour of these essays steal upon their consciousness, catching them unawares, and moving them where the strident tones of grand passion or high tragedy would probably fail.

But thoughts do not always pass with such calm ease through the writer's mind. Sometimes they burn with a white and passionate heat that, by reason of its very intensity, makes expression more difficult. We are all conscious of such thoughts, but with most of us they are accompanied by a feeling of utter incompetence and incoherence. The commonplaces of life we can utter, but these rare and burning ideas find us dumb. We cannot express them even to ourselves, and so they pass. But here and there is one to whom is given the incommunicable gift of controlling and marshalling such thoughts so as to give them coherent and glorious expression in measured speech. Ordered by the strict limitations of rhythm, and obedient to the recurrences of rime and metre, the unruly ideas are fashioned into a lyric, just as scattered particles, straying here and there, are drawn together and fused into crystalline beauty. The difference, indeed, is one of temperature. The metal bar, cold or lukewarm, will do anywhere, but heat it to melting-point and you must confine it within the rigid limits of the mould or see it at length but an amorphous splash at your feet.

So lyric and essay are both pre-eminently expressions of personality, but whereas one is the embodiment of rare moments of passion and exaltation, the other is the expression of those quiet everyday moods when one is at leisure and peace, yet not all at ease. The mind, vaguely seeking for better things, unfolds and particularizes its own most intimate longings. Just because it is so apt an expression of everyday personality the essay is one of the most elusive of literary forms. Its easy, unobtrusive rhythm, its subtle recurrences, its quiet humour, are not obvious to the casual beholder as are the corresponding traits in drama, novel, or sonnet. But they are there nevertheless, and well repay the search. It would be wrong, too, to imagine that the essay is merely a tepid affair subsisting solely on the dead level of the commonplace. If it keeps largely to the commonplace, it is only that it may reveal its beauty, as when Mrs Rhys directs our admiring gaze to the pig-sty. The essay has, it should be remembered, its own sublimities ; as when Leigh Hunt muses upon the deaths of little children, or Edward Thomas conjures up the spirit that dwells in a neglected London garden.

When we come to look at the essays of to-day we find, in the wealth of material at our disposal, all those characteristics that we have been noticing clearly set forth. There is the gentle dissatisfaction with things as they are ; the quiet determination to depose existing idols. Mr J. Middleton Murry, in an acute piece of criticism, has pointed out that each generation lives by slaughtering the ideals of its parents. Thus we move—whether by way of progress or not we cannot here argue. At all events, the revolt against what is conveniently labelled Victorianism, a revolt of which we shall find many evidences in these essays, is not a mere whim, but an expression of the instinct for self-preservation. We must show that we are alive and different. The man who will judge decisively between our parents and ourselves will come in a later age, when the heat of the struggle will have cooled. Meanwhile, without attempting to anticipate that judgment, we may notice one or two unmistakable features. The ideals of one age always seem topsy-turvy to the next. And each will take a boyish delight in overturning the older notions, discarding them altogether or setting them, as it thinks, right way up. Dixon Scott pillories the early-riser as an immoral person ; Mr G. K. Chesterton holds up detective stories as a branch of literature worthy of our highest admiration ; Vernon Lee shows how much may be gained by losing a train ; and Roger Wray replaces the old autumn legend by one more virile and pleasing to youth.

This basic dissatisfaction with existing ideals shows itself in various guises other than the boyish way of turning them upside down. Just as Montaigne had his tower of refuge, so every essayist finds a means of occasional escape from the exigent " here and now." Some shrink into themselves and give us intimate bits of self-revelation, or retire to the library, to finger lovingly their favourite volumes. We see this exemplified in much of the work of Edward Thomas and in that of George Gissing writing as " Henry Ryecroft." Others look for romance and, finding it not, seek places that are more promising. Mr Belloc, for instance, takes us to Delft and shows us its beauty, characteristically adding, " And to think that you can get to a place like that for less than a pound ! " Faery pleasures are not so far removed after all as we are apt to imagine : while we spend large sums in compassing the ends of the earth, lo, romance is at our doors ! Others teach the same lesson in varying ways.

" Alpha of the Plough " spreads out a map before us and climbs the dizzy heights over again. Mr St John Adcock repeoples the dingy byways of London with quaintly picturesque figures, so converting a monotonous walk into a pageant. Mr E. V. Lucas makes even the days of the week take on a new significance. Preferences apparently idle and trifling are given a royal importance. For the nonce the essayist is king, and without question we accept his lightest word and put our trust in his shadow. All existing ideas of relative values are cheerfully set aside. We lose a train, but care not. Rather are we pleased to discover that the loss has been the means of opening a new door in our consciousness of what is beautiful and significant.

In one way or another all these essays converge on criticism—the criticism of life and letters, of ideals and practice. We are taught to try all things and to hold fast to the good, but we are warned not to accept preconceived notions of what is good. Life in all its many phases comes within the essayist's purview, and not the least important of these phases is that manifestation of life at its highest which we know as literature—a revelation of those yearnings which would otherwise remain hidden. So we get these " familiar studies of men and books "—fragments which for all their brevity and easy informality will enable us to take stock of ourselves and our surroundings, to separate the accidental from the permanent, and to distinguish between the reality and the illusion.

We are not likely at this time of day to make the mistake of supposing that the essay is an easy form because its main features are less pronounced than those of other kinds of literature. To do that would be like imagining that blank verse is a medium necessarily more suited to the literary novice than riming couplets. The mistake has been made, however. Crabbe once said that the essay was the most popular mode of writing because " it suits the writer who has neither talent nor ingenuity to pursue his enquiries farther," and, being quite impartial in the use of his lash, he added that it also suits " the generality of readers who are amused with variety and superficiality." There is no need to argue that question. We know that to write an essay with grace and distinction is one of the most difficult of literary tasks. And because that fact is now generally recognized not a few educationists are suggesting that it is altogether too difficult an exercise for the schoolroom. Dialogue, descriptive sketches, the short story, and the more elementary verse-forms all have, they say with truth, a technique which is much more readily mastered than that of the essay, lacking as it does those salient features upon which a beginner may fasten. So they would banish it entirely. It is true that nothing too bad can be said about that peculiarly artificial product of the classroom, the schoolboy essay. Those painful little disquisitions on Coal, the Uses of Money, Newspapers, or the Post Office never gave a moment of pleasure to anybody, which shows that they are not properly essays at all, and therefore do not affect the main question. A boy will read a modern essay with an interest which Addison is incapable of arousing. He has not yet obtained that comprehension of the setting which will enable him to appreciate the point and beauty of Addison's quiet humour. That will come later, and everything may be lost by attempting to force the pace. But to the writing of Dixon Scott or Filson Young, as represented in this volume, he will need no introduction. It is live ; it deals with problems that he has experienced ; it is just what he has often thought himself, but could never express. And the sight of a master-craftsman doing with such apparent ease what the reader could not do for himself will unfailingly produce in him the *cacoëthes scribendi*. Give him a cognate subject on which to try his hand, and he will need no urging to write. And while the results will be crude and ineffective probably, they will be true essays—spontaneous attempts at self-expression that will leave those who make them stronger and better for the exercise. So a plea may be entered, not for the retention of the essay in school, for in too many cases it has hitherto been a stranger there, but for its introduction and use as the most natural way of expressing our relationship to the world as we know it.

YOUTH AND OLD AGE

ON PIRATES

RICHARD MIDDLETON

OF the nameless classics which were of so much concern to all of us when we were young, the most important were certainly those salt and boisterous volumes that told of pirates. It was in vain for kindly relatives to give us books on Nelson and his like, for their craft, beautiful though they might be to the eye, had ever the moralities lurking between decks, and if we met them it was only that we might make their crews walk the plank, and add new stories of crime and pressure by the crimson vessel with the sinister flag, which it was our pleasure to command.

And yet the books that gave us this splendid dominion, where are they now? In truth, I cannot say. Examination of recent boys' books has convinced me that the old spirit is lacking, for if pirates are there, it is only as the hapless victims of horrible British crews with every virtue save that one which youth should cherish most, the revolutionary spirit. Who would be a midshipman when he might be a pirate? Yet all the books would have it so, and even Mr Kenneth Grahame, who knows everything that is worth knowing, does not always take the right side in such matters. The grown-up books are equally unsatisfactory to the inquiring mind. Treasure Island, which is sometimes loosely referred to as if it were a horn-book for young pirates, hardly touches the main problems of pirate life at all. Stevenson's consideration

ON PIRATES

RICHARD MIDDLETON

OF the nameless classics which were of so much concern to all of us when we were young, the most important were certainly those salt and blusterous volumes that told of pirates. It was in vain for kindly relatives to give us books on Nelson and his like ; for their craft, beautiful though they might be to the eye, had ever the moralities lurking between decks, and if we met them it was only that we might make their crews walk the plank, and add new stores of guns and treasure to the crimson vessel with the sinister flag which it was our pleasure to command.

And yet the books that gave us this splendid dominion, where are they now ? In truth, I cannot say. Examination of recent boys' books has convinced me that the old spirit is lacking, for if pirates are there, it is only as the hapless victims of horrible British crews with every virtue save that one which youth should cherish most, the revolutionary spirit. Who would be a midshipman when he might be a pirate ? Yet all the books would have it so, and even Mr Kenneth Grahame, who knows everything that is worth knowing, does not always take the right side in such matters. The grown-up books are equally unsatisfactory to the enquiring mind. *Treasure Island*, which is sometimes loosely referred to as if it were a horn-book for young pirates, hardly touches the main problems of pirate life at all. Stevenson's consideration for "youth and the fond parient" made him leave out all oaths. No ships are taken, no lovely females captured, nobody walks the plank, and Captain John Silver, for all the maimed strength and masterfulness that Henley suggested to the author, falls lamentably short of what a pirate should be. Captain Teach, of the *Sarah*, in the *Master of Ballantrae*, is better, and there were the makings of a very good pirate captain in the master himself, but this section of the book is too short to supply our requirements. The book must be all pirates. Defoe's *Captain Singleton* repents, and is therefore disqualified, and Marryat's *Pirate* is, as Stevenson said, "written in sand with a saltspoon." Mr Clark Russell, in one of his romances, ingeniously melts a pirate who has been frozen for a couple of centuries into life, but though he promises well at first, his is but a torpid ferocity, and ends, as it began, in words. Nor are the histories of the pirates more satisfying. Captain Johnson's *History of Notorious Pirates* I have not seen, but any one who wishes to lose an illusion can read the trial of William Kidd and a few of his companions in the State trials of the year 1701. The captain of the *Adventure Galley* appears to have done little to merit the name of pirate beyond killing his gunner with a bucket, and the miserable results of his pilferings bear no relationship to the enormous hoard associated with his name in *The Gold Bug* of Poe, though there is certainly a familiar note in finding included among his captives a number of barrels of sugar-candy, which were divided in shares among the crew, the captain himself having forty shares. The Turkish pirates mentioned in *Purchas* cut a very poor figure. You can read there how four English youths overcame a prize crew of thirteen men who had been put in the ship *Jacob*. In a storm they slew the pirate captain, for with the handle of a pump "they gave him such a palt on the pate as made his brains forsake the possession of his head." They then killed three of the other pirates with "cuttle-axes," and brought the ship safely into Spain, "where they sold the nine Turkes for galley-slaves for a good summe of money, and as I thinke, a great deale more than they were worth." Not thus would the chronicles have described the pirates who fought and caroused with such splendid devotion in my youth. To die beneath the handle of a pump is an unworthy end for a pirate captain. The *History of the Buccaneers of America*, written by a brother of Fanny Burney, a book which was the subject of one of Mr Andrew Lang's appreciative essays, is nearer the mark, for among other notable fellows mentioned therein is one François L'Olonnois, who put to death the whole crew of a Spanish ship, ninety men, by beheading them, performing himself the office of executioner. One of the gentlemen in this book turned buccaneer in order to pay his debts, while it is told of another that he shot one of his crew in church for behaving irreverently during Mass. Sir Henry Morgan and Richard Sawkins performed some pretty feats of piracy, but their main energies were concerned in the sacking of towns, and the whole book suffers from an unaccountable prejudice which the author displays against the brave and hard-working villains of whom he writes.

In truth, these real pirates are disappointing men to meet. They are usually lacking in fierceness and in fidelity to the pirate ideals of courage and faithfulness to their comrades, while the fine nobility of character which was never absent from those other pirates is unknown in the historical kind. Few, if

23

any, of them merit the old Portuguese punishment for pirates, which consisted in hanging them from the yards of their own ship, and setting the latter to drift with the winds and waves without rudder or sails, an example for rogues and a source of considerable danger to honest mariners.

If that were a fitting end for great knaves, the meaner ruffians must be content with the pump-handle and the bucket.

It is hard if our hearts may not go out to those gloomy vessels, with their cargoes of gold and courage and rum, that sail, it seems, the mental seas of youth no more. Were they really bad for us, those sanguinary tussles, those star-lit nights of dissipation? A pinafore would wipe away a deal of blood, and the rum, though we might drink it boiling like Quilp, in no wise lessened our interest in home-made cake. But these regrets are of yesterday, and to-day I must draw what consolation I may from the kindly comment of Mr Lang : " Alluring as the pirate's profession is, we must not forget that it had a seamy side, and was by no means all rum and pieces-of-eight. And there is something repulsive to a generous nature in roasting men because they will not show you where to steal hogs."

From " The Day before Yesterday "

THE SECRET DRAWER

KENNETH GRAHAME

IT must surely have served as a boudoir for the ladies of old time, this little-used, rarely-entered chamber where the neglected old bureau stood. There was something very feminine in the faint hues of its faded brocades, in the rose and blue of such bits of china as yet remained, and in the delicate, old-world fragrance of pot-pourri from the great bowl—blue and white, with funny holes in its cover—that stood on the bureau's flat top. Modern aunts disdained this out-of-the-way, backwater, upstairs room, preferring to do their accounts and grapple with their correspondence in some central position more in the whirl of things, whence one eye could be kept on the carriage-drive, while the other was alert for malingering servants and marauding children. Those aunts of a former generation—I sometimes felt—would have suited our habits better. But even by us children, to whom few places were private or reserved, the room was visited but rarely. To be sure, there was nothing in particular in it that we coveted or required—only a few spindle-legged, gilt-backed chairs ; an old harp on which, so the legend ran, Aunt Eliza herself used once to play in years remote, unchronicled ; a corner cupboard with a few pieces of china ; and the old bureau. But one other thing the room possessed peculiar to itself : a certain sense of privacy—a power of making the intruder feel that he *was* intruding—perhaps even a faculty of hinting that some one might have been sitting on those chairs, writing at the bureau, or fingering the china just a second before one entered. No such violent word as 'haunted' could possibly apply to this pleasant old-fashioned chamber, which indeed we all rather liked ; but there was no doubt it was reserved and stand-offish, keeping itself to itself.

Uncle Thomas was the first to draw my attention to the possibilities of the old bureau. He was pottering about the house one afternoon, having ordered me to keep at his heels for company—he was a man who hated to be left one minute alone—when his eye fell on it. " H'm ! Sheraton ! " he remarked. (He had a smattering of most things, this uncle, especially the vocabularies.) Then he let down the flap, and examined the empty pigeon-holes and dusty panelling. " Fine bit of inlay," he went on ; " good work, all of it. I know the sort. There's a secret drawer in there somewhere." Then, as I breathlessly drew near, he suddenly exclaimed, " By Jove, I do want to smoke ! " And wheeling round, he abruptly fled for the garden, leaving me with the cup dashed from my lips. What a strange thing, I mused, was this smoking, that takes a man suddenly—be he in the court, the camp, or the grove—grips him like an Afreet, and whirls him off to do its imperious behests ! Would it be even so with myself, I wondered, in those unknown grown-up years to come ?

But I had no time to waste in vain speculations. My whole being was still vibrating to those magic syllables ' secret drawer ' ; and that particular chord had been touched that never fails to thrill responsive to such words as *cave, trap-door, sliding-panel, bullion, ingots,* or *Spanish dollars.* For, besides its own special bliss, who ever heard of a secret drawer with nothing in it? And oh, I did want money so badly! I mentally ran over the list of demands which were pressing me the most imperiously.

First, there was the pipe I wanted to give George Jannaway. George, who was Martha's young man, was a shepherd, and a great ally of mine; and the last fair he was at, when he bought his sweetheart fairings, as a right-minded shepherd should, he had purchased a lovely snake expressly for me—one of the wooden sort, with joints, waggling deliciously in the hand; with yellow spots on a green ground, sticky and strong-smelling, as a fresh-painted snake ought to be; and with a red-flannel tongue pasted cunningly into its jaws. I loved it much, and took it to bed with me every night till what time its spinal cord was loosed and it fell apart, and went the way of all mortal joys. I thought it very nice of George to think of me at the fair, and that's why I wanted to give him a pipe. When the young year was chill and lambing-time was on, George inhabited a little wooden house on wheels, far out on the wintry downs, and saw no faces but such as were sheepish and woolly and mute; and when he and Martha were married, she was going to carry his dinner out to him every day, two miles; and after it, perhaps he would smoke my pipe. It seemed an idyllic sort of existence for both the parties concerned; but a pipe of quality, a pipe fitted to be part of such a life as this, could not be procured (so Martha informed me) for a smaller sum than eighteenpence. And meantime——

Then there was the fourpence I owed Edward; not that he was bothering me for it, but I knew he was in need of it himself to pay back Selina, who wanted it to make up a sum of two shillings to buy Harold an ironclad for his approaching birthday—H.M.S.

Majestic, now lying uselessly careened in the toy-shop window, just when her country had such sore need of her.

And then there was that boy in the village who had caught a young squirrel, and I had never possessed one ; and he wanted a shilling for it, but I knew that for ninepence in cash—— But what was the good of these sorry, threadbare reflections ? I had wants enough to exhaust any possible find of bullion, even if it amount to half a sovereign. My only hope now lay in the magic drawer ; and here I was, standing and letting the precious minutes slip by ! Whether ' findings ' of this sort could, morally speaking, be considered ' keepings ' was a point that did not occur to me.

The room was very still as I approached the bureau ; possessed, it seemed to be, by a sort of hush of expectation. The faint odour of orris-root that floated forth as I let down the flap seemed to identify itself with the yellows and browns of the old wood, till hue and scent were of one quality and interchangeable. Even so, ere this, the pot-pourri had mixed itself with the tints of the old brocade, and brocade and pot-pourri had long been one. With expectant fingers I explored the empty pigeon-holes and sounded the depths of the softly-sliding drawers. No books that I knew of gave any general recipe for a quest like this ; but the glory, should I succeed unaided, would be all the greater.

To him who is destined to arrive, the fates never fail to afford on the way their small encouragements. In less than two minutes I had come across a rusty button-hook. This was truly magnificent. In the nursery there existed, indeed, a general button-hook, common to either sex ; but none of us possessed a private and special button-hook, to lend or to refuse, as suited the high humour of the moment. I pocketed the treasure carefully, and proceeded. At the back of another drawer three old foreign stamps told me I was surely on the highroad to fortune.

Following on these bracing incentives came a dull, blank period of unrewarded search. In vain I removed all the drawers and felt over every inch of the smooth surfaces from front to back. Never a knob, spring, or projection met the thrilling finger-tips ; unyielding the old bureau stood, stoutly guarding its secret, if secret it really had. I began to grow weary and disheartened. This was not the first time that Uncle Thomas had proved shallow, uninformed—a guide into blind alleys where the echoes mocked you. Was it any good persisting longer ? Was anything any good whatever ? In my mind I began to review past disappointments, and life seemed one long record of failure and of non-arrival. Disillusioned and depressed I left my work and went to the window. The light was ebbing from the room, and seemed outside to be collecting itself on the horizon for its concentrated effort of sunset. Far down in the garden, Uncle Thomas was holding Edward in the air reversed, and smacking him. Edward, gurgling hysterically, was striking blind fists in the direction where he judged his uncle's stomach should rightly be ; the contents of his pockets—a motley show—were strewing the lawn. Somehow, though I had been put through a similar performance myself an hour or two ago, it all seemed very far away and cut off from me.

Westwards, the clouds were massing themselves in a low violet bank ; below them, to north and south, as far round as eye could reach, a narrow streak of gold ran out and stretched away, straight along the horizon. Somewhere very far off a horn was blowing, clear and thin ; it sounded like the golden streak grown audible, while the gold seemed the visible sound. It pricked my ebbing courage, this blended strain of music and colour. I turned for a last effort ; and Fortune thereupon, as if half ashamed of the unworthy game she had been playing with me, relented, opening her clenched fist. Hardly had I put my hand once more to the obdurate wood, when with a sort of small sigh, almost a sob—as it were—of relief, the secret drawer sprang open.

I drew it out and carried it to the window, to examine it in the failing light. Too hopeless had I gradually grown in my dispiriting search to expect very much ; and yet at a glance I saw that my basket of glass lay in shivers at my feet. No ingots or dollars were here, to crown me the little Monte Cristo of a week. Outside, the distant horn had ceased its gnat-song, the gold was paling to primrose, and everything was lonely and still. Within, my confident little castles were tumbling down like so many card-houses, leaving me stripped of estate, both real and personal, and dominated by the depressing reaction.

And yet, as I looked again at the small collection that lay within that drawer of disillusions, some warmth crept back to my heart as I recognized that a kindred spirit to my own had been at the making of it. Two tarnished gilt buttons—naval, apparently ; a portrait of a monarch unknown to me, cut from some antique print and deftly coloured by hand in just my own bold style of brushwork ; some foreign copper coins, thicker and clumsier of make than those I hoarded myself ; and a list of birds' eggs, with names of the places where they had been found. Also a ferret's muzzle, and a twist of tarry string, still faintly aromatic ! It was a real boy's hoard, then, that I had happened upon. He, too, had found out the secret drawer, this happy-starred young person ; and here he had stowed away his treasures, one by one, and had cherished them secretly awhile ; and then—what ? Well, one would never know now the reason why these priceless possessions lay still here unreclaimed ; but across the void stretch of years I seemed to touch hands a moment with my little comrade of seasons— how many seasons ?—long since dead.

I restored the drawer, with its contents, to the trusty bureau, and heard the spring click with a certain satisfaction. Some other boy, perhaps, would some day release that spring again. I trusted he would be equally appreciative. As I opened the door to go, I could hear, from the nursery at the end of the passage, shouts and yells, telling that the hunt was up. Bears, apparently, or bandits, were on the evening bill of fare, judging by the character of the noises. In another minute I would be in the thick of it, in all the warmth and light and laughter. And yet—what a long way off it all seemed, both in space and time, to me yet lingering on the threshold of that old-world chamber !

From " The Golden Age "

31

LANDFALL AND DEPARTURE

JOSEPH CONRAD

LANDFALL and Departure mark the rhythmical swing of a seaman's life and of a ship's career. From land to land is the most concise definition of a ship's earthly fate.

A 'Departure' is not what a vain people of landsmen may think. The term 'Landfall' is more easily understood; you fall in with the land, and it is a matter of a quick eye and of a clear atmosphere. The Departure is not the ship's going away from her port any more than the Landfall can be looked upon as the synonym of arrival. But there is this difference in the Departure: that the term does not imply so much a sea event as a definite act entailing a process—the precise observation of certain landmarks by means of the compass card.

Your Landfall, be it a peculiarly-shaped mountain, a rocky headland, or a stretch of sand-dunes, you meet at first with a single glance. Further recognition will follow in due course; but essentially a Landfall, good or bad, is made and done with at the first cry of " Land ho ! " The Departure is distinctly a ceremony of navigation. A ship may have left her port some time before; she may have been at sea, in the fullest sense of the phrase, for days; but, for all that, as long as the coast she was about to leave remained in sight, a southern-going ship of yesterday had not in the sailor's sense begun the enterprise of a passage.

The taking of Departure, if not the last sight of

the land, is, perhaps, the last professional recognition of the land on the part of a sailor. It is the technical, as distinguished from the sentimental, ' good-bye.' Henceforth he has done with the coast astern of his ship. It is a matter personal to the man. It is not the ship that takes her Departure ; the seaman takes his Departure by means of cross-bearings which fix the place of the first tiny pencil-cross on the white expanse of the track-chart, where the ship's position at noon shall be marked by just such another tiny pencil-cross for every day of her passage. And there may be sixty, eighty, any number of these crosses on the ship's track from land to land. The greatest number in my experience was a hundred and thirty of such crosses from the pilot station at the Sand Heads in the Bay of Bengal to the Scilly's light. A bad passage. . . .

A Departure, the last professional sight of land, is always good, or at least good enough. For, even if the weather be thick, it does not matter much to a ship having all the open sea before her bows. A Landfall may be good or bad. You encompass the earth with one particular spot of it in your eye. In all the devious tracings the course of a sailing-ship leaves upon the white paper of a chart, she is always aiming for that one little spot—maybe a small island in the ocean, a single headland upon the long coast of a continent, a lighthouse on a bluff, or simply the peaked form of a mountain like an ant-heap afloat upon the waters. But if you have sighted it on the expected bearing, then that Landfall is good. Fogs, snow-storms, gales thick with clouds and rain—those are the enemies of good Landfalls.

Some commanders of ships take their Departure

from the home coast sadly, in a spirit of grief and discontent. They have a wife, children perhaps, some affection at any rate, or perhaps only some pet vice, that must be left behind for a year or more. I remember only one man who walked his deck with a springy step, and gave the first course of the passage in an elated voice. But he, as I learned afterwards, was leaving nothing behind him, except a welter of debts and threats of legal proceedings.

On the other hand, I have known many captains who, directly their ship had left the narrow waters of the Channel, would disappear from the sight of their ship's company altogether for some three days or more. They would take a long dive, as it were, into their state-room, only to emerge a few days afterwards with a more or less serene brow. Those were the men easy to get on with. Besides, such a complete retirement seemed to imply a satisfactory amount of trust in their officers, and to be trusted displeases no seaman worthy of the name.

On my first voyage as chief mate with good Captain MacW—— I remember that I felt quite flattered, and went blithely about my duties, myself a commander for all practical purposes. Still, whatever the greatness of my illusion, the fact remained that the real commander was there, backing up my self-confidence, though invisible to my eyes behind a maple-wood veneered cabin-door with a white china handle.

That is the time, after your Departure is taken, when the spirit of your commander communes with you in a muffled voice, as if from the *sanctum sanctorum* of a temple ; because, call her a temple or a ' hell afloat '—as some ships have been called—the captain's state-room is surely the august place in every vessel.

The good MacW—— would not even come out to

his meals, and fed solitarily in his holy of holies from a tray covered with a white napkin. Our steward used to bend an ironic glance at the perfectly empty plates he was bringing out from there. This grief for his home, which overcomes so many married seamen, did not deprive Captain MacW—— of his legitimate appetite. In fact, the steward would almost invariably come up to me, sitting in the captain's chair at the head of the table, to say in a grave murmur, " The captain asks for one more slice of meat and two potatoes." We, his officers, could hear him moving about in his berth, or lightly snoring, or fetching deep sighs, or splashing and blowing in his bath-room ; and we made our reports to him through the keyhole, as it were. It was the crowning achievement of his amiable character that the answers we got were given in a quite mild and friendly tone. Some commanders in their periods of seclusion are constantly grumpy, and seem to resent the mere sound of your voice as an injury and an insult.

But a grumpy recluse cannot worry his subordinates : whereas the man in whom the sense of duty is strong (or, perhaps, only the sense of self-importance), and who persists in airing on deck his moroseness all day— and perhaps half the night—becomes a grievous infliction. He walks the poop darting gloomy glances, as though he wished to poison the sea, and snaps your head off savagely whenever you happen to blunder within earshot. And these vagaries are the harder to bear patiently, as becomes a man and an officer, because no sailor is really good-tempered during the first few days of a voyage. There are regrets, memories, the instinctive longing for the departed idleness, the instinctive hate of all work. Besides, things have a knack of going wrong at the start, especially in the matter of irritating trifles. And there is the abiding thought of a whole year of more or less hard life before one, because there was hardly a southern-going voyage in the yesterday of the sea which meant anything less than a twelvemonth. Yes ; it needed a few days after the taking of your Departure for a ship's company to shake down into their places, and for the soothing deep-water ship routine to establish its beneficent sway.

It is a great doctor for sore hearts and sore heads, too, your ship's routine, which I have seen soothe— at least for a time—the most turbulent of spirits. There is health in it, and peace, and satisfaction of the accomplished round ; for each day of the ship's life seems to close a circle within the wide ring of the sea horizon. It borrows a certain dignity of sameness from the majestic monotony of the sea. He who loves the sea loves also the ship's routine.

Nowhere else than upon the sea do the days, weeks, and months fall away quicker into the past. They seem to be left astern as easily as the light air-bubbles in the swirls of the ship's wake, and vanish into a great silence in which your ship moves on with a sort of magical effort. They pass away, the days, the weeks, the months. Nothing but a gale can disturb the orderly life of the ship ; and the spell of unshaken monotony that seems to have fallen upon the very voices of her men is broken only by the near prospect of a Landfall.

Then is the spirit of the ship's commander stirred strongly again. But it is not moved to seek seclusion, and to remain, hidden and inert, shut up in a small cabin with the solace of a good bodily appetite. When about to make the land, the spirit of the ship's commander is tormented by an unconquerable restlessness. It seems unable to abide for many seconds together

36

in the holy of holies of the captain's state-room ; it will out on deck and gaze ahead, through straining eyes, as the appointed moment comes nearer. It is kept vigorously upon the stretch of excessive vigilance. Meantime the body of the ship's commander is being enfeebled by want of appetite ; at least, such is my experience, though ' enfeebled ' is perhaps not exactly the word. I might say, rather, that it is spiritualized by a disregard for food, sleep, and all the ordinary comforts, such as they are, of sea life. In one or two cases I have known that detachment from the grosser needs of existence remain regrettably incomplete in the matter of drink.

But these two cases were, properly speaking, patho-logical cases, and the only two in all my sea experience. In one of these two instances of a craving for stimulants, developed from sheer anxiety, I cannot assert that the man's seamanlike qualities were impaired in the least. It was a very anxious case, too, the land being made suddenly, close-to, on a wrong bearing, in thick weather, and during a fresh on-shore gale. Going below to speak to him soon after, I was unlucky enough to catch my captain in the very act of hasty cork-drawing. The sight, I may say, gave me an awful scare. I was well aware of the morbidly sensitive nature of the man. Fortunately, I managed to draw back unseen, and, taking care to stamp heavily with my sea-boots at the foot of the cabin stairs, I made my second entry. But for this unexpected glimpse, no act of his during the next twenty-four hours could have given me the slightest suspicion that all was not well with his nerve.

Quite another case, and having nothing to do with drink, was that of poor Captain B——. He used to

37

suffer from sick headaches, in his young days, every time he was approaching a coast. Well over fifty years of age when I knew him, short, stout, dignified, perhaps a little pompous, he was a man of a singularly well-informed mind, the least sailor-like in outward aspect, but certainly one of the best seamen whom it has been my good luck to serve under. He was a Plymouth man, I think, the son of a country doctor, and both his elder boys were studying medicine. He commanded a big London ship, fairly well known in her day. I thought no end of him, and that is why I remember with a peculiar satisfaction the last words he spoke to me on board his ship after an eighteen months' voyage. It was in the dock in Dundee, where we had brought a full cargo of jute from Calcutta. We had been paid off that morning, and I had come on board to take my sea-chest away, and to say good-bye. In his slightly lofty but courteous way he inquired what were my plans. I replied that I intended leaving for London by the afternoon train, and thought of going up for examination to get my master's certificate. I had just enough service for that. He commended me for not wasting any time, with such an evident interest in my case that I was quite surprised ; then, rising from his chair, he said :

" Have you a ship in view after you have passed ? "

I answered that I had nothing whatever in view.

He shook hands with me, and pronounced the memorable words :

" If you happen to be in want of employment, remember that as long as I have a ship you have a ship too."

In the way of compliment there is nothing to beat this from a ship's captain to his second mate at the end of a voyage, when the work is over and the subordinate is done with. And there is a pathos in that memory, for the poor fellow never went to sea again after all. He was already ailing when we passed St Helena ; was laid up for a time when we were off the Western Islands, but got out of bed to make his Landfall. He managed to keep up on deck as far as the Downs, where, giving his orders in an exhausted voice, he anchored for a few hours to send a wire to his wife and take aboard a North Sea pilot to help him sail the ship up the East coast. He had not felt equal to the task by himself, for it is the sort of thing that keeps a deep-water man on his feet pretty well night and day.

When we arrived in Dundee, Mrs B—— was already there, waiting to take him home. We travelled up to London by the same train ; but by the time I had managed to get through with my examination the ship had sailed on her next voyage without him, and, instead of joining her again, I went by request to see my old commander in his home. This is the only one of my captains I have ever visited in that way. He was out of bed by then, " quite convalescent," as he declared, making a few tottering steps to meet me at the sitting-room door. Evidently he was reluctant to take his final cross-bearings of this earth for a Departure on the only voyage to an unknown destination a sailor ever undertakes. And it was all very nice—the large, sunny room ; his deep easy chair in a bow window, with pillows and a foot-stool ; the quiet, watchful care of the elderly, gentle woman who had borne him five children, and had not, perhaps, lived with him more than full five years out of the thirty or so of their married life. There was also another woman there in a plain black dress, quite grey-haired, sitting very erect on her chair with some sewing, from which she snatched side-glances in his direction, and uttering not a single word during all the time of my call. Even when, in due course, I carried over to her a cup of tea, she only nodded at me silently, with the faintest ghost of a smile on her tight-set lips. I imagine she must have been a maiden sister of Mrs B—— come to help nurse her brother-in-law. His youngest boy, a late-comer, a great cricketer it seemed, twelve years old or thereabouts, chattered enthusiastically of the exploits of W. G. Grace. And I remember his eldest son, a newly-fledged doctor, who took me out to smoke in the garden, and shaking his head with professional gravity, but with genuine concern, muttered : " Yes, but he doesn't get back his appetite. I don't like that—I don't like that at all." The last sight of Captain B—— I had was as he nodded his head to me out of the bow window when I turned round to close the front gate.

It was a distinct and complete impression, something that I don't know whether to call a Landfall or a Departure. Certainly he had gazed at times very fixedly before him with the Landfall's vigilant look, this sea-captain seated incongruously in a deep-backed chair. He had not then talked to me of employment, of ships, of being ready to take another command ; but he had discoursed of his early days, in the abundant but thin flow of an invalid's talk. The women looked worried, but sat still, and I learned more of him in that interview than in the whole eighteen months we had sailed together. It appeared he had ' served his time ' in the copper-ore trade, the famous copper-ore trade of old days between Swansea and the Chilian coast, coal out and ore in, deep-loaded both ways, as

if in wanton defiance of the great Cape Horn seas—
a work, this, for staunch ships, and a great school of
staunchness for West-Country seamen. A whole fleet
of copper-bottomed barques, as strong in rib and
planking, as well-found in gear, as ever was sent upon
the seas, manned by hardy crews and commanded by
young masters, was engaged in that long-defunct trade.
" That was the school I was trained in," he said to
me almost boastfully, lying back amongst his pillows
with a rug over his legs. And it was in that trade
that he obtained his first command at a very early
age. It was then that he mentioned to me how, as
a young commander, he was always ill for a few days
before making land after a long passage. But this
sort of sickness used to pass off with the first sight of
a familiar landmark. Afterwards, he added, as he
grew older, all that nervousness wore off completely ;
and I observed his weary eyes gaze steadily ahead,
as if there had been nothing between him and the
straight line of sea and sky, where whatever a seaman
is looking for is bound first to appear. But I have
also seen his eyes rest fondly upon the faces in the
room, upon the pictures on the wall, upon all the
familiar objects of that home, whose abiding and clear
image must have flashed often on his memory in times
of stress and anxiety at sea. Was he looking out for
a strange Landfall, or taking with an untroubled mind
the bearings for his last Departure ?

It is hard to say ; for in that voyage from which
no man returns, Landfall and Departure are instan-
taneous, merging together into one moment of supreme
and final attention. Certainly I do not remember
observing any sign of faltering in the set expression
of his wasted face, no hint of the nervous anxiety of
a young commander about to make land on an

uncharted shore. He had had too much experience of Departures and Landfalls. And had he not ' served his time ' in the famous copper-ore trade out of the Bristol Channel, the work of the staunchest ships afloat, and the school of staunch seamen ?

From " The Mirror of the Sea "

GOING AWAY AND ARRIVING

FILSON YOUNG

THE act of Going Away, in the case of a whole
family making an annual migration, is a very
important part of a holiday. In the case of
simple people who have neither great establishments
or large means, it is a thing fraught with a certain
amount of careful apprehension ; to the elders it is
a serious matter, complicated by questions of packing,
of dealings with servants, or arrangements for shutting
up or carefully maintaining the house during their
absence ; but for children it is quite another thing.
It is the most exciting part of the holiday, in which
the joys of travel and adventure are combined in
a highly concentrated form. It is surrounded by rites
and ceremonies, and crowned with the knowledge that
beyond it lie the delights of the holiday itself. To
appreciate the true joys of Going Away one must be
a child in a family whose annual migration is a thing
long looked forward to as the supreme delight of the
year.

My own memory of Going Away in this manner
lies like a golden haze on the most distant part of life
that I can remember. I associate it with that sense of
exhausted summer experienced in large towns towards
the end of July ; with an approaching emptiness and
suspension of the ordinary affairs of life, and with the
alien's sense of quitting the place of his bondage and
returning to his native land. For England, although
the greater part of my year was spent in it, was

43

associated in my youth with the drab side of life; with going to school, and with a disagreeable sense of false position caused by living constantly among rich and, if the truth be told, somewhat Philistine people, whose simple way it was to estimate others by the amount of money which they had; whom superiority of attainment or of cultivation rendered uncomfortable, and who were glad to find any ground from which they could look down on their superiors. And as the end of July approached we, as children, had a growing sense that we had dwelt too long in Mesech and had our habitation in the tents of Kedar. We were going back to our own land and our own people, and we were glad.

Our Going Away took place very properly on a Monday. The Saturday preceding it was a day of disturbance and unrest, when the ordinary order of things was suspended, and one was thrilled by the sight of the various large trunks standing about in the fairways of corridors and landings. It was on Saturday, or sometimes even on Friday, that we began to repeat a rhyme or chant used only on these occasions. It was as follows:

> "This time three days where shall we be?
> In the steamer going to ——."

The missing word supplied the rhyme; and it was considered creditable and effective if one of us, by making elaborate calculation, could suddenly foreshadow one of the more thrilling moments of the journey by saying:

> "This time twenty-five hours where shall we be?
> Standing-on-the-quay-waiting-for-the-mail-car,
>   going to ——."

Saturday evening passed in a kind of wretched

reaction and serious searching of heart as to how the whole of Sunday and Monday could possibly be got through. Church on Sunday was a little exciting because of the thinned condition of the congregation ; one had an infinite pity for the wretched handful who should remain at the mercy of a succession of casual and unknown ministrants. All packing was of course suspended on Sunday ; the trunks gaped invitingly, and sometimes a toy would be surreptitiously inserted among the folds of garments, only to be discovered and ejected on the following day. On Sunday evening there was a touching and somewhat sentimental feeling in the air, stimulated by the long sunshine slanting in through the windows, my father's last sermon, the familiar hymns dedicated by custom to this occasion, and (in one mind at least) associated not with the Deity, but with cabs and railway trains. One could almost have wept. And so to bed, and another sick night of suspense.

We did not leave till about seven in the evening ; but for my part I was always ready and waiting to get into my overcoat by about nine in the morning. Things really began to happen in the morning. Our excitement was constantly being quelled by elders, who walked about with furrowed brows and attempted to keep calm. Servants were engaged upon unfamiliar jobs, and we took our meals with our loins girded, noting an absence of familiar table furniture. Various humble dependants came to the house to be paid, and as we spoke to them of our imminent departure we were filled, I know not why, with a sense of pathos. We felt sorry for them, that they should thus be looking on us for the last time ; and we had a strange thrilling sense of importance, as of people who should claim the attention and the privileges of the death-bed.

As the afternoon wore on there was a difficulty in breathing and total loss of appetite, which, strange to say, was treated almost as an offence The moment when the first trunk was brought downstairs was generally the scene of a demonstration and, probably, of a reprimand ; and it was at this time that agonizing secret discussions began as to how we should sit in the 'bus, who, if any, should go on the box, whether it would be a fine night, and if we should be allowed to stay up late on the steamer. Half an hour before the time of departure the hideous chill of apprehension arose as to what would happen if the 'bus did not come, and the scout detailed to station himself on the road, scanning every vehicle, received one bitter disappointment after another. But at last it arrived, being greeted, according to ritual, with a quotation from an early story-book, " It comes, it rolls up to the door."

Now indeed we were in the very act and article of departure. One could have embraced the driver as he came to help down with the boxes ; we wanted to draw him aside and tell him about the joys that were waiting for us ; for surely he must be aware that this was no ordinary station job, but the homeward flight of remarkable people to the most wonderful paradise on earth. This was one of the occasions on which one shook hands with servants, and was strangely aware of the texture of their skin. And at last, every parcel being counted, and every child tightly clinging to some minor piece of luggage, the door was shut with a bang, the wheels scraped the road, and we were off, hoping to pass on the road some of our acquaintances who were not going away.

Followed the more awful excitement of the railway station, when we were brigaded into various parties and given posts to guard while the business of taking tickets and seats was transacted. There was no play about it now ; we were off in earnest amid the grim realities of trains and engines ; and our excitement took an almost fearful thrill, as though we had started some tremendous machine which we could not stop. The great delight of the railway journey was the obvious light-heartedness of my father ; his method of counting the luggage to see that it was all there ; the tones in which he announced the stations which were passed, which would not have seemed real if anyone else had spoken them ; and it was part of the ritual, all unknown to him, that as we approached our port of embarkation he should let down the window and make some remark on the state of the weather or the sea. For a more sober interest now began to overcast our excitements ; we were not all good sailors ; and on the state of the weather would depend our happiness or misery for the next eight hours. But I remember these occasions chiefly as being associated with calm weather, and long sunsets, and the faint, salt smell of the sea across the darkness.

The next thrill on the pilgrimage was when, disembarking from the train and beginning to tramp through a succession of echoing boarded passages, we first caught sight of the legend in huge letters : TO THE STEAMER. I do not know why such notices should enter so deeply into one's sense of life ; but so long as I live I shall remember the almost intolerable tremor of being with which I read these legends, and with what a sense of glorious fate I followed the pointing wooden hand with which they were punctuated. And then at last the gangway, and the deck of the steamer, and the lights shining from the companion-way, and the weird smell which made one clench one's teeth as one descended the stairs (for this was before the day of universal electric lights and fans), the finding of one's cabin and the depositing therein of one's small effects, the desire to be in every part of the ship at once lest one should miss anything, the glorious vibration of the foghorn's note in the pit of one's stomach when it announced our departure, and the moment at which one could say " We are off." And then the tramping up and down the deck, the watching of the winking buoys sliding by, the returning to peep down the companion ladder, and the coming back to find that one's teeth were still firmly clenched. Every one of these experiences was a joy in itself. And down in the saloon was a pleasant clatter of knives and forks, and the appetizing smells of hot meats, after which my young stomach lusted, although I was obliged to be content with an expurgated meal of tea and toast and jam.

And then once more on deck, we men, tightly buttoned up now, one's mother and sisters safely tucked away in their cabins whence good and reassuring news came of their estate, to walk up and down in the lee of the most interesting, fascinating, and all-powerful father in holiday mood, looking at the blinking lighthouse that seemed to come no nearer, until the wind began to bite and the eyes, in spite of all the efforts of the will, to close. To turn in was delayed as long as possible, for it meant the end of Going Away ; there was but a bridge of sleep before one would enter into to-morrow with all its joys.

But if Going Away was the most glorious part of the holidays of childhood, Arriving was the most purely joyous. The excitement of Going Away was tinged with the apprehension which, pleasant or unpleasant, is inseparable from the beginning of any great enterprise, and was shadowed by a sense of perils and adventures by land and sea to be encountered before the end was reached. But on arriving these things were all behind us ; it was a crescendo of pleasures ; they did not end, but were simply merged in a succession of joys, a vista of delight of which even the visible horizon did not mark the end. In short, Going Away happened at night, and Arriving happened in the morning ; and in that statement is contained the whole essential difference between the two.

Arriving began by one's waking up in the small hours of the morning and wondering where one was, and gradually becoming aware that one was indeed in the cabin of the ship and travelling in the midst of the sea. The great question was how soon one could get up. The view from the porthole probably revealed only a grey waste of waters. One hardly dared to look at the time for fear it should be some dreadful hour like three or four o'clock—a hopeless hour at which it was quite useless to get up. One lay trying to go to sleep again, or, failing that, determined to lie still for an hour by sheer effort of will ; and when one looked at the clock again it was but five minutes later. Sometimes one would try to persuade oneself that four o'clock was quite a reasonable hour to get up, and having dressed, find one's way up on decks that were either deserted and very wet, or else in process of being washed down, so that there was no dry spot to sit upon. No land being visible, and the air being probably bitterly cold, and the sun not risen, the most sanguine temperament failed to support such conditions, and one would come down again and make another effort to sleep, repeating these experiments until one did sleep in earnest, and woke up with a shock to find that the green shores of Ireland

were visible, that the sun had risen, and that other
people had been up for quite a long time. How sweet
the air was, how green seemed the familiar shores
of one's native land! There were greetings to be
exchanged, notes to be compared on the experiences
of the night, absorbing interests connected with the
arrival of the steamer alongside the quay and—joy
of joys—the sight of the yellow wheels of the conveyance which was to carry us on the last thirty miles
of our journey. This was nothing more nor less than
a long car, a kind of vehicle unknown except in Ireland,
and, in sober truth, nothing more luxurious than a
species of spring dray with wooden flaps over the
wheels and a kind of knife-board arrangement on
which four or six people sat facing outwards on either
side, the luggage being piled in the middle. But the
fiery chariot of Elijah could not have seemed to us a
more delectable and luxurious and splendid conveyance.

And now we were all packed and tucked in behind
rugs and aprons, and rattling over the stony streets
of the town and out into the country road, with the
morning sunshine slanting still low across it, and the
air still sweet from the dews and the showers of the
night, and the hedgerows fragrant and bright with
wild roses and dog-daisies. We had thirty miles to
cover, with changes of horses three times, and the joy
of the road before us. The first thing I remember
when once well out on the road was the production of
baskets and packets of biscuits and sandwiches; and
my strongest association with this part of the road
is the slightly metallic taste of milk drunk out of the
cup of a flask, and the difficulty of imbibing it from
the narrow end of the cup while seated on a jolting
vehicle. And after that I think I generally slept or
dozed for about an hour; dozed deliciously, leaning

against some protecting shoulder, with an under-current of the gritty sound of wheels along the road, of Irish voices heard in pauses by the roadside. Then, refreshed by sleep, one would wake to an absorbed interest in the affairs of the journey; for our vehicle carried the mails for thirty miles, and carried many other things as well; so that the driver, as we rounded a bend of the road, would suddenly throw a fish at the door of a house, and give a bundle of newspapers to some old woman who had walked a couple of miles down a side road to receive them. At one corner there was always a dog, a black retriever, who waited for his master's newspaper, and could be seen soberly trotting off with it until the bend of the road hid him from sight. Then there was a beggar who frequented the road, Jimmy Leary, of whom we were terrified, and the sight of him stumping along in his picturesque tatters, or pausing, as we passed, to raise his lined face and shake his knarled stick at us, thrilled us with a sense of perils encountered. Then there were the halts to change horses, and the sight of men drinking porter in some little wayside public-house; and my views of life at that time must have been very strict, for I remember feeling rather frightened that in such a happy country, and on such a beautiful morning, men should be found wicked and abandoned enough to commit this sin.

Half-way along the road, just after it passes through the town of Newtownards, takes a sudden bend and comes out on one of the most fragrant shores in the world. One moment you are under trees, going by a moss-grown chapel and market-house, and the next you are out in the open with the stony beach close to you, the intoxicating smell of seaweed, and the sound of waves washing against stones—no muddy lake water, but the veritable sea itself, clear and green and transparent against the rocks and pebbles of the beach. Need I tell you what the moment of that vision meant to us in this succession of delights? For these were our own waters, the shores of our own lough, which we were to follow in all their twistings and turnings for some fifteen miles, and well-nigh to the open sea itself. Great was the competition to sit on the shore side of the car; so great indeed that turns had to be taken, and at stopping-places there was much lifting down and hoisting up as these exchanges were effected.

Two more changes of horses after this, and we were out on the last ten miles, mostly inland again, for we were to lose sight of the sea until it burst upon us at the very doors of our home. Now the excitement became almost sickening as we strained our eyes along the road to mark the familiar objects; and as we neared the village of our destination familiar faces began to appear on the road, and we recognized them with a thrill of wonder that they should exist so unchanged during our absence. Now began the long wall of the demesne, with a curtseying figure at the first lodge gate; and at the end of the wall, under a tunnel of trees, the pump and the first white cottages of the long village street. The horses were whipped up, and with a glorious commotion we entered on the last stage of our triumphal progress. The upper halves of the house doors were opened, and old women with mutches on their heads looked out upon us, shading their eyes with their hands. Now we have passed the baker's, that functionary himself, perpetually white, and living, as it were, in a mist of flour, standing behind his counter; now past the wonderful shop of sweets and mysteries, with the

name 'Anderson' in crusted white letters (one of
them missing) over the lintel; now another shop, the
source of the most delicious ginger-bread, with its
little proprietress nodding and waving to us from the
door; now, with a last crack of the whip, and scat-
tering of poultry from under the very wheels, into the
market square itself, in front of the post-office, with
familiar faces waiting to greet us. But even yet we
had not finished; the greater joy was to come. The
mails have been taken off, the parcels and odd luggage
discharged, and with a grating of brakes we turn away
down the steep street, where the masts of ships show
over the roofs of houses, round the corner, beside
the pump, along the wall of an old castle, and suddenly
the view is open—to me the most sacred and beautiful
view in the world; a view of beach and harbour and
sea, with our own craft at her moorings in the fore-
ground, and the swift sliding tide beyond, and across
it green wooded shores trimmed with a brown line of
seaweed, and the blue mountains in the distance.
That was the culmination; but a few yards more and
the wheels had come to rest, and we jumped down on
to the gravel sweep into the arms waiting to receive
us. Yet it was not the beloved kinsfolk whose presence
and welcome most thrilled us, but the sturdy, bearded,
blue-jerseyed figure, commodore and admiral of our
small fleet of boats, who stood waiting to take part
in the welcome, and, incidentally, to help with the
luggage. That he should be really alive and existing
before us in the very flesh was the crowning miracle
and delight of our journey. When we had found him
we had Arrived.

Going Away and Arriving—how closely the whole
of existence fits itself between those two adventures!
When you stand in the mid-sea of life, far away from

its beginnings, and apparently far from its ending, you realize how many things you have gone away from, and how comparatively few you seem to have arrived at. Yet I like to think that they are but the two halves of one whole, and that if Going Away is the chief joy of youthful life, Arriving is the special pleasure and privilege of age ; and that even though the horizons of youth are grown dim and misty in the distance, for people who have grown old wisely the land they are approaching grows more and more clearly defined, and from being a strange and unknown, becomes a familiar and welcoming country ; on whose soft shore they look forward to lying down for a long rest, with the noise of the waters over which they have passed lulling them to a pleasant and dreamless sleep.

From " Letters from Solitude "

A HERMITAGE IN SIGHT

MAURICE HEWLETT

I HOPE that I have secured for myself a haven, a yet more impenetrable shade than this, against the time when, having seen four generations of men, two behind and two beyond, I may consider in silence what is likely to be the end of it all. It is true that I am getting old, but I am not yet prepared for a lodge in the wilderness. My present house has a wall on the village street. The post-office is a matter of crossing the road ; the church is at the bottom of a meadow. I like all that, because I like all my neighbours and the sound of their voices. At eleven o'clock in the morning I can hear the children let out from school, " as shrill as swifts in upper air." That, too, I like. But the time will come when silence is best, and, as I say, I believe that I have found the very place. I have had my eye upon it for years, and seldom a month passes but I am there. A small black dog and I once saw Oreads there, or said we did, and in print at that. This very year the farm to which it belongs came into the market, and was sold ; the purchaser will treat with me. I have described it once, nay twice, and won't do it again. Enough to say that it is the butt end of a deep green combe in the Downs, that it is sheltered from every wind, faces the south, and is below an ancient road, now a grass track, and the remains of what is called a British village on the ordnance maps, a great ramparted square with half a dozen gateways and two

55

mist-pools within its ambit. All about it lie the
neolithic dead, of whose race, as Glaucus told Diomede,
" I boast myself to be."

We are all Iberians here, or so I love to believe,
grounding myself upon the learned Dr Beddoes—a
swarthy people, dark-haired, grey-eyed, rather under
than over the mean height. The aboriginal strain has
proved itself stronger than the Frisian, and the Danish
type does not appear at all. There are English names
among us, of course, such as Gurd, which is Gurth as
pronounced by a Norman ; but it is understood that
we are neolithic chiefly on the distaff side. The theory
that each successive wave of invasion demolished the
existing inhabitants is absurd. Not even the Germans
do that ; nor have the Turks succeeded in obliterating
the Armenian nation. No—in turn our oncoming
hordes, Celts, Romans, English, Danes, enslaved the
men and married, or at least mated with, the women.
And so we are descended, and (let me at this hour of
victory be allowed to say) a marvellous people we are.
For tenacity, patience, and obedience to the law—not
of men, but of nature—I don't suppose there is another
such people in the world. Those characteristics, for
which neither Celt nor Roman, Teuton nor Dane, as
we know them now, is remarkable, I set to the score
of the neolithic race, whose physical features are
equally enduring.

When you get what seems like a clear case in either
sex, you have a very handsome person.

The most beautiful woman I ever saw in my days
was scrubbing a kitchen floor on her knees, when I
saw her first—not a hundred miles from here. Pure
Iberian, so far as one can judge—olive skin, black
hair, grey-green eyes. Otherwise—colouring apart—
the Venus de Milo, no less. I don't say that she was

very intelligent. I wonder if the Venus was. But she was obedient to the law of her being—that I do know, and it is a matter of faith with me that Aphrodite can have been no less so.

Neither a quick-witted nor an imaginative race are we ; but we have the roots of poetry in us, and the roots of other arts, for we have reverence for what is above and beyond us. Custom, too, we worship, and decency and order. We fight unwillingly, and are very slow to anger ; but we never let go. Witness the last four dreadful years ; witness Europe from Mons to Gallipoli. The British private, soldier or sailor, has been the backbone of the fight for freedom. But I am a long way from my valley in the Downs.

I shall first of all sink a well, for one must have water, even if one is going to die. Then I shall make a mist-pool—that art is not lost yet—because as well as water to drink I like water to look upon. Lastly, I will build a hermitage of puddled chalk and straw, and thatch it with reeds, if I can get them. It will consist of a single room thirty feet long. It will have a gallery at each end, attained by a ladder. In each gallery shall be a bed, and the appurtenance thereof, one for use and one for a co-hermit or hermitess, if such there be. I leave that open. There must be a stoop, of course. Nothing enclosed. No flowers, by request. The sheep shall nibble to the very threshold. I don't forget that there is a fox-earth in the spinney attached. I saw a vixen and her cubs there one morning as clearly as I see this paper. She barked at me once or twice, sitting high on her haunches, but the children played on without a glance at me. They were playing at catch-as-catch-can— with a full-grown hare. Sheer fun. No after-thoughts. I watched them for twenty minutes.

If I grow anything there at all I shall confine my part of the business to planting, and let Nature do the rest. It may be absolutely necessary to keep the sheep off for a year or two, and the rabbits—but that is all. And what I do plant shall be deciduous, so that I may have the yearly miracle to expect. It is a mighty eater of time—and there won't be much of that left probably ; yet a joy which no man who has ever begotten anything, baby or poem, can deny himself.

If anybody wants to see what Nature can do in the way of a season's growth, I can tell him how to go to work. Let him plant on the bank of a running water a root of *Gunnera manicata*. Let him then wait ten years, observing these directions faithfully. Every fall, after the first frost—that frost which blackens his dahlias—let him cover the crown of his *Gunnera* with one of its own leaves. Pile some stable-stuff over that, and then heap upon all the leaf-sweepings of that part of the garden. Growth starts in mid-April and proceeds by a foot a week. Mine, which is about ten years old now, is thirty-five feet in circumference, nearly twelve feet high, has flowers two-feet-six in length, and in a hot summer has grown leaves seven feet across. You can go under one of them in a shower of rain and be as dry as in church. And all that done in five months. The plant is a rhubarb of sorts and comes from Chili. I should like to see it over there on the marge of some monstrous river. In another order, the *Ipomœa* (Morning Glory), which comes from East Africa, runs it close. I had one seed in Sussex which completely overflowed a garden wall, smothering everything upon it. A kind of Jack's beanstalk, and every morning starred with turquoise blue trumpets of ravishing beauty, which were dead at noon. The poor thing was constrained to be a

58

hierondule, gave no seed. Nature is the prodigal's foster-mother.

I have a plant whose seed is much more beautiful than its flower. By the way, I have two, for the Spindle Tree is in seed, which has a quite insignificant blossom. But the plant I mean is a wild peony, which I dug up in a brake on the slopes of Helikon. It is a single white, whose flower lasts, perhaps, three days. It makes a large seed-pod, which burst a short time ago, and revealed blue-black seeds sheathed in coralline forms of the most absolute vermilion. You could see them fifty yards away. It seems to have no purpose in life but to pack the seeds—or perhaps, they are beacons for the birds. I took pains to be beforehand with the birds, having no desire to see Greek peonies in my neighbours' gardens. The seeds are safely bestowed, though their fate has not been Jonah's. There's a spinney of elder-trees in the combe of my hermitage, which, I am told, was planted entirely by magpies. And I suppose it was wood-pigeons who planted two ilex-trees on the top of the Guinigi tower in Lucca ; and some bird or other, once more, which is answerable for a fine fig-tree growing in the parapet of the bridge at Cordova, in no soil whatsoever. It was loaded with fruit when I saw it. But fig-trees are like poets ; if you want them to sing you must torture their roots. The parallel wobbles, but it will be understood.

From "In a Green Shade"

ACCORDING TO TASTE

A BROTHER OF ST FRANCIS

GRACE RHYS

W HEN talking to a wise friend a while ago I told her of the feeling of horror which had invaded me when watching a hippopotamus.

" Indeed," said she, " you do not need to go to the hippopotamus for a sensation. Look at a pig ! There is something due in the face of a pig. To think the same power should have created it that created a star ! "

Those who love beauty and peace are often tempted to scamp their thinking, to avoid the elemental terrors that bring night into the mind. Yet if the fearful things of life are there, why not pluck up heart and look at them ? Better have no Bluebeard's chamber in the mind. Better go boldly in and see what hangs by the wall. So salt, so medicinal is Truth, that even the bitterest draught may be made wholesome to the gentlest soul. So I would recommend anyone who can bear to think to leave the flower garden and go down and spend an hour by the pigsty.

There lies our friend in the sun upon the straw, blinking his clever little eye. Half friendly is his look (He does not know that I—Heaven forgive me!— sometimes have bacon for breakfast!). Plainly, with that gashed mouth, those dreadful cheeks, and that sprawl of his, he belongs to an older world; that older world, when first the mud and slime rose and moved, and, roaring, found a voice: aye, and no doubt enjoyed life, and in harsh and fearful sounds praised the Creator at the spinning.

A BROTHER OF ST FRANCIS

GRACE RHYS

WHEN talking to a wise friend a while ago I told her of the feeling of horror which had invaded me when watching a hippopotamus.

"Indeed," said she, "you do not need to go to the hippopotamus for a sensation. Look at a pig! There is something dire in the face of a pig. To think the same power should have created it that created a star!"

Those who love beauty and peace are often tempted to scamp their thinking, to avoid the elemental terrors that bring night into the mind. Yet if the fearful things of life are there, why not pluck up heart and look at them? Better have no Bluebeard's chamber in the mind. Better go boldly in and see what hangs by the wall. So salt, so medicinal is Truth, that even the bitterest draught may be made wholesome to the gentlest soul. So I would recommend anyone who can bear to think to leave the flower garden and go down and spend an hour by the pigstye.

There lies our friend in the sun upon the straw, blinking his clever little eye. Half friendly is his look. (He does not know that I—Heaven forgive me!—sometimes have bacon for breakfast!) Plainly, with that gashed mouth, those dreadful cheeks, and that sprawl of his, he belongs to an older world; that older world when first the mud and slime rose and moved, and, roaring, found a voice: aye, and no doubt enjoyed life, and in harsh and fearful sounds praised the Creator at the sunrising.

To prove the origin of the pig, let him out, and he will celebrate it by making straight for the nearest mud and diving into it. So strange is his aspect, so unreal to me, that it is almost as if the sunshine falling upon him might dissolve him, and resolve him into his original element. But no ; there he is, perfectly real ; as real as the good Christians and philosophers who will eventually eat him. While he lies there let me reflect in all charity on the disagreeable things I have heard about him.

He is dirty, people say. Nay, is he as dirty (or, at least, as complicated in his dirt) as his brother man can be ? Let those who know the dens of London give the answer. Leave the pig to himself, and he is not so bad. He knows his mother mud is cleansing ; he rolls partly because he loves her and partly because he wishes to be clean.

He is greedy ? In my mind's eye there rises the picture of human gormandizers, fat-necked, with half-buried eyes and toddling step. How long since the giant Gluttony was slain ? or does he still keep his monstrous *table d'hôte*.

The pig pushes his brother from the trough ? Why, that is a commonplace of our life. There is a whole school of so-called philosophers and political economists busied in elevating the pig's shove into a social and political necessity.

He screams horribly if you touch him or his share of victuals ? I have heard a polite gathering of the best people turn senseless and rave at a mild suggestion of Christian Socialism. He is bitter-tempered ? God knows, so are we. He has carnal desires ? The worst sinner is man. He will fight ? Look to the under-side of war. He is cruel ? Well, boys do queer things sometimes. For the rest, read the blacker pages of history ; not as they are served up for the schoolroom by private national vanity, but after the facts.

If a cow or a sheep is sick or wounded and the pig can get at it, he will worry it to death ? So does tyranny with subject peoples.

He loves to lie in the sun among his brothers, idle and at his ease ? Aye, but suppose this one called himself a lord pig and lay in the sun with a necklace of gold about his throat and jewels in his ears, having found means to drive his brethren (merry little pigs and all) out of the sun for his own benefit, what should we say of him then ?

No ; he has none of our cold cunning. He is all simplicity. I am told it is possible to love him. I know a kindly Frenchwoman who takes her pig for an airing on the sands of St Michel-en-Grève every summer afternoon. Knitting, she walks along, and calls gaily and endearingly to the delighted creature ; he follows at a word, gambolling with flapping ears over the ribs of sand, pasturing on shrimps and seaweed while he enjoys the salt air.

Clearly, then, the pig is our good little brother, and we have no right to be disgusted at him. Clearly our own feet are planted in the clay. Clearly the same Voice once called to our ears while yet unformed. Clearly we, too, have arisen from that fearful bed, and the slime of it clings to us still. Cleanse ourselves as we may, and repenting, renew the whiteness of our garments, we and the nations are for ever slipping back into the native element. What a fearful command the " Be ye perfect " to earth-born creatures, but half-emerged, the star upon their foreheads bespattered and dimmed ! But let us (even those of us who have courage to know the worst of man) take heart. In the terror of our origin, in the struggle

B

to stand upon our feet, to cleanse ourselves, and cast an eye heavenward, our glory is come by. The darker our naissance, the greater the terrors that have brooded round that strife, the more august and puissant shines the angel in man.

From " About Many Things "

ESSAYS OF TO-DAY

GOLDEN FRUIT

A. A. MILNE

OF the fruits of the year I give my vote to the orange. In the first place it is a perennial—if not in actual fact, at least in the greengrocer's shop. On the days when dessert is a name given to a handful of chocolates and a little preserved ginger, when *macédoine de fruits* is the title bestowed on two prunes and a piece of rhubarb, then the orange, however sour, comes nobly to the rescue ; and on those other days of plenty when cherries and strawberries and raspberries and gooseberries riot together upon the table, the orange, sweeter than ever, is still there to hold its own. Bread and butter, beef and mutton, eggs and bacon, are not more necessary to an ordered existence than the orange.

It is well that the commonest fruit should be also the best. Of the virtues of the orange I have not room fully to speak. It has properties of health-giving, as that it cures influenza and establishes the complexion. It is clean, for whoever handles it on its way to your table, but handles its outer covering, its top coat, which is left in the hall. It is round, and forms an excellent substitute with the young for a cricket ball. The pips can be flicked at your enemies, and quite a small piece of peel makes a slide for an old gentleman.

But all this would count nothing had not the orange such delightful qualities of taste. I dare not let myself go upon this subject. I am a slave to its sweetness. I grudge every marriage in that it means a fresh supply of orange blossom, the promise of so much golden fruit cut short. However, the world must go on.

Next to the orange I place the cherry. The cherry is a companionable fruit. You can eat it while you are reading or talking, and you can go on and on, absent-mindedly as it were, though you must mind not to swallow the stone. The trouble of disengaging this from the fruit is just sufficient to make the fruit taste sweeter for the labour. The stalk keeps you from soiling your fingers; it enables you also to play bob cherry. Lastly it is by means of cherries that one penetrates the great mysteries of life—when and whom you will marry, and whether she really loves you or is taking you for your worldly prospects. (I may add here that I know a girl who can tie a knot in the stalk of a cherry with her tongue. It is a tricky business, and I am doubtful whether to add it to the virtues of the cherry or not.)

There are only two ways of eating strawberries. One is neat in the strawberry bed, and the other is mashed on the plate. The first method generally requires us to take up a bent position under a net—in a hot sun very uncomfortable, and at any time fatal to the hair. The second method takes us into the privacy of the home, for it demands a dressing-gown and no spectators. For these reasons I think the strawberry an overrated fruit. Yet I must say that I like to see one floating in cider cup. It gives a note of richness to the affair, and excuses any shortcomings in the lunch itself.

Raspberries are a good fruit gone wrong. A raspberry by itself might indeed be the best fruit of all; but it is almost impossible to find it alone. I do not refer to its attachment to the red currant ; rather to the attachment to it of so many of our dumb little friends. The instinct of the lower creatures for the best is well shown in the case of the raspberry. If it is to be eaten it must be picked by the hand, well shaken, and then taken.

When you engage a gardener, the first thing to do is to come to an understanding with him about the peaches. The best way of settling the matter is to give him the carrots and the black currants and the rhubarb for himself, to allow him a free hand with the groundsel and the walnut trees, and to insist in return for this that you should pick the peaches when and how you like. If he is a gentleman he will consent. Supposing that some satisfactory arrangement were come to, and supposing also that you had a silver-bladed pocket-knife with which you could peel them in the open air, then peaches would come very high in the list of fruits. But the conditions are difficult.

Gooseberries burst at the wrong end and smother you ; melons—as the nigger boy discovered—make your ears sticky ; currants, when you have removed the skin and extracted the seeds, are unsatisfying ; blackberries have the faults of raspberries without their virtues ; plums are never ripe. Yet all these fruits are excellent in their season. Their faults are faults which we can forgive during a slight acquaintance, which indeed seem but pleasant little idiosyncrasies in the stranger. But we could not live with them.

Yet with the orange we do live year in and year out. That speaks well for the orange. The fact is that there is an honesty about the orange which appeals to all of us. If it is going to be bad—for the best of us are bad sometimes—it begins to be bad

69

from the outside, not from the inside. How many a pear which presents a blooming face to the world is rotten at the core. How many an innocent-looking apple is harbouring a worm in the bud. But the orange has no secret faults. Its outside is a mirror of its inside, and if you are quick you can tell the shopman so before he slips it into the bag.

From " Not That It Matters "

OF TIMES AND SEASONS

THE DOODLE DOO

DIXON SCOTT

IN a very little book which has just been published an anonymous thinker tackles a very big problem —one of the most leaden and inveterate, indeed, of all the problems that go to make up the burden of the mystery of things : the problem that crouches hideously on every pillow in the world, that fouls every dawn with its presence, that robs sleep of half its virtue, and makes midnight festivals, be they never so innocent, mere hollow mockeries and gawds. We refer, of course, to the problem of Getting Up. We all have to get up ; we all have to get up every day ; and it is to a renewed consideration of that appalling and inevitable diurnal agony that the writer of this little book invites his readers. Invites them, too, in the most uncompromising fashion. Witness his rich title, *The Early Bird* : a title whose deep allusiveness not the most phlegmatic of readers will be able to resist. Witness, again, the piece of poignant symbolism appended to the title, which makes his dolorous subject-matter superlatively plain : a striking and convincing representation of a Crowing Cock. Could any more fitting or impressive emblem have been utilized ? Mr Barrie, that fine mystic and philosopher, knew its puissance when he used it with such grim effect in his great symbolical tragedy of *Peter Pan*. He desired, the reader will recollect, to crush that defiant and blood-boltered miscreant Hook beneath the weight of some intolerable doom, and he could

73

think of no more powerful engine than the dreadful long-drawn cry of the Doodle Doo.

But while it is with imaginations of this high order that our author's title-page inclines us to associate him, the book that follows ranks him, as a philosopher, on a vastly inferior level. For he is one of those self-mortifying fanatics who believe that to tighten bonds is to lighten burdens, that to intensify the agony is to minimize the hurt, that the solution of this great Problem of Getting Up is—to get up earlier ! Turning the pages with a fluttering eagerness, hoping against hope that here at last may be some way of escape from the diurnal agony, what does the reader descry ? He descries, written again and again in flaring majuscules, the astounding phrase, " Rise In Summer At Five, In Winter At Six." In the name of Morpheus, what phantasy is this ? Why should we scourge ourselves thus gratuitously ? Because, responds the author proudly, because the farmer does. But we—we are not Farmers ; we are civilians— merchants, chemists, numismatists, office-boys ; why should we fling aside the resources of our hardly-won civilization—the 8.30 express, the swift electric car— in order to vie with some thrice miserable bucolics ? Because the sparrows twitter and the starlings pipe at five o'clock in the summer, urges our friend. Are we, then, to be hounded into flagellation by a lot of gibbering birds ? But it is better for your health, he runs on. 'Tis a retort that smacks of foolishness. Since when was health to be captured by curtailing sleep ? What has become of all our " Nature's sweet restorer " beliefs ? But you must make the sleep up the night before, he protests ; and there, we think, we have him on the hip.

For why should one deliberately squander a couple

of hours of fireside domesticity, of earnest study, of friendly intercourse, of patronage of the English Drama, for the sake of strolling emptily about an unwarmed garden, or crouching drearily over an ash-filled grate, an hour and a half before breakfast announces the true beginning of the day ? There are only two possible answers. Of these, one is " *O vanitas, O mores.*" It is probably sheer vanity, colossal and detestable egotism, that induces you, Mr Anonymous Self-Mortifier, to make that aimless pilgrimage among a lot of unintelligent sparrows. You hope, secretly, that your neighbour's blind may suddenly run up, that your neighbour may be consumed with admiration for your extraordinary energy. The night before, no doubt, when you were stealing stodgily to bed, he was busy among his friends, playing his due, sociable part, pursuing some course of study, benefiting the world by writing articles on Doodle Doos. You shirked these things ; you stole hoggishly to bed ; and now, since you have failed to achieve a legitimate distinction, you hope to become adventitiously distinctive. You would steal a march on your fellows ; and that, a march without a goal. And if you protest that you have a goal you simply take refuge in the other answer, the deplorable argument which the vulgar believe they finely enforce when they say that " The early bird catches the worm." It is an argument whose essential baseness is easily disclosed. For the man who goes out into the world with that motto in his head, goes out with the deliberate intention of shirking his first duty as a worker. He goes out determined not to make something, but to take something. He is not going to create, he is going to appropriate. He is not going to rely on a just reward for his own personal capacities ; he is going to get up before Justice is awakened, and while the world's back is turned to him, and steal, not only a march, but everything unguarded that his march may lead him to. He is a tramp; and all tramps are lazy. And the mark and measure of his secret and essential laziness is the fact that he gets up a stealthy hour and a half before his fellows.

From "A Number of Things"

THE TOWN WEEK

E. V. LUCAS

IT is odd that 'Mondayish' is the only word which the days of the week have given us; since Monday is not alone in possessing a positive and peculiar character. Why not 'Tuesdayish' or 'Wednesdayish'? Each word would convey as much meaning to me, 'Tuesdayish' in particular, for Monday's cardinal and reprehensible error of beginning the business week seems to me almost a virtue compared with Tuesday's utter flatness. To begin a new week is no fault at all, though tradition has branded it as one. To begin is a noble accomplishment; but to continue dully, to be the tame follower of a courageous beginner, to be the second day in a week of action, as in Tuesday's case—that is deplorable, if you like.

Monday can be flat enough, but in a different way from Tuesday. Monday is flat because one has been idling, perhaps unconsciously absorbing notions of living like the lilies; because so many days must pass before the week ends; because yesterday is no more. But Tuesday has the sheer essential flatness of nonentity; Tuesday is nothing. If you would know how absolutely nothing it is, go to a week-end hotel at, say Brighton, and stay on after the Saturday-to-Monday population has flitted. On Tuesday you touch the depths. So does the menu—no *chef* ever exerted himself for a Tuesday guest. Tuesday is also very difficult to spell, many otherwise cultured ladies putting the *e* before the *u*; and why not? What right has Tuesday to any preference?

With all its faults, Monday has a positive character. Monday brings a feeling of revolt ; Tuesday, the base craven, reconciles us to the machine. I am not surprised that the recent American revivalists held no meetings on Mondays. It was a mark of their astuteness ; they knew that the wear and tear of overcoming the Monday feeling of the greater part of their audience would exhaust them before their magnetism began to have play ; while a similarly stubborn difficulty would confront them in the remaining portion sunk in apathy by the thought that to-morrow would be Tuesday. It is this presage of certain tedium which has robbed Monday evening of its " glittering star." Yet since nothing so becomes a flat day as the death of it, Tuesday evening's glittering star (it is Wordsworth's phrase) is of the brightest— for is not the dreary day nearly done, and is not to-morrow Wednesday the bland ?

With Wednesday, the week stirs itself, turns over, begins to wake. There are matinées on Wednesday ; on Wednesdays some of the more genial weekly papers come out. The very word has a good honest round air—Wednesday. Things, adventures, might happen very naturally on Wednesday ; but that nothing ever happened on a Tuesday I am convinced. In summer Wednesday has often close finishes at Lord's, and it is a day on which one's friends are pretty sure to be accessible. On Monday they may not have returned from the country ; on Friday they have begun to go out of town again ; but on Wednesday they are here, at home—are solid. I am sure it is my favourite day.

(Even politicians, so slow as a rule to recognize the kindlier, more generous, side of life, realized for many years that Wednesday was a day on which they had no right to conduct their acrimonious business for

more than an hour or so. Much of the failure of the
last Government may be traced to their atheistical
decision no longer to remember Wednesday to keep
it holy.)

On Thursday the week falls back a little ; the
stirring of Wednesday is forgotten ; there is a return
to the folding of the hands. I am not sure that
Thursday has not become the real day of rest. That
it is a good honest day is the most that can be said
for it. It is certainly not Thor's day any longer—if
my reading of the character of the blacksmith-god is
true. There is nothing strong and downright and
fine about it. Compared with Tuesday's small beer,
Thursday is almost champagne ; but none the less
they are related. One can group them together. If
I were a business man, I should, I am certain, sell my
shares at a loss on Monday and at a profit on Wednesday and Friday, but on Tuesday and Thursday I
should get for them exactly what I gave.

I group Friday with Wednesday as a day that can
be friendly to me, but it has not Wednesday's quality.
Wednesday is calm, assured, urbane ; Friday allows
itself to be a little flurried and excited. Wednesday
stands alone ; Friday to some extent throws in its
lot with Saturday. Friday is too busy. Too many
papers come out, too many bags are packed, on
Friday. But herein, of course, is some of its virtue ;
it is the beginning of the end, the forerunner of Saturday and Sunday. If anticipation, as the moralists say,
is better than the realization, Friday is perhaps the
best day of the week, for one spends much of it in
thinking of the morrow and what of good it should
bring forth. Friday's greatest merit is perhaps that
it paves the way to Saturday and the cessation of work.
That it ever was really unlucky I greatly doubt.

And so we come to Saturday and Sunday. But here the analyst falters, for Saturday and Sunday pass from the region of definable days. Monday and Tuesday, Wednesday and Thursday and Friday, these are days with a character fixed more or less for all. But Saturday and Sunday are what we individually make of them. In one family they are friends, associates ; in another as ill-assorted as Socrates and Xantippe. For most of us Saturday is not exactly a day at all, it is a collection of hours, part work, part pleasure, and all restlessness. It is a day that we plan for, and therefore it is often a failure. I have no distinct and unvarying impression of Saturday, except that trains are full and late and shops shut too early.

Sunday even more than Saturday is different as people are different. To the godly it is a day of low tones, its minutes go by muffled ; to the children of the godly it is eternity. To the ungodly it is a day jeopardized by an interest in barometers that is almost too poignant. To one man it is an interruption of the week ; to another it is the week itself, and all the rest of the days are but preparations for it. One cannot analyze Saturday and Sunday.

But Monday ? There we are on solid ground again. Monday—but I have discussed Monday already : that is one of its principal characteristics, that it is always coming round again, pretending to be new. It is always the same in reality.

From " Fireside and Sunshine "

ON CHRISTMAS

ROBERT LYND

THERE is a cant of Christmas, and there is a cant of anti-Christmas. There are some people who want to throw their arms round you simply because it is Christmas ; there are other people who want to strangle you simply because it is Christmas. Thus between those who appreciate and those who depreciate Christmas, it is difficult for an ordinary man to escape bruises. As I grow older, I confess, I accept Christmas more philosophically than I used to do. There was a time when it seemed a dangerous institution, like home life or going to church. One felt that in undermining its joys one was making a breach in the defences of an ancient hypocrisy. Still more, one resented the steady boredom of the day— the boredom of a day from which one had been led to expect larger ecstasies than a surfeit of dishes and the explosion of crackers can give. One might have enjoyed it well enough, perhaps, if one had not had the feeling that it was one's duty to be happy. But to be deliberately happy for a whole day was a task as exhausting as deliberately hopping with one's feet tied. It was not that one wanted to be unhappy. It was merely that one desired one's liberty to be either as happy or as miserable as one pleased.

Remembering these early hostilities, I will not bid anyone be happy or merry or jolly on Christmas Day, except as the turkey and plum-pudding move them. At the same time, I cannot let the festival pass without recanting my childish insolence towards the holly and mistletoe. I have been converted to Christmas as thoroughly almost as that prince of individualists, Scrooge. I can now pull a cracker with any man ; I can accept gifts without actual discourtesy ; and if the flame goes out before the plum-pudding reaches me, I am as mortified as can be. The Christmas tree shines with the host of the stars, and I can even forgive my neighbour who plays " While shepherds watched " all day long on the gramophone. The Salvation Army, which plays the same tune and one or two others all through the small hours on the trombone and the cornet-à-piston, is a severer test of endurance. But even that one can grin and bear when one remembers that the Salvationist bandsmen are but a sort of melancholy herald angels. The solitary figure in the Christmas procession, indeed, whom one hates with a boiling and bubbling hatred, is the postman who does not call. In Utopia the postman does not miss a letter-box on Christmas Day. Or on any other day.

It would be affectation to pretend, however, that one has suddenly developed a craving for plum-pudding and cracker-mottoes in one's middle age. One's reconcilement with Christmas is due neither to one's stomach nor to a taste for the wit and wisdom of cracker manufacturers. It is simply that one has come to enjoy a season of lordly inutility, when for the space of a day or two the cash-nexus hangs upon the world as light as air. It is no small thing to have this upsetting of the tyrannies, if it is only for a few hours. The heathen, as we call them, realized this even before the birth of Christ, and had the Saturnalia and other festivals of the kind in which a communism of licence ruled, if not a communism of gentleness. It is still an instinct in many Christian places to turn Christmas into a general orgy—to make it a day on which one bows down and worships the human maw.

(And there are worse things in the world than brandy-sauce.) On the other hand, there is also the instinct to make of the day a door into a new world of neighbourliness. It is the only day in the year on which many men speak humanly to their servants and open their eyes to the cheerful lives of children and simple people. Hypercritical youth will deny that man has a right to confine his neighbourliness to a single day in the year any more than he has a right to confine his sanctity to the Sabbath. But we who have ceased to exact miracles from human nature are glad to have even a single day as a beginning. Socialism, we may admit, depends upon the extension of the Christmas festival into the rest of the year. It demands that the relations between man and man shall be, as far as possible, not shop-keeping relations, but Christmas relations. In other words, it aims at a society in which the little conquests of gain will cease to be the chief end of time, and men will no more think of cheating each other than Romeo would think of cheating Juliet. Nor is there any other side of the new civilization which will be more difficult to build than this. This is the very spirit of the new city. Without it the rest would be but a chaos of stones and mortar—a Gehenna of purposeless machinery.

It is an extraordinary fact that the rediscovery of Christmas in the nineteenth century was not followed sooner by the rediscovery of the limitations of individualism. Dickens himself, the incarnation of Christmas, did not realize till quite late in life what a denial modern civilization is of the Christmas spirit. Even in *Hard Times*, where, as Mr Shaw pointed out, he expresses the insurrection of the human conscience against a Manchesterized society, he offers us no hope except from the spread of a sort of Tory benevolence.

Perhaps, however, it does not matter how you label benevolence so long as it is the real thing and is not merely another name for that most insidious form of egotism—patronage. That Dickens was pugnaciously benevolent in all his work—except when he was writing about Dissenters and Americans—was one of the most fortunate accidents in the popular literature of the nineteenth century. He did not, perhaps, dramatize the secret mystery of human brotherhood—the brotherhood of saint and fool and criminal and ordinary man—as Tolstoi and Dostoevsky have done in some of their work. But he dramatized goodwill with a thoroughness never attempted before in England.

On the whole it may be doubted whether the Christmas spirit has not grown stronger and deeper since the time of Dickens. Only a few years ago it seemed as though it were dying. People began to detest even Christmas cards as something more Victorian than the *Idylls of the King*. But here the old enthusiasm is back again, and we can no more kill Christmas than the lion could kill Androcles. Perhaps the popularization of Italian art, as well as Dickens, has something to do with it. Our imagination cannot escape from the Virgin and the Child, and we are like children ourselves in the inquisitiveness with which we peer into that magic stable where the ass and the cow worship and the shepherds and the kings and the little angels in their nightgowns are on their knees. There has come back a gaiety, a playfulness, into the picture, such as our grandfathers might have thought irreverent, but their grandfathers' grandfathers, on the other hand, would have seen to be perfectly natural. The cult of the child has, perhaps, been overdone in recent years, and we have brought our mawkishness and our morbid analysis even to the side of the cradle. At the same time, no one has yet been able to point out a way by which we can escape from the obsession of rates and taxes, of profit and loss, except by the recovery of the child's vision. Without that vision, religion itself becomes a matter of profit and loss. With that vision the dullest world blossoms with flowers; even truisms cease to be meaningless; and Christmas is itself again. Out of the drowning of the world have we made a toy for the nursery, and the birth of the King of Glory has become the theme of a song for infants.

One of the most exquisite pictures in literature is that of the three ships that come sailing into Bethlehem " on Christmas Day, in the morning"; and not less childishly beautiful is that other short carol:

> There comes a ship far sailing then,
> Saint Michael was the steersman,
> Saint John sat in the horn;
> Our Lord harped, our Lady sang,
> And all the bells of Heaven they rang,
> On Christ's Sunday at morn.

One sees the same childish imagination at work in the old English carol, " Hail, comely and clean," in which the three shepherds come to the inn stable with their gifts, the first with " a bob of cherries " for the new-born baby, the second with a bird, and the third with a tennis-ball. " Hail," cries the third shepherd—

> " Hail, darling dear, full of godheed!
> I pray Thee be near, when that I have need.
> Hail! sweet Thy cheer! My heart would bleed
> To see Thee sit here in so poor weed,
> With no pennies.
> Hail! put forth Thy dall!
> I bring Thee but a ball,
> Have and play Thee withal,
> And go to the tennis."

These songs, it may be, are more popular to-day than they were fifty years ago—partly owing to the decline of the old-fashioned suspicious sort of Protestantism, which saw the Pope behind every bush—including the holly-bush. One remembers how Protestants of the old school used to denounce even Raphael's grave Madonnas as trash of Popery. "I'll have no Popish pictures in my house," declared a man I know to his son, who had brought home the Sistine Madonna to hang on his walls ; and the picture had to be given away to a friend. Similarly the observance of Christmas Day was regarded in some places as a Popish superstition. One old Protestant clergyman many years ago used to make the rounds of his friends and parishioners on Christmas morning to wish them the compliments of the day. It was his custom, however, to pray with each of them, and in the course of his prayers to explain that he must not be regarded as taking Christmas Day seriously. "Lord," he would pray, "we are not gathered here in any superstitious spirit, as the Roman Catholics are, under the delusion that Thy Son was born in Bethlehem on the twenty-fifth of December. Hast not Thou told us in Thy Holy Book that on the night on which Thy Son was born the shepherds watched their flocks by night in the open air ? And Thou knowest, O Lord, that in the fierce and inclement weather of December, with its biting frosts and its whirling snows, this would not have been possible, and can be but a Popish invention." But, having set himself right with God, he was human enough to proceed on his journey of good wishes. Noble intolerance like his is now, I believe, dead. To-day even a Plymouth Brother may wreathe his brow with mistletoe, and a Presbyterian may wish you a merry Christmas without the sky or the Shorter Catechism falling.

From " The Book of This and That "

ESSAYS OF TO-DAY

LOSING ONE'S TRAIN

VERNON LEE

THE clocks up at the villa must have been all wrong, or else my watch did not go with them, or else I had not looked often enough at it while rambling about the town on my way to the station. Certain it is that when I got there, at the gallop of my cab-horse, the express was gone. There is something hatefully inexorable about expresses : it is useless to run after them, even in Italy. The next train took an hour and a quarter instead of forty minutes to cover the nineteen miles between Pistoia and Florence. Moreover, that next train was not till eight in the evening, and it was now half-past five.

I felt all it was proper to feel on the occasion, and said, if anything, rather more. Missing a train is a terrible business, even if you miss nothing else in consequence ; and the inner disarray, the blow and wrench to thoughts and feelings, is most often far worse than any mere upsetting of arrangements. A chasm suddenly gapes between present and future, and the river of life flows backwards, if but for a second. It is most fit and natural to lose one's temper ; but the throwing out of so much moral ballast does not help one to overtake that train. I mention this, lest I should pass for heartless ; and now proceed to say that, after a few minutes given to wrath and lamentation, I called the cab back and went in search of a certain very ancient church, containing a very ancient pulpit, which I had never

87

succeeded in seeing before. Exactly as on previous occasions, when I got to the farm where the key of that church was kept, the key had gone to town in the pocket of the peasant. He would be back, no doubt, at nightfall. But I had not very much expected the church to be open, so I felt perfectly indifferent at not seeing the pulpit—nay, if anything, a little relieved, as one does sometimes when friends prove *not at home*.

I walked up a long steep track to the little battered, black, fast-locked church, which stands all alone under some oak trees. The track was through thin hillside woods. Such divine woods ! young oak and acacia, and an undergrowth of grass and ferns, of full-blown roses thrown across the grass ; and here and there, dark in that pale young green, a cypress. The freshness of evening came all of a sudden, and with it a scent of every kind of leaf and herb and fern, and the sweetness of the ripening corn all round. And when I got to the ridge, slippery with dry cut grass, what should I see in front of me, over the olive-yards and the wooded slopes, but the walls and towers of Serra-valle, which have beckoned to my fancy almost ever since my childhood. I sat there a long while in the June sunset and very nearly missed the second train, which it had seemed intolerable to wait for.

This is an allegory, and I commend its application to the wise and gentle reader. There are more of such symbolical trains lost than real ones, even by the most travelled mortals, Odysseus or a bag-man. And such losing of trains is not inevitably a blessing. I have often written about life with optimistic heartlessness, because life, on the whole, has been uncommonly kind to me, and because one is nearer the truth when cheerful than when depressed. But this is the place for a brief interlude of pessimism. For it

is all very well to make the best of losing trains when
we have time, cabs, and a fine view at hand ; and
when in losing the train we lose nothing else, except
our temper. But surely 'tis no ingratitude towards
life's great mercies and blessings to discriminate them
from life's buffets and bruisings. And methinks that
the teaching of courage or resignation might fitly
begin by the recognition of the many cases where only
courage or resignation avails, because they are
thoroughly bad. There is something stupid and
underbred at times in the attitude of saints and
stoics—at least in their books. When Rachel weepeth
for her children, we have no business to come round
hawking our consolation ; we should stand aside,
unless we can cradle her to sleep in our arms. And
if we refuse to weep, 'tis not because there is not
matter enough for weeping, but because we require
our strength and serenity to carry her through her
trouble. Pain, dear cheerful friends, is pain ; and
grief, grief ; and if our own complete human efficiency
requires the acquaintance thereof, 'tis because the
knowledge of their violence and of their wiles is needed
for our own protection and the helping of other folk.
Evil comes from the gods, no doubt ; but so do all
things ; and to extract good from it—the great Prome-
theus-feat of man—is not to evil's credit, but to the
credit of good. The contrary doctrine is a poison to
the spirit, though a poison of medicinal use in moments
of anguish, a bromide or an opiate.

I am speaking, therefore, only of such contingencies
as will bear comparison, without silly stoicism, to the
missing of a train. Much of the good such disappointments may contain is of the nature of education, and
most of it a matter of mere novelty. Without suspect-
ing it, we are all suffering from lack of new departures ;

and life would no doubt be better if we tried a few more things, and gave the hidden, neglected possibilities a greater chance. Change as such is often fruitful of improvement, exposing to renovating air and rains the hard, exhausted soil of our souls, turning up new layers and helping on life's chemistry. The thwarting of our cherished plans is beneficial, because our plans are often mere routine, born not of wisdom, but of inertness. In our endless treadmill of activity, in our ceaseless rumination, we are, as a fact, neither acting nor thinking ; and life, secretly at a standstill, ceases to produce any good. There was no reason for taking that express and getting back two or three hours sooner to my house : no one required me, nothing needed doing. Yet, unless I had lost that train I should not have dreamed of taking that walk, of making that little journey of discovery, in a delightful unknown place.

There is another source of good hidden in disappointment. For it is disappointment rather than age (age getting the credit for what it merely witnesses) which teaches us to work into life's scheme certain facts, frequently difficult of acceptance ; trying to make them, as all reality should be, causes of strength rather than of weakness. Painful facts ? Or rather, perhaps, only painful contradictions to certain pleasant delusions, founded on nothing save their pleasantness, and taken for granted—who knows how long ?— without proof and without questioning. Facts concerning not merely success, love, personal contact, but also one's own powers and possibilities for good, what the world is able to receive at one's hands, as much as of what the world can give to one.

But the knowledge which disappointment gives, to those wishing to learn from it, has a higher usefulness than practical application. It constitutes a view of life, a certain contemplative attitude which, in its active resignation, in its domination of reality by intelligent acquiescence, gives continuity, peace, and dignity. And here my allegory finds its completion. For what compensated me after my lost train and all my worry and vexation of spirit ? Nothing to put in my pocket or swell my luggage, not even a kingdom, such as made up for the loss of poor Saul's asses ; but an impression of sunset freshness and sweetness among ripening corn and delicate leaves, and a view, unexpected, solemn, and charming, with those long-forgotten distant walls and towers which I shall never reach, and which have beckoned to me from my childhood.

Such is the allegory, or morality, of the Lost Train.

From " Hortus Vitæ "

AUTUMN

ROGER WRAY

SPRING is a serenade, but autumn is a nocturne. In the waning of the year, the world is full of sombre solemnity and a pathetic sense of old age. I have gleaned this information by reading poems on the subject.

> The melancholy days are come, the saddest of the year,
> Of wailing winds, and naked woods, and meadows brown
> and sere.

So begins the dirge of William Cullen Bryant.

> Yes, the year is growing old,
> And his eye is pale and bleared.

This is from Longfellow, and the poet proceeds to compare autumn to the insane old King Lear. Wordsworth speaks of the " pensive " beauty of autumn, but to Shelley—

> The year
> On the earth, her deathbed, in a shroud of leaves dead
> Is lying.

And Hood's admirable little poem ends :

> But here the autumn melancholy dwells,
> And sighs her tearful spells,
> Among the sunless shadows of the plain.

All of which is most impressive ; and reading it to an accompaniment of minor music, rendered by wind-demons in the keyhole, it convinced me absolutely. Accordingly, when I went a long ramble through the countryside this morning I was fully prepared to observe the sad tokens of Nature's senility and decay.

But a glorious surprise met me at the outset, and changed my mood from lamentation to exultation. I passed from the dismal poetic fiction to the actual glowing fact; from mournful reverie to mighty revelry. And all the predictions of the gloomy poets were scattered like the autumn leaves. For who can look at the blaze of autumn colours and declare them solemn? Who can drink deep draughts of the autumn gales and talk about senility?

Autumn is youthful, mirthful, frolicsome—the child of summer's joy—and on every side there are suggestions of juvenility and mischief. While spring is a careful artist who paints each flower with delicate workmanship, autumn flings whole pots of paint about in wildest carelessness. The crimson and scarlet colours reserved for roses and tulips are splashed on the brambles till every bush is aflame, and the old creeper-covered house blushes like a sunset.

The violet paint is smeared grotesquely on the riotous foliage; daffodil and crocus dyes are emptied over limes and chestnuts. Our eyes surfeit themselves on the gorgeous feast of colours—purple, mauve, vermilion, saffron, russet, silver, copper, bronze, and old gold. The leaves are dipped and soaked in fiery hues, and the mischievous 'artist' will never rest till he has used up every drop. Yet Shelley gazed at the pantomime-woods and declared (amid all the pomp and pageantry) that the year was on her deathbed, and this was her shroud!

Why do the poets feel that autumn is ancient? He romps over the earth, chasing the puppy-like gales, making them scamper over the mirrored pools, and ruffling their surface till the water-reeds hiss him away.

He revels in boisterous gaiety, playing pranks like a schoolboy on the first day of his holidays. He turns on the rain-taps to try the effect ; he daubs a few toadstools blood-red ; he switches on summer sunshine for an hour, and then lets loose a tempest. He torments the stately trees, tears their foliage off in handfuls, rocks them backwards and forwards till they groan, and then scampers away for a brief interval leaving heavenly peace behind him. The fallen leaves are set racing down the lane. With madcap destructiveness he wastes his own handiwork, stripping the finery from the woods and forests. The bare trees sigh and shiver, but he mocks them with howls and caterwaulings. Then he sets the bracken afire and pauses to admire the October tints. Finally, with deceptive golden sunshine, he tempts the sage out of doors, suddenly drenches him, and drives him home saturated to the skin. The sage thereupon changes his raiment, and murmurs about the solemnity of the dying year and the pensive beauties of autumn !

The whole spirit of autumn is frolicsome and changeful as that of an eager child. The 'solemn tints' are the grotesque hues of the harlequin, and the 'mournful winds' are suggestive of young giants playing leapfrog over the tree-tops. The lengthening period of darkness is a reminder of the long sleep of a healthy child, and when the sun awakes each autumn morning he rubs his misty eyes and wonders what antics he will see before bed-time.

Spring is a lovely maiden ; Summer a radiant bride ; but Autumn is a tomboy whose occasional quietness is more alarming than his noisiest escapades.

IN THOSE DAYS

SOME LONDON MEMORIES

A. ST. JOHN ADCOCK

I HAVE read so much about vanished London that I can sometimes nearly persuade myself that I have personal recollections of streets and odd corners of it which I know as a fact passed out of visible existence long before I was born. They may indeed—for I realize them so clearly—be actual recollections of a former existence when I occupied another body and walked about in knee breeches and a cocked hat. Anyhow, there are moods in which, loitering past the Law Courts, for instance, I seem to have memories of a much narrower Strand, and of that ancient Butcher's Row which filled the same line of frontage there in the remote days of the first George—that huddled row of toppling peaked gabled shops that Gay pictures in his Trivia as having strings of combs and other merchandise dangling from their low penthouses into the faces of those who passed by on the strip of broken pavement. And I am satisfied that Bell Yard is one of the identical greenmarket lanes that Gay describes in his poem as opening on the Strand hereabouts and being occasionally choked with colliers' carts.

Before it had sobered into the dull, colourless respectable lane it is to-day, Bell Yard was a frowsy, squalid, decaying thoroughfare of antiquated houses, some of which must have been coeval with the quaint shops of Butcher's Row. I knew it then, when the Law Courts were as fresh as they were called the

SOME LONDON MEMORIES

A. ST JOHN ADCOCK

I HAVE read so much about vanished London that I can sometimes nearly persuade myself that I have personal recollections of streets and odd corners of it which I know as a fact passed out of visible existence long before I was born. They may, indeed—for I realize them so clearly—be actual recollections of a former existence when I occupied another body and walked about in knee breeches and a cocked hat. Anyhow, there are moods in which, loitering past the Law Courts, for instance, I seem to have memories of a much narrower Strand, and of that ancient Butcher's Row which filled the same line of frontage there in the remote days of the first George—that huddled row of toppling, peaked, gabled shops that Gay pictures in his *Trivia* as having strings of combs and other merchandise dangling from their low penthouses into the faces of those who passed by on the strip of broken pavement. And I am satisfied that Bell Yard is one of the identical attenuated lanes that Gay describes in his poem as opening on the Strand hereabouts and being occasionally choked with colliers' carts.

Before it had sobered into the dull, colourless, respectable lane it is to-day, Bell Yard was a frowsy, slummy, decaying thoroughfare of antiquated houses, some of which must have been coeval with the quaint shops of Butcher's Row. I knew it then, when the Law Courts were so fresh that they were called the

New Law Courts, and the builders were still busy about them. The western side of Bell Yard had already been wiped out to leave the Courts a breathing space, and the surviving side was faced by stacks of bricks and a general litter of building material.

One of those frowsy Bell Yard shops sold second-hand furniture and shoddy curios ; above it there lodged a certain solicitor who was a Commissioner for Oaths, and I, having an affidavit to make in connexion with some legal proceedings, was recommended to patronize him because he was driving a brisk trade by illegally competing with other Commissioners and swearing affidavits for a shilling instead of eighteen-pence. Entering by a musty, pinched side door, I mounted a groaning staircase behind the back wall of the shop. Stairs and flooring were soft and crumbly under the feet ; the air smelt of dry rot ; and when I opened a door on the second floor it let me into a dirty, neglected, stuffy little room that contained nothing but piles of worm-eaten boxes, a nest of mouldy pigeon-holes, a crippled chair with straw stuffing sticking out of it shamelessly, a bow-legged table strewn with soiled papers, and seated at it a blinking, snuffy, damaged-looking old man with untidy grey hair. He must have been eighty at least : a worn, furtive, spectacled, disreputable old sinner who had outlived his practice and derived a shuffling liveli-hood wholly from administering oaths at less than the statutory fee.

I gave him my affidavit, and he mechanically handed me an amazingly dilapidated small volume tied round with tape that had once been pink. As he filled up and signed his part of the document, he ejaculated nothing more of the customary form of oath than a " So help you God. Kiss the book ! " and I confess

I kissed the cleanest part of it warily. Its leather covers were worn to a spongy, yellow nap ; its leaves protruded torn and ragged edges round all four sides of it.

" I suppose," I remarked in jest, " this really is a Testament ? "

He glanced across at the book strangely, as if he had not noticed it for some time ; took it from my hand, plucked at the bow of the tape, and the whole thing tumbled to pieces.

" There you are," he muttered, fluttering the flimsy pages. " Matthew—Mark—What more do you want ? "

He turned to the fly-leaf, and moving a grubby forefinger under an inscription there began to chuckle inanely.

" Look at that ! See ? " he said, pushing it towards me across the table and gurgling and chuckling softly, with his finger keeping the place as I read. There was his name written in thin, sloping, faded characters, and beneath it : " With fondest love from Annie " ; then the name of some country-sounding place and a date that was more than half a century gone. " I was a good boy then," he chuckled. " My sweetheart gave me that. She married somebody else, though, and Lord knows where she is now—but there you are—it's a Testament right enough ! "

He shook it together, and began twisting the tape round it again, and I was still sufficiently young to be oddly touched by the thought of that little country girl, grown old or in her grave, and this insensate old rascal, in pursuit of shillings, letting her sacred gift out to be desecrated by alien lips.

But that is typical of all London. Scrape its new paint, or sweep aside its accumulated dust, and you are sure to uncover something of shattered or forgotten romance.

When I first went up and down Fleet Street, a small boy of twelve, Temple Bar was standing where now the Griffin ramps, and I recall lingering late one night to watch the workmen pulling down the Bar by the flare of many naphtha lamps, with the weird arm of a giant crane groping high into the dark above them and thrusting down its iron claws to pick off the loosened stones and lower them into the road. The grim, ancient barrier had been shored up with stout beams throughout my brief acquaintance with it ; its narrow gateways on the pavements pleased me, and I had grown accustomed to seeing the buses crawling slowly in and out under its wider central arch, but I knew little more of its history than that the heads of traitors used to be spiked on its roof, or I might have been conscious that the shadows of Dr Johnson, of Goldsmith, of Lamb, and other of the immortals, paused beside me there that night, and looked wistfully on with me at the woeful demolition.

So on sentimental grounds I have resented the presence of the Griffin ever since he made his appearance on that site. On the same grounds I shall never be reconciled to the improvements that have been made in Cheapside. There is a lofty, pompous stone building—a bank or insurance office—opposite the Mansion House, at the corner of Prince's Street and Poultry—that I regard with invincible dislike because it has shut out the cosy, picturesque old London tavern that once upon a time belonged there : a sleepy, rural-looking hostelry, it had a bumpy, red-tiled roof, two steps leading down into its sanded bar, and on the edge of the kerb opposite was a standpipe with several squat green buckets clustered around it. Beside the standpipe, a rheumaticky, antiquated man dozed on a stool in the sun, when it was summer, and in winter stamped up and down wrapped in an over-coat, some mufflers and old sacking to keep out the cold. At intervals he would stoop to the tap and set the water gushing into the buckets, and slop it over the pavement, and proceed to quench the thirst of the bus horses that made this their stopping place, whilst the driver climbed from his seat, descended the two steps into the bar, and quenched his own.

That such a leisurely business could ever have been transacted here, close under the eye of the Mansion House, seems incredible when you push and struggle at this corner among the swarming, roaring, congested, sternly practical traffic to-day; but I saw it and know that it was; and occasionally now, when I traverse the empty stretch of Cheapside towards midnight, when the whole place is eerily quiet and unreal in the lamplight and the starlight, I round the bend of the Poultry and come within sight of that corner of Prince's Street keenly prepared to discover that, at such a witching hour, the comfortable old inn has reasserted itself and the stone insurance premises have shredded away smoke-like and left it unveiled to the night.

London is statelier, more magnificent than it used to be, but what it has gained in splendour it has lost in homeliness and in picturesqueness. Anybody strolling along Holborn can see and admire the imposing new buildings that have sprung up there in the last few years, but I would gladly give half a dozen of the largest of them, if they were mine, to be able to restore to that Holborn byway, Brooke Street, the common little house in whose attic Chatterton died. I would even give two or three of them to bring back that curious old milk shop which snoozed until recently in the yard at the top of Brooke Street—

a crazy wooden shop that, in its youth, basked amid
fields, but, when I knew it, was hemmed in by squalid
courts and alleys, and its green pastures buried under
cobbles and paving stones, though it still kept above
its door a mellow, dim, three-century-old signboard
with browsing cattle painted on it and an announcement that new milk was supplied from its own cows
which were milked twice daily at hours that were
duly specified.

Some day, when Kingsway is a fine, respectably
finished thoroughfare, nobody will remember the
squalor of its predecessor, Clare Market, nor the
indescribable atmosphere of romance that brooded
over its dense, unwholesome, glamorous tangle of
mean streets. Soon there will be nobody who can
rightly remember Old Serjeants' Inn and the broad
archway that opened into it out of Chancery Lane ;
and it troubles me sometimes to wonder what has
become of the grotesque old ghost who had his home
under that archway.

When I first knew London, you went through the
arch, across the Inn, and round to the left to get to
a row of low buildings that extended along a terrace
overlooking the garden-square of Clifford's Inn. These
dwellings were those Judges' Chambers described in
Pickwick—where the lawyers' clerks used to gather
and raise a babel with shouting the names of the firms
whose representatives they wanted to meet on business ;
and in those days there always stood under the arch
an obese, triple-chinned, shabby, elderly man who
watched the stream of lawyers' clerks hurrying by all
the morning, and when he could catch the eye of one
of them he would duck, and duck ingratiatingly, and
thrust forth a grimy hand to offer a pinch from his
snuff-box. I never saw him do anything else, but I

fancy he must have picked up a scanty income by carrying messages for chance clients. I saw him there like that for several years; then one day he was absent from his post, and he never materialized again; but every time I went in under the arch ever after I was aware of him, though others might not have noticed that anything was there, and I knew that if I let him catch my eye he would duck dolefully and offer me an impalpable snuff-box. And now the arch itself is no more and I can know him no longer.

A day will come, too, when nobody will remember the sundial, the flowers and the pleasant garden that Clement's Inn and New Inn used to share between them; nobody will remember the dingy, secretive Wych Street, haunted with rumours of Jack Sheppard, nor the narrow lane of Holywell Street, with its dusky treasure-caverns of old book-shops on both sides of the way. But at present there are, of course, thousands who, like myself, can walk up that maimed section of the Strand where the hoardings are, just beyond St Clement's Church, and still feel the stones of Holywell Street under their feet and be conscious of the shadowy, book-crammed shops brooding to right and left of them.

Oddly enough, though, I can never realize the place thus in winter or dull weather; but often if I pass Clement's Church when all the Strand is flooded with sunlight I hear a sound of ghostly music beginning— the sobbing of a harp, the wail of a cornet, the shrilling of a flute—and straightway, a little beyond the church, I see the sign of the Rising Sun Inn facing me again, and the cramped, crooked alley of Holywell Street yawning near beside it; and a minute later I am passing up that grove of book-shops, the music growing louder and louder, as I have heard it on many a long-gone sunny Saturday afternoon, until I come in sight of the players : three broken, derelict men standing in the shallow bay that gives space for carts to pass each other. Dim-eyed old scholars, all manner of haunters of the second-hand book-shops are lingering to listen, or unconsciously giving an ear to the melody as they saunter from shop to shop poring over the books ; and there—though the shopkeepers are scattered about London and you may notice familiar names of some of them above windows in Charing Cross Road—there so long as I live those three forlorn musicians will always be playing in the sunshine, and until their playing is ended, whatever may be built upon its site, the old street can never pass altogether away.

From " Modern Grub Street "

THE LAST GLEEMAN

W. B. YEATS

MICHAEL MORAN was born about 1794 off Black Pitts, in the Liberties of Dublin, in Faddle Alley. A fortnight after birth he went stone blind from illness, and became thereby a blessing to his parents, who were soon able to send him to rhyme and beg at street corners and at the bridges over the Liffey. They may well have wished that their quiver were full of such as he, for, free from the interruption of sight, his mind became a perfect echoing chamber, where every movement of the day and every change of public passion whispered itself into rhyme or quaint saying. By the time he had grown to manhood he was the admitted rector of all the ballad-mongers of the Liberties. Madden, the weaver, Kearney, the blind fiddler from Wicklow, Martin from Meath, M'Bride from heaven knows where, and that M'Grane, who in after days, when the true Moran was no more, strutted in borrowed plumes, or rather in borrowed rags, and gave out that there had never been any Moran but himself, and many another, did homage before him, and held him chief of all their tribe. Nor despite his blindness did he find any difficulty in getting a wife, but rather was able to pick and choose, for he was just that mixture of ragamuffin and of genius which is dear to the heart of woman, who, perhaps because she is wholly conventional herself, loves the unexpected, the crooked, the bewildering. Nor did he lack despite his rags many excellent things, for it is remembered that he ever loved caper sauce, going so far indeed in his honest indignation at its absence upon one occasion as to fling a leg of mutton at his wife. He was not, however, much to look at, with his coarse frieze coat with its cape and scalloped edge, his old corduroy trousers and great brogues, and his stout stick made fast to his wrist by a thong of leather : and he would have been a woeful shock to the gleeman MacConglinne could that friend of kings have beheld him in prophetic vision from the pillar stone at Cork. And yet though the short cloak and the leather wallet were no more, he was a true gleeman, being alike poet, jester, and newsman of the people. In the morning when he had finished his breakfast, his wife or some neighbour would read the newspaper to him, and read on and on until he interrupted with, " That'll do—I have me meditations " ; and from these meditations would come the day's store of jest and rhyme. He had the whole Middle Ages under his frieze coat.

He had not, however, MacConglinne's hatred of the Church and clergy, for when the fruit of his meditations did not ripen well, or when the crowd called for something more solid, he would recite or sing a metrical tale or ballad of saint or martyr or of Biblical adventure. He would stand at a street corner, and when a crowd had gathered would begin in some such fashion as follows (I copy the record of one who knew him) : " Gather round me, boys, gather round me. Boys, am I standin' in puddle ? am I standin' in wet ? " Thereon several boys would cry, " Ah, no ! yez not ! yer in a nice dry place. Go on with *St Mary* ; go on with *Moses* "—each calling for his favourite tale. Then Moran, with a suspicious wriggle of his body and a clutch at his rags, would burst out with, " All me buzzim friends are turned backbiters ; " and after a final " If yez don't drop your coddin' and deversion I'll lave some of yez a case," by way of warning to the boys, begin his recitation, or perhaps still delay, to ask, " Is there a crowd around me now ? Any blackguard heretic around me ? " The best-known of his religious tales was *St Mary of Egypt*, a long poem of exceeding solemnity, condensed from the much longer work of a certain Bishop Coyle. It told how a fast woman of Egypt, Mary by name, followed pilgrims to Jerusalem for no good purpose, and then, turning penitent on finding herself withheld from entering the Temple by supernatural interference, fled to the desert and spent the remainder of her life in solitary penance. When at last she was at the point of death, God sent Bishop Zozimus to hear her confession, give her the last sacrament, and with the help of a lion, whom He sent also, dig her grave. The poem has the intolerable cadence of the eighteenth century, but was so popular and so often called for that Moran was soon nicknamed Zozimus, and by that name is he remembered. He had also a poem of his own called *Moses*, which went a little nearer poetry without going very near. But he could ill brook solemnity, and before long parodied his own verses in the following ragamuffin fashion :

In Egypt's land, contagious to the Nile,
King Pharaoh's daughter went to bathe in style.
She tuk her dip, then walked unto the land,
To dry her royal pelt she ran along the strand.
A bulrush tripped her, whereupon she saw
A smiling babby in a wad o' straw.
She tuk it up, and said with accents mild,
" Tare-and-agers, girls, which av yez owns the child ? "

His humorous rhymes were, however, more often

quips and cranks at the expense of his contemporaries. It was his delight, for instance, to remind a certain shoemaker, noted alike for display of wealth and for personal uncleanness, of his inconsiderable origin in a song of which but the first stanza has come down to us :

> At the dirty end of Dirty Lane,
> Liv'd a dirty cobbler, Dick Maclane ;
> His wife was in the old king's reign
>> A stout brave orange-woman.
> On Essex Bridge she strained her throat,
> And six-a-penny was her note.
> But Dikey wore a bran-new coat,
>> He got among the yeomen.
> He was a bigot, like his clan,
> And in the streets he wildly sang,
>> O Roly, toly, toly raid, with his old jade.

He had troubles of divers kinds, and numerous inter-lopers to face and put down. Once an officious peeler arrested him as a vagabond, but was triumphantly routed amid the laughter of the court, when Moran reminded his Worship of the precedent set by Homer, who was also, he declared, a poet, and a blind man, and a beggarman. He had to face a more serious difficulty as his fame grew. Various imitators started up upon all sides. A certain actor, for instance, made as many guineas as Moran did shillings by mimicking his sayings and his songs and his get-up upon the stage. One night this actor was at supper with some friends, when a dispute arose as to whether his mimicry was overdone or not. It was agreed to settle it by an appeal to the mob. A forty-shilling supper at a famous coffee-house was to be the wager. The actor took up his station at Essex Bridge, a great haunt of Moran's, and soon gathered a small crowd. He had scarce got through " In Egypt's land, contagious to the Nile," when Moran himself came up, followed by another crowd. The crowds met in great excitement and laughter. "Good Christians," cried the pretender, "is it possible that any man would mock the poor dark man like that?"

"Who's that? It's some imposhterer," replied Moran.

"Begone, you wretch! it's you'ze the imposhterer. Don't you fear the light of heaven being struck from your eyes for mocking the poor dark man?"

"Saints and angels, is there no protection against this? You're a most inhuman blaguard to try to deprive me of my honest bread this way," replied poor Moran.

"And you, you wretch, won't you let me go on with the beautiful poem. Christian people, in your charity won't you beat this man away? he's taking advantage of my darkness."

The pretender, seeing that he was having the best of it, thanked the people for their sympathy and protection, and went on with the poem, Moran listening for a time in bewildered silence. After a while Moran protested again with:

"Is it possible that none of yez can know me? Don't yez see it's myself; and that's some one else?"

"Before I proceed any further in this lovely story," interrupted the pretender, "I call on yez to contribute your charitable donations to help me to go on."

"Have you no sowl to be saved, you mocker of heaven?" cried Moran, put completely beside himself by this last injury. "Would you rob the poor as well as desave the world? O, was ever such wickedness known."

"I leave it to yourselves, my friends," said the pretender, "to give to the real dark man, that you all know so well, and save me from that schemer," and with that he collected some pennies and half-pence. While he was doing so, Moran started his *Mary of Egypt*, but the indignant crowd seizing his stick were about to belabour him, when they fell back bewildered anew by his close resemblance to himself. The pretender now called to them to " just give him a grip of that villain, and he'd soon let him know who the imposhterer, was ! " They led him over to Moran, but instead of closing with him he thrust a few shillings into his hand, and turning to the crowd explained to them he was indeed but an actor, and that he had just gained a wager, and so departed amid much enthusiasm, to eat the supper he had won.

In April, 1846, word was sent to the priest that Michael Moran was dying. He found him at 15 (now 14½) Patrick Street, on a straw bed, in a room full of ragged ballad-singers come to cheer his last moments. After his death the ballad-singers, with many fiddles and the like, came again and gave him a fine wake, each adding to the merriment whatever he knew in the way of rann, tale, old saw, or quaint rhyme. He had had his day, had said his prayers and made his confession, and why should they not give him a hearty send-off ? The funeral took place the next day. A good party of his admirers and friends got into the hearse with the coffin, for the day was wet and nasty. They had not gone far when one of them burst out with " It's cruel cowld, isn't it ? " " Garra'," replied another, " we'll all be as stiff as the corpse when we get to the berrin-ground." " Bad cess to him," said a third ; " I wish he'd held out another month until the weather got dacent." A man called Carroll thereupon produced a half-pint of whiskey, and they all drank to the soul of the departed. Unhappily,

however, the hearse was over-weighted, and they had
not reached the cemetery before the spring broke,
and the bottle with it.

Moran must have felt strange and out of place in
that other kingdom he was entering, perhaps while
his friends were drinking in his honour. Let us hope
that some kindly middle region was found for him,
where he can call dishevelled angels about him with
some new and more rhythmical form of his old

> " Gather round me, boys, will yez
>   Gather round me ?
> And hear what I have to say
>   Before ould Salley brings me
> My bread and jug of tay ; "

and fling outrageous quips and cranks at cherubim
and seraphim. Perhaps he may have found and
gathered, ragamuffin though he be, the Lily of High
Truth, the Rose of Far-sight Beauty, for whose lack
so many of the writers of Ireland, whether famous or
forgotten, have been futile as the blown froth upon
the shore.

From " The Celtic Twilight "

THE SPIRIT OF PLACE

DELFT

HILAIRE BELLOC

DELFT is the most charming town in the world.
It is one of the neat cities: trim, small, packed,
self-contained. A good woman in early middle
age, careful of her dress, combined, orderly, not without
a sober beauty—such a woman on her way to church
of a Sunday morning is not more pleasing than Delft.
It is on the verge of monotony, yet still individual;
in one style, yet suggesting many centuries of activity.
There is a full harmony of many colours, yet the
memory the place leaves is of a united, warm, and
generous tone. Were you suddenly put down in Delft,
you would know very well that the vast and luxuriant
meadows of Holland surrounded it, so much are its air,
houses, and habits those of men inspired by the fields.

Delft is very quiet, as befits a town so many of whose
streets are ordered lanes of water, yet one is inspired
all the while by the voices of children, and the place
is strongly alive. Over its sky there follow in stately
order the great white clouds of summer, and at evening
the haze is lit just barely from below with that transforming level light which is the joy and inspiration
of the Netherlands. Against such an expanse stands
up for ever one of the gigantic but delicate belfries,
round which these towns are gathered. For Holland,
it seems is not a country of villages, but of compact
clean towns, standing scattered over a great waste of
grass like the sea.

This belfry of Delft is a thing by itself in Europe,

DELFT

HILAIRE BELLOC

DELFT is the most charming town in the world. It is one of the neat cities: trim, small, packed, self-contained. A good woman in early middle age, careful of her dress, combined, orderly, not without a sober beauty—such a woman on her way to church of a Sunday morning is not more pleasing than Delft. It is on the verge of monotony, yet still individual; in one style, yet suggesting many centuries of activity. There is a full harmony of many colours, yet the memory the place leaves is of a united, warm, and generous tone. Were you suddenly put down in Delft, you would know very well that the vast and luxuriant meadows of Holland surrounded it, so much are its air, houses, and habits those of men inspired by the fields.

Delft is very quiet, as befits a town so many of whose streets are ordered lanes of water, yet one is inspired all the while by the voices of children, and the place is strongly alive. Over its sky there follow in stately order the great white clouds of summer, and at evening the haze is lit just barely from below with that transforming level light which is the joy and inspiration of the Netherlands. Against such an expanse stands up for ever one of the gigantic but delicate belfries, round which these towns are gathered. For Holland, it seems, is not a country of villages, but of compact, clean towns, standing scattered over a great waste of grass like the sea.

This belfry of Delft is a thing by itself in Europe,

and all these truths can be said of it by a man who sees it for the first time : first, that its enormous height is drawn up, as it were, and enhanced by every chance stroke that the instinct of its slow builders lit upon ; for these men of the infinite flats love the contrast of such pinnacles, and they have made in the labour of about a thousand years a landscape of their own by building, just as they have made by ceaseless labour a rich pasture and home out of those solitary marshes of the delta.

Secondly, that height is enhanced by something which you will not see, save in the low countries between the hills of Ardennes and the yellow seas— I mean brick Gothic ; for the Gothic which you and I know is built up of stone, and, even so, produces every effect of depth and distance ; but the Gothic of the Netherlands is often built curiously of bricks, and the bricks are so thin that it needs a whole host of them in an infinity of fine lines to cover a hundred feet of wall. They fill the blank spaces with their repeated detail ; they make the style (which even in stone is full of chances and particular corners) most intricate, and—if one may use so exaggerated a meta-phor—' populous.' Above all, they lead the eye up and up, making a comparison and measure of their tiny bands until the domination of a buttress or a tower is exaggerated to the enormous. Now the belfry of Delft, though all the upper part is of stone, yet it stands on a great pedestal (as it were) of brick—a pedestal higher than the houses, and in this base are pierced two towering, broad, and single ogives, empty and wonder-ful and full of that untragic sadness which you may find also in the drooping and wide eyes of extreme old age.

Thirdly, the very structure of the thing is bells. Here the bells are more than the soul of a Christian spire; they are its body too, its whole self. An army of them fills up all the space between the delicate supports and framework of the upper parts; for I know not how many feet, in order, diminishing in actual size and in the perspective also of that triumphant elevation, stand ranks on ranks of bells from the solemn to the wild, from the large to the small; a hundred or two hundred or a thousand. There is here the prodigality of Brabant and Hainaut and the Batavian blood, a generosity and a productivity in bells without stint, the man who designed it saying: " Since we are to have bells, let us have bells: not measured out, calculated, expensive, and prudent bells, but careless bells, self-answering multitudinous bells; bells without fear, bells excessive and bells innumerable; bells worthy of the ecstasies that are best thrown out and published in the clashing of bells. For bells are single, like real pleasures, and we will combine such a great number that they shall be like the happy and complex life of a man. In a word, let us be noble and scatter our bells and reap a harvest till our town is famous for its bells." So now all the spire is more than clothed with them; they are more than stuff or ornament; they are an outer and yet sensitive armour, all of bells.

Nor is the wealth of these bells in their number only, but also in their use; for they are not reserved in any way, but ring tunes and add harmonies at every half and quarter and at all the hours both by night and by day. Nor must you imagine that there is any obsession of noise through this; they are far too high and melodious, and, what is more, too thoroughly a part of all the spirit of Delft to be more than a perpetual and half-forgotten impression of continual music; they render its air sacred and fill it with something so akin to an uplifted silence as to leave one—when one has passed from their influence—asking what balm that was which soothed all the harshness of sound about one.

Round that tower and that voice the town hangs industrious and subdued—a family. Its waters, its intimate canals, its boats for travel, and its slight plashing of bows in the place of wheels, entered the spirit of the traveller and gave him for one long day the Right of Burgess. In autumn, in the early after-noon—the very season for those walls—it was easy for him to be filled with a restrained but united chorus, the under-voices of the city, droning and murmuring perpetually of Peace and of Labour and of the wild rose—Content. . . .

Peace, labour, and content—three very good words, and summing up, perhaps, the goal of all mankind. Of course, there is a problem everywhere, and it would be heresy to say that the people of Delft have solved it. It is Matter of Breviary that the progress of our lives is but asymptotic to true joy ; we can approach it nearer and nearer, but we can never reach it.

Nevertheless, I say that in this excellent city, though it is outside Eden, you may, when the wind is in the right quarter, receive in distant and rare appeals the scent and air of Paradise ; the soul is filled.

To this emotion there corresponds and shall here be quoted a very noble verse, which runs—or rather glides—as follows :

> Satiety, that momentary flower
> Stretched to an hour—
> These are her gifts which all mankind may use,
> And all refuse.

Or words to that effect. And to think that you can get to a place like that for less than a pound !

From " Hills and the Sea "

NIAGARA FALLS

RUPERT BROOKE

SAMUEL BUTLER has a lot to answer for. But for him, a modern traveller could spend his time peacefully admiring the scenery instead of feeling himself bound to dog the simple and grotesque of the world for the sake of their too-human comments. It is his fault if a peasant's *naïveté* has come to outweigh the beauty of rivers, and the remarks of clergymen are more than mountains. It is very restful to give up all effort at observing human nature and drawing social and political deductions from trifles, and to let oneself relapse into wide-mouthed worship of the wonders of nature. And this is very easy at Niagara. Niagara means nothing. It is not leading anywhere. It does not result from anything. It throws no light on the effects of Protection, nor on the Facility for Divorce in America, nor on Corruption in Public Life, nor on Canadian Character, nor even on the Navy Bill. It is merely a great deal of water falling over some cliffs. But it is very remarkably that. The human race, apt as a child to destroy what it admires, has done its best to surround the Falls with every distraction, incongruity, and vulgarity. Hotels, power-houses, bridges, trams, picture postcards, sham legends, stalls, booths, rifle-galleries, and side-shows frame them about. And there are Touts. Niagara is the central home and breeding-place for all the touts of earth. There are touts insinuating, and touts raucous, greasy touts, brazen touts, and upper-class, refined, gentlemanly,

take-you-by-the-arm touts ; touts who intimidate and
touts who wheedle ; professionals, amateurs, and
dilettanti, male and female ; touts who would photo-
graph you with your arm round a young lady against
a faked background of the sublimest cataract, touts
who would bully you into cars, char-à-bancs, elevators,
or tunnels, or deceive you into a carriage and pair,
touts who would sell you picture postcards, moccasins,
sham Indian beadwork, blankets, tee-pees, and crock-
ery ; and touts, finally, who have no apparent object
in the world, but just purely, simply, merely, inces-
santly, indefatigably, and ineffugibly—to tout. And
in the midst of all this, overwhelming it all, are the
Falls. He who sees them instantly forgets humanity.
They are not very high, but they are overpowering.
They are divided by an island into two parts, the
Canadian and the American.

Half a mile or so above the Falls, on either side,
the water of the great stream begins to run more
swiftly and in confusion. It descends with ever-
growing speed. It begins chattering and leaping,
breaking into a thousand ripples, throwing up joyful
fingers of spray. Sometimes it is divided by islands
and rocks, sometimes the eye can see nothing but a
waste of laughing, springing, foamy waves, turning,
crossing, even seeming to stand for an instant erect,
but always borne impetuously forward like a crowd
of triumphant feasters. Sit down close by it, and
you see a fragment of the torrent against the sky,
mottled, steely, and foaming, leaping onward in far-
flung criss-cross strands of water. Perpetually the
eye is on the point of descrying a pattern in this
weaving, and perpetually it is cheated by change. In
one place part of the flood plunges over a ledge a few
feet high and a quarter of a mile or so long, in a uniform

and stable curve. It gives an impression of almost
military concerted movement, grown suddenly out of
confusion. But it is swiftly lost again in the multitudinous tossing merriment. Here and there a rock
close to the surface is marked by a white wave that
faces backwards and seems to be rushing madly up-
stream, but is really stationary in the headlong charge.
But for these signs of reluctance, the waters seem to
fling themselves on with some foreknowledge of their
fate, in an ever wilder frenzy. But it is no Maeter-
linckian prescience. They prove, rather, that Greek
belief that the great crashes are preceded by a louder
merriment and a wilder gaiety. Leaping in the sunlight, careless, entwining, clamorously joyful, the waves
riot on towards the verge.

But there they change. As they turn to the sheer
descent, the white and blue and slate-colour, in the
heart of the Canadian Falls at least, blend and deepen
to a rich, wonderful, luminous green. On the edge
of disaster the river seems to gather herself, to pause,
to lift a head noble in ruin, and then, with a slow
grandeur, to plunge into the eternal thunder and white
chaos below. Where the stream runs shallower it is
a kind of violet colour, but both violet and green fray
and frill to white as they fall. The mass of water,
striking some ever-hidden base of rock, leaps up the
whole two hundred feet again in pinnacles and domes
of spray. The spray falls back into the lower river
once more ; all but a little that fines to foam and
white mist, which drifts in layers along the air, graining
it, and wanders out on the wind over the trees and
gardens and houses, and so vanishes.

The manager of one of the great power-stations on
the banks of the river above the Falls told me that
the centre of the river-bed at the Canadian Falls is

deep and of a saucer shape. So it may be possible to fill this up to a uniform depth, and divert a lot of water for the power-houses. And this, he said, would supply the need for more power, which will certainly soon arise, without taking away from the beauty of Niagara. This is a handsome concession of the utilitarians to ordinary sightseers. Yet, I doubt if we shall be satisfied. The real secret of the beauty and terror of the Falls is not their height or width, but the feeling of colossal power and of unintelligible disaster caused by the plunge of that vast body of water. If that were taken away, there would be little visible change ; but the heart would be gone.

The American Falls do not inspire this feeling in the same way as the Canadian. It is because they are less in volume, and because the water does not fall so much into one place. By comparison their beauty is almost delicate and fragile. They are extraordinarily level, one long curtain of lacework and woven foam. Seen from opposite, when the sun is on them, they are blindingly white, and the clouds of spray show dark against them. With both Falls the colour of the water is the ever-altering wonder. Greens and blues, purples and whites, melt into one another, fade, and come again, and change with the changing sun. Sometimes they are as richly diaphanous as a precious stone, and glow from within with a deep, inexplicable light. Sometimes the white intricacies of dropping foam become opaque and creamy. And always there are the rainbows. If you come suddenly upon the Falls from above, a great double rainbow, very vivid, spanning the extent of spray from top to bottom, is the first thing you see. If you wander along the cliff opposite, a bow springs into being in the American Falls, accompanies you courteously on your walk, dwindles and dies as the mist ends, and awakens again as you reach the Canadian tumult. And the bold traveller who attempts the trip under the American Falls sees, when he dare open his eyes to anything, tiny baby rainbows, some four or five yards in span, leaping from rock to rock among the foam, and gambolling beside him, barely out of hand's reach, as he goes. One I saw in that place was a complete circle, such as I have never seen before, and so near that I could put my foot on it. It is a terrifying journey, beneath and behind the Falls. The senses are battered and bewildered by the thunder of the water and the assault of wind and spray; or rather, the sound is not of falling water, but merely of falling; a noise of unspecified ruin. So, if you are close behind the endless clamour, the sight cannot recognize liquid in the masses that hurl past. You are dimly and pitifully aware that sheets of light and darkness are falling in great curves in front of you. Dull omnipresent foam washes the face. Farther away, in the roar and hissing, clouds of spray seem literally to slide down some invisible plane of air.

Beyond the foot of the Falls the river is like a slipping floor of marble, green with veins of dirty white, made by the scum that was foam. It slides very quietly and slowly down for a mile or two, sullenly exhausted. Then it turns to a dull sage green, and hurries more swiftly, smooth and ominous. As the walls of the ravine close in, trouble stirs, and the waters boil and eddy. These are the lower rapids, a sight more terrifying than the Falls, because less intelligible. Close in its bands of rock, the river surges tumultuously forward, writhing and leaping as if inspired by a demon. It is pressed by the straits into a visibly convex form. Great planes of water slide past. Sometimes it is thrown up into a pinnacle of foam higher than a house, or leaps with incredible speed from the crest of one vast wave to another, along the shining curve between, like the spring of a wild beast. Its motion continually suggests muscular action. The power manifest in these rapids moves one with a different sense of awe and terror from that of the Falls. Here the inhuman life and strength are spontaneous, active, almost resolute ; masculine vigour compared with the passive, gigantic power, female, helpless and overwhelming, of the Falls. A place of fear.

One is drawn back, strangely, to a contemplation of the Falls, at every hour, and especially by night, when the cloud of spray becomes an immense visible ghost, straining and wavering high above the river, white and pathetic and translucent. The Victorian lies very close below the surface in every man. There one can sit and let great cloudy thoughts of destiny and the passage of empires drift through the mind ; for such dreams are at home by Niagara. I could not get out of my mind the thought of a friend, who said that the rainbows over the Falls were like the arts and beauty and goodness, with regard to the stream of life—caused by it, thrown upon its spray, but unable to stay or direct or affect it, and ceasing when it ceased. In all comparisons that rise in the heart, the river, with its multitudinous waves and its single current, likens itself to a life, whether of an individual or of a community. A man's life is of many flashing moments, and yet one stream ; a nation's flows through all its citizens, and yet is more than they. In such places, one is aware, with an almost insupportable and yet comforting certitude, that both men and nations are hurried onwards to their ruin or ending as inevitably as this dark flood. Some go down to it unreluctant, and meet it, like the river, not without nobility. And, as incessant, as inevitable, and as unavailing as the spray that hangs over the Falls, is the white cloud of human crying. . . . With some such thoughts does the platitudinous heart win from the confusion and thunder of Niagara a peace that the quietest plains or most stable hills can never give.

From " Letters from America "

THE SOUL OF A CATHEDRAL

SIR JAMES YOXALL

TO wander gives you to meet strange folk, and I once saw Huysmans, the man who knew cathedrals best and most. Pallid and dark and racial—Hispano-Flamand—he sat enthroned the Sir Oracle of a cabaret, toping his absinthe as if it were wine-and-water, and talking, talking, talking and theorizing in the most irreverential way. Nothing was sacred to sapper Huysmans, then; his art had become as a morbid mirror, reflecting only the unholy and the unclean. His was the doomed type which begins by being æsthetical and grows anti-ethical, dares every paradox and waxes irrational, courts insanity and achieves it, slides down the sensuous into the gross, and—Apollo becoming Apollyon—descends to very hell.

But *he* emerged, and a miracle he felt his retrieval to be. He tried to atone, he wrote *La Cathédrale*, he died in a lay-brother's cassock and *une odeur de misère et bigoterie*, statuettes of saints on the table beside his bed. Extremes *do* meet sometimes, and without explosions of mirth, even. Let us thank Heaven for that, since what is worse than cynical laughter? Let hyænas laugh at a Huysmans, *I* will not; we should regard such things with at least a wistful tolerance. There is truth in the old Arminian dogma of the " change of heart "; the chronicle of sudden conversions runs right down from St Paul to St Augustine, and then to the latest rescue by the Salvation Army.

" The heart is deceitful above all things," I know, but do you suppose there are many conscious hypocrites in the world? There are not, O Sneerwell! The heart can be so many things at once, God wot; the heart deceives itself so readily, the heart is such an unconscious sophist; and in every man there are many more personalities and entities than Stevenson or Oliver Wendell Holmes counted up. I doubt the alleged hypocrisy of even Louis XI, the " low voluptuary " with " the dozen little paltry figures of saints stamped in lead " around the band of his hat. And I doubt it of Huysmans. *Beaucoup d'âmes, beaucoup de gants*—sometimes one must put on one's gloves to shake hands, however; I mention Huysmans here because he it was of all men who understood cathedrals most intimately and reverently; strange to say, it was he who wrote, *L'archéologie et l'architecture nous ont revelé simplement l'organisme, les corps, des cathédrales. Qui nous en dira l'âme?*

Long before I read that I had felt that great churches have souls. I, so to speak, have collected cathedrals; France is a very Palestine of them, the true Gothic was born in the Ile de France, and I have studied every cathedral in that travel-land of my predilection. One knows, of course, by wanderings otherwhere, the Comacine, the Byzantine, and the Rhenish altar-houses; and Belgium can teach us something about cathedrals which France or Germany cannot do. For Belgium shows the synthetist *why* these vast religious monuments ceased to be built. Seat yourselves on the Arabian carpet a moment and hie with me to Louvain; let us stand between the Town Hall there and what was meant to be a great cathedral church. Look how the Hôtel de Ville, begun in 1447 only, was steadily and quickly finished to its ultimate crocket and least finial ; now turn and gaze at its neighbour the church, founded *anno humanæ salutis* 1423, half a century earlier than the completion of the Hôtel de Ville ; the church remains unfinished yet. Regard that decrepit old fane understandingly, therefore. Custom and convention began it at a time when custom and convention were modifying ; when the Gothic was becoming effete and the cathedral-building Age of Faith was waning away. In the Louvain of that time it was no longer Seigneur, priest, and serf alone ; the clergy and the feudal officers—viscount and bailli— felt power and prerogative slipping from their grasp ; commerce, law, science, the civic feeling, were lifting their heads ; a new aristocracy, the city magnates, was coming into status ; burgomaster, *échevin*, and councillor—professors, doctors, municipal and judiciary officers—had begun to count ; and it was the young enthusiasm and pride of the burgher-spirit which planned and finished in one jet that sumptuous old Town Hall. Religion itself was not dying, I know, but certainly the votive and blindly-accepting concept of religion, which made cathedral-building feasible, had begun to languish, with symptoms of phthisis indeed, as though entering upon the patient agony of a slow decline. A century later, in France and England came the axe and hammer work of iconoclasm, and cathedral-building has dozed and nodded since then, as do the snuffy red canons at Rheims over their prayers of an afternoon. A few vast churches have risen since then, I allow, but they are bodies only, empty of soul. St Paul's in the City is one of them ; St Peter's at Rome is another ; there is a pseudo-Gothic pseudo-Cathedral at Orléans ; there is one at Boulogne ; and null and mortuary places they are, even at their ceremonious best. If you pass from the Twelfth-century minster at Exeter to the Nineteenth-century fane at Truro, or from Westminster Abbey to the huge Byzantine pile amidst the Pimlico flats, you feel that the *anima* is missing, that the vital spark was never kindled there.

But the aged cathedrals, the true antiques, born in due time and escaping the spoiler—old English minsters, for example, that stand so firmly planted, or lay their four limbs of chancel, nave, and transepts so possessingly and inveterately on the sod—*they* have a soul. Greybeards inalienably religious they are, that have ceased to be superstitious but remain devout ; in all the world elsewhere there are, I think, no orisons so sweet, so befitting, so sublime, as those of which old English cathedrals are the always-echoing shrines. I can bow the head or the knee in many hallowed places, thank God—in the Roman basilica, the Gothic minster, the stucco chapel, and the brick Little Bethel ; perhaps the best forms and services for any of us are those by which our spiritual exaltation is best excited ; it is my faith that " God fulfils himself in many ways " of worship, the orthodox as much as the others, and the new as well as the old. Yet so far as architecture and the *religio loci* can aid one to feel devout, the Gothic is, I think, most helpful ; solemnity, consecration, and awe are more present in Lincoln Cathedral than in St Peter's or St Paul's. And there is Gothic and Gothic, remember ; the Fifteenth-century Gothic in France became depraved. Old English Gothic is mighty and stately, but homely too ; majestic in immobility, broad, wide, and permanent, four-square to all the winds that blow. In France the great ogival arches lift themselves more loftily, but more narrowly also, than does the Gothic here ; laterally cramped and vertically exaggerate, the cathedral at Beauvais, and

I

at Amiens, even, suggests the Chicago sky-scraper somewhat. Width as well as height is needful in a home of the spirit ; your fanatic has seldom much breadth to his soul.

At certain hours the old Cathedrals speak, in music. Enter " as the bells are tolling to Mass and all seems undulating and heaving beneath their swing." At first the bells all sound together ; there is a French folk-song which renders the intermingled rhythms and tones of the great bass bourdon and the merry tenor bells—

Orléans, Beaugency,
Notre-Dame de Cléry,
Vendôme,
Vendôme !

But soon the bells which also ring for marriages and festivals fall silent ; the couplets chime awhile ; and then it is the deep solitary call of the great bass bourdon which keeps on. That huge oscillating urn of bronze as green as malachite sends forth its grave and simple intonations, to hover and undulate and brood above the city, and be echoed from every listening spire. Then, when that holy convocation ceases, hark to the organ, high in the centre of the rood !—the University of instruments begins its symphonies of psalm. Comes next the tenuous silver summons of the altar-bell, and the human voice is vibrant ; for centuries the sonorous old wood and stone has thrilled to this same appeal. The plain-song follows ; the unison symbolizes our common humanity, our identical plea. The *schola cantorum* sing, letting their voices go in masses ; intonings soar to the firmament of vaulting, strike the acoustic focus, and set the whole fabric athrob, a litany in stone. These are the breath and speech of the beautiful awful place, but these are not all. For near the altar you perceive a pulsing heart of movement, and the Cathedral begins to seem to you a living organism—" a great harmonious mass full of life down to the minutest parts," as Goethe at Strasbourg declared ; another minute of musing, and you know that this mighty body has a soul.

The soul of an archetypal cathedral of the Thirteenth century speaks in symbols. The Gothic is Romantic, no doubt ; it lacks the severity, restraint, and discipline of the Greek and Romanesque ; it is individual, special, idiocratic and original, as all good work in art or literature must be. It has its *differentia*, I know, but just as a Gothic cathedral is *not* " petrified religion," as Coleridge said it was, it is *not* " embodied caprice," as certain of the neo-Classicists have declared. In it, *au contraire*, all is figure, token, emblem, type, and sign, wrought out in a marvellous system and tenour of meaning, a labyrinth but not a maze of thoughts, expressed in a complexity of forms. The Gothic blends liberty with self-restraint, audacity with prudence, science with emotion : it is logic poesied. The church is cruciform, but that is rudimental ; the thinking-out of the construction went far beyond that. For look you, the Lady Chapel, midway in the curve of the apse, is the lap of mourning Mary ; the high altar is the head of her Son there pillowed, and the chapels of the chevet—*chevet*, the very word means pillow—ray thence like the thorns of the dolorous crown. In English cathedrals you do not find this particular symbol of the coronal ; here the east front is nearly always rectangular ; but everywhere you find the Mary chapel. The embodied appeal of Mary the woman, Mary the mother, was far too eloquent for any Roman Catholic cathedral-builder to omit ; in France and Belgium a hundred times I have noted how men will worship the Mother who are dull to the claims of the Son. And think for a moment what a woman's call to women, what a poignant anthropomorphic appeal, the figure of Mary makes to those of her stricken sex ! To the Woman and Mother with the *Bambino* in her arms I have seen Italian women lift eyes tear-blind, and gropingly reach up, to touch the stony but down-held fingers ; as in the night of a great sorrow a man may take for solace the hand of his familiar friend. I think that is why Notre-Dame is the favourite ascription of cathedrals abroad. There is one strange omission ; nowhere in cathedrals have I found a *symbol* of the Christ-*child* ; the cathedral Christ is always a Man of Sorrows, always grown up and acquainted with grief.

Not even in France, however, where the mother is the natural head of the family, were cathedrals ever Mariolatrous in conception. For proof of that, consider the rest of the ground-plan ; it is the *corpus Domini*. The transepts represent the outstretched arms of the Crucified, and the pinnacles of the transept gables typify the nails in the hands. Looking up the vast hollow cross of a cathedral from its foot, you can see that the axes of the chancel and apsis deflect from the medial line of the nave ; it does not lie quite straight ; even so, thought the monks who planned it, did the head of Christ on the Roman gallows at Golgotha droop sidelong. Narrow is the opening at the altar-screen, as is the neck between the clavicles. And into the very breast of the church is thrust the tall spear of the *flèche*.

In the chancel windows the predominant hues are grey and red, to represent " the water and the blood." Doubly emblematic is the high altar, for were not the earliest altars also tombs ? The chancel is darkened, as was the hill of Calvary in the hour of the Passion ;

there is symbol as well as beauty in that stormy purple glass. Beneath the chancel the crypt crouches low, almost prostrate, like the humblest worshippers; the crypt is Romanesque, for it recalls the earliest Christendom, and its chapels are small and dark because small and dark were the shrines in the Catacombs. To ascend from the charnel-house in the crypt to the loftiness and space and light of the sanctuary gives a symbol of the Resurrection. The crypt is secret and subterranean, but upon and above that place of fearful and clandestine prayer the great Temple of the Faith now rises boldly—upstands with splendid front— dares Cæsar, reaches towards the Christians' God; with " flame of line and curve " aspiring, thinning away its mortal body of stone, opening wider eyes of glass, dematerializing, spiritualizing, lifting its sky-y-pointing spires like the hands of an apostle, heavenwards; bursting like flower from calyx, out of the old furtive devotion into exultant lauds; and openly incarnating its soul.

That the very body and edifice of a cathedral should be imbued with symbol, *lucidus ordo*, need cause the cold critic no wonder. That was the intention, the cathedral was thus designed, to that end it was constructed; it was to image on earth its counterpart laid up in heaven, and the interpretations here given must not be considered *post hoc*. In its Greek sense the word ' symbol ' meant bringing-together and uniting; a cathedral typified the sacred body joined to the living Christ again, the Word anew made flesh, the *Logos* descended into the Church to be its soul. In ground-plan, elevation, and detail this symbolism was systematically set forth. The pride and fervour of Christian Ecclesiasticism, which began to tower in the Ninth century and culminated in the Thirteenth, had at disposal all the lore of that branch of metaphysics which is called theology, and a cathedral became a treatise on orthodoxy, in stone. A hundred times more thought than an architect now gives to the purpose and fitness of a set of municipal offices was spent on the planning and illustration of a Thirteenth-century cathedral; it was a deliberate and considered derivative from the intelligent religious spirit of the time. In its creation two sciences, architecture and theology, wrought side by side; master-builders erected it physically, but churchmen devised it intellectually; in point of fact, the master-builder was often a priest himself. Each new cathedral as it arose became a lesson and incentive for the next, and the power to figure forth the Christian Idea in stone and wood and glass grew abler from generation to generation, just as the offerings of the faithful became more profuse. Consider, indeed, not the cathedrals only, but the fine old parish churches which stud the Eastern Counties here, from Holderness down through East Anglia to the Thames. Why were they built so huge? And whence came the money for such costly edifices? Too large for their parochial purpose they must always have been; the village populations have not so shrunk as all that. I know that the pious founder's purpose counts for much in this matter, and it might not be unfair to say the greater the crime to be expiated the bigger the building—the heavier the load of sin the founder felt the larger the church he offered to God. But the main resource for cathedral-building was the offerings of the pilgrim devout. And thus, with lavish contributions of money and wageless labour, with a wealth of stored and funded tradition and gradually-gathered theological and architectural skill at disposal, the greatest of the cathedrals came into being, and to vastness and magnificence of edifice a fulness of meaning was given.

A cathedral was meant to be lofty and universal ; it was to lift itself as a divine work and image of the Infinite. The very mass of it was to figure the Mount of the Ascension, with—you see this best at Milan— disciples on its summit watching that celestial flight ; the very armorials of the French guild of stone-cutters tell of that ; they are " In azure, an ascension of the Son of God from a mountain, the whole in gold." A cathedral must be high and aspiring, it must reach towards Heaven, leaving cottage, shop and market far below—an obvious symbol. It must be huge ; it must show a splendour of space ; at Rheims, Paris, Amiens, or York the cathedral church is forty or fifty times the size of the Temple of Minerva on the Acropolis Hill, or of the Maison Carrée at Nîmes. Of the same Maison Carrée Arthur Young wrote, a century ago, " the most elegant, light, and pleasing building I ever beheld " ; and there in France it stood, a model for what in the Eighteenth century had come to be the distinctive French taste in architecture. The Madeleine at Paris, indeed, begun in 1764, was built in imitation of the late-Roman adaptation of the Greculan style, as seen in the Maison Carrée at Nîmes. But bishops and canons in the Twelfth and Thirteenth centuries did not think it befitting that a chief house of God should be " elegant, light, and pleasing," or small. A village church might be small and low—it was only the church of a parish ; an Abbey chapel, the church of the monks, might be low and splendid ; but the cathedral was to be the church of all the parishes, and of all the monks and nuns and priests, and the people as a whole ; it must be magnificent, resonant, tall and vast, it must symbolize something of the large span and scope of Heaven itself; it must lift " a thicket of airy spires "—the Holy Thorn.

A cathedral was to be universal and all-accessible, a place for the solitary at moments, at other times the scene of gatherings immense. It might be a Gethsemane retreat, whither individuals could go for peace and shade and rest, for hallowed silence, for a refuge from life's fitful fever, and a shelter from the huxtering world outside; but it was also to be a place of assemblies, great as the crowd which listened to Christ on the Mount. A cathedral was to be a microcosmos, ample enough for all the population of the city, yet separated into a score of different regions; as Hegel first pointed out—this chapel for low Mass, that for baptism, yonder the funeral rites of eld, and here the wedlock of youth, concurrently going on. Some of the drawings by Prout show us these multifarious uses of a cathedral eighty years ago; on festival Sundays abroad you may see them in the real, even yet. The old cathedrals abroad never stood isolated in stately precincts; only in England did they get their green surrounding close.

The cathedral was to be one yet divers, like the Trinity; there must be no wearisome and unnatural uniformity. Is Nature ever uniform? Non-natural indeed is the geometrical symmetry which was sought for in the pagan temples of Greece and Rome. Here in the Gothic the infinite variety of Nature was to be imitated; though balance and proportion as elements of beauty and seemliness were not forgotten, they were made to serve, they were not permitted to rule. All riches, all arts, all devices, all splendours were to be focussed in what was to be a nucleus of the world, and a central symbol of the Faith. Lofty, vast, comprehensive, diverse, and splendid the cathedral, therefore;

and into this intellectualized body began to be born a soul.

Let us study some part of the symbolism in detail ; from the curtilage of the western façade let us mount the great spread of the steps which lead to our imaginary archetype of cathedrals—for there is none left perfect now in reality, alas. The steps in that flight are many and easy, to prefigure the continuous and practicable effort of the sinner towards better things ; and the steps are wide and inviting, offering room and approach for all.

On the platform at the top of them rises—outside the church proper itself—the narthex or antechamber, a place of probation and decision ; penitents and catechumens waited there. The need for decision between perdition and salvation is manifested in the sculpture which fills the tympanum of the central portal, and in the angry light of the window there ; for they represent the Judgment Day, a scene of terror more than joy. It is never too late to flee from the wrath to come, however—indeed the western is the principal entrance to the cathedral—and the rays of even a setting sun can enter there. But the three occidental doorways differ from each other, and the southern and northern portals differ from all, for there are many paths to the Cross. Inside the doorways stand basins of holy-water, offering the lustrations which purify on entering or fortify on quitting   And the font stands near the narthex, baptizing the neophyte into the Church.

Let us pass up the nave, to the choir and the sanctuary around the high altar. Thither the Stations of the Cross go guidingly, for this is the mystical path from Earth towards Heaven. The nave is Earth, but Earth may be redeemed and magnified ; glorious in the clerestory windows of the nave are the robes and emblems of prophets, apostles, priests, saints, warriors for the Cross and monarchs *fidei defensores*, the Church Militant to wit. Lower than these, yet exalted, is the circumambulatory of the churchmen, the triforium, *tres fores* under an arch—three in one, the Trinity symbolized. If the nave is Earth, the chancel and sanctuary are Heaven ; and we pass the transepts to reach the sanctum, for though there be many paths to the Cross, by the Cross is the one way to Heaven.

Use and wont can so lamentably harden and formalize even the noblest observances ! Mentally, the theologians and the architects of the Thirteenth century lived in a world of abstractions ; realities to them were the mere appearances and representations of ideas ; number and order and hierarchism seemed to them the important laws of Nature ; and symbols and emblems were to them almost as sacred as the concepts represented. But to us ? " Eleving Deans has I sot under, sir," a cathedral servant is said to have said ; " Eleving of 'em, man and boy, but I'm a living Christian yet ! " So also, too often, the tourist and sightseer, in his hand a red-backed volume that is no book of prayers or *Imitatio Christi*, but the merest Baedeker, will tramp up the nave at Chartres or Milan in a way he would not dare at Ely or York. " *Where* is that picture I've got to see ? " he asks himself, as he turns the guide-book pages. " Chapel in the south transept ? Which *is* the south transept ? Why on earth can't they label 'em ? Must ask a beadle, I s'pose. Here you ? Hi ! " No soul in that Cathedral for him. Even the smallest preliminary study of architecture and symbology quickens and enlivens travel for us ; we see the things we look for, as a rule.

So let *us* perceive in the three steps which rise from

the nave to the chancel level the three degrees of the
spiritual life ; in the gnomon of the clock see Christ,
in the hours the twelve apostles ; in the *vaisseau* or
nef of the nave, a vessel dim and aromatic as a ship
of spices, the ark in which the Church rides safely
through the Flood and the storms of time. Let *us*
remember why the lectern is shaped like an eagle, the
natural enemy of the serpent, and the bird of John
the Evangelist ; are not the two outspread wings the
symbol of the two Testaments which rest upon them ?
The cross, the nails, the crown of thorns are everywhere ; lifted in air at the summit of St Ouen's at
Rouen is the crown of glory itself. *We* will note that
the choir and sanctuary, enclosed by walls and a
jubé or grille, form the Holy of Holies, and are therefore
the part of the church the most decorated, with
sculpture which illustrates the life of the Lord. Lifting
our heads, we see that the windows here show forth
the Passion ; their light falls fullest and most glorious
upon the high altar, for there was radiance on the
summit of the Cross.

A soul of meaning is evident in the mere staining of
the windows, for the eyes of the devout should be
dulled to the carnal and marketing sights of the world
outside ; nowhere in the Thirteenth century did any
cathedral window contain any white transparent glass.
Consider the rose-window—the *reondes verrières*, under
the *croisée d'augive*, as Twelfth-century architects
phrased it—all coruscating with coloured light ; they
figure forth the *Rosa Mystica* of the Litany and the
Rose of Sharon, but they symbolize other meanings
too. The great flower of glass at Évreux holds at
its heart, as it were, a cluster of blood-dipt thorns, it
is the *rosa dolorosa* ; the northern rosace at Limoges
shows at its centre, amidst a thousand petals all

glorious with intensest hues, a Christ who blesses and then calms a very storm of splendour; at Sens and at Chartres the western round windows represent the Last Judgment, lit by Gehenna flames. Sometimes the rose-window is a wheel-window, the vision of Ezekiel; one of the windows at Amiens is a figure of the 'wheel of Fortune' itself. In the blue rosace of Notre-Dame de Paris a great circle of glass, built up of fragments each a different tint or tone of blue, lifts to the north, unchanging with the passing hours, its figure and mirror of the firmament, its blues of the sea, of the peacock's feather, or lapis-lazuli and tur-quoise, of the pansy and periwinkle and lavender and violet; and then of the final, the thinning and watchet azure of ether, the path to Heaven. A chaplet and rosary of rose-windows might be gathered and strung.

Nowhere in the old days, I say, was bare white glass, or even the ribbed grey or green or pink 'leaded lights' which play substitute nowadays, to be seen in a cathedral; internally the great old houses of prayer and praise were bathed with " deepened glories, streaming from off the sun like seraph's wings "; the light which fell within them shone prismatic, in a rainbow of eternal hope. Glass-stainers of the Renais-sance, and mid-Victorian bunglers of course, mis-understood and debased it, but in the old days the windows showed a Christian heraldry, each hue repre-senting a gem, and each gem some attribute or moral quality, some King in Israel, or some canonized saint. Over the south-west portal the window depicts the Tree of Jesse, the stem of David, and casts its mosaic light from the Old Dispensation to the New. As the day closes the western glow becomes most splendid; it is hope in the end of one's life. Richest of all is the glass which gives to the sanctuary and the apse especial splendour, to glorify the drooping head, the thorny crown. In the seven chapels of the chevet there are seven rose-windows, purple or rosy-red ; the seven joys of Mary, and her seven woes. And look how the light of the tall windows in the central lantern tower falls on the pulpit beneath, like inspiration ; the pulpit is carved into a semblance of Mount Carmel, the hill of combat against unbelief and lustings after false gods.

Within and without the beautiful awful place is sculptured and painted and blazoned into endless allegory, image, personification, picture or present-ment ; and in the old days there was a mundane reason for that. The glass, the frescoes, the oil-paintings, the brasses and bronzes, the wrought iron, the carvings and the tapestries, were as books for the illiterate devout ; *libri idiotarum,* St Augustine called them—a worshipper knew his cathedral images and emblems as middle-class children here knew their " Peep of Day " book forty years ago. The cathedral was a Bible—*biblia pauperum*—the Old Testament was figured without, the New Testament within. The very titles of the pavements gave teaching as the worshippers trod them ; the wave-patterns imaged the Sea of Glass, the fish were an emblem of baptism, the winding and convoluted maze showed the difficult journey of life. The animal world and the vegetable world were brought in, to share in the cosmos of the cathedral : teeming with life and variety is the sculp-ture on capitals and arcadings, it is almost the wild luxuriance of Nature herself. And there was meaning in the Gothic flora ; it was not acanthine, classically monotonous, and symmetrically inane. The vine and its branches are shown for Christ and His followers ; the palm stands for victory and for justice, the cypress typifies the Just made ready for their death. Here, too, are animals in stone ; the Lamb of God, the goat, the Lion of Judah, the serpent accursed ; and birds, the raven, and the dove. The oxen which drew the great blocks of granite across the plain to the site of the cathedral are sculptured here, and not for ornament only ; - man, woman, child, angel, muse, sibyl, and musician are shown. Five thousand statues and statuettes stand here, each the image of some living thing, some being, concept, quality, or state. Even crimes and vices are personified, to show comprehensiveness and pardon, and that " it takes all sorts to make a world." Hell and the fiends themselves are not omitted ; witness the cynical gargoyles, and the " Devils of Notre-Dame." Here, too, are effigies of all trades, arts, crafts, and occupations, the whole story of mankind, the fall of Adam, and human regeneration ; here are the chronicles and parables of God.

The Cathedral is indeed all parable, all " earthly story with a heavenly meaning," told in silver-grey stone. The mysteries of theology are set forth, the hieratic forms and numbers are rendered. Three portals under one arch—the Trinity ; two piers to the arch—the Testaments ; seven pillars of the reredos—the Roman sacraments ; twenty-two nave windows—the Kings of the House of Judah ; twelve pinnacles—the Minor Prophets. The Roman sacraments were imaged in the seven towers which a cathedral in its perfection possessed. The buttresses are mystical in their number ; and the finials, and the crockets too. Three bays, each with three arches, each arch surmounted by three windows, each window itself triune ; three portals, each with three doors ; three aisles in each transept, three piers in each aisle—the Trinity is typified throughout. And in this "temple where Time has wed Eternity" the Eternal is figured in the ever-burning sanctuary lamp.

It is this, all this, this solemn and enraptured beauty of symbol and spectacle, which in a great Gothic church gives you emotions that in a St Peter's or a St Paul's you can seldom know; compared with all this the Byzantine, the Lombardic, and the unmitigated Norman, seem lay, meaningless, and void of soul. For round and horseshoe arches bound the eye; the ogival and pointed lead the gaze above. See in the Gothic how the flying-buttresses, those bold trajectories in freestone, loop the azure as they spring away from earth. The Gothic was no "frenzy of the vertical," madly using the force of gravitation without aim; the towers, the spires, the *flèches* typify man's call to spurn the world and soar. I do not decry the Norman, I do not say that the Romanesque was never made a style deeply religious; the noble fane at Soissons, and the hallowed little *Dom* at Avignon— nay, the vast Romanesque dome of the sky itself— forbid a judgment so harsh. But to my mind, from all but the true Thirteenth-century Gothic—from St Mark's at Venice, even, the one cathedral wholly dedicated to Christ—there is missing the perfectness of beauty, the richness of meaning, the universal fitness and completeness, the instinctive awe and wordless sanctity which is to our archetypal church its soul. Alone in a Gothic cathedral one can forget the architect's calculations, the master-builder's care, the toils and tools of carpenters and masons, and feel as if sturdy pillar and indomitable arch, sun-steeped window and piercing pinnacle, are the natural expression of a living will, the clothing of a spirit which lives and breathes in all. Here dwells the consummate outward and visible sign of the worshipping soul : a cathedral is an intellectual prayer. It was no mere matter of structural consequence that pillars should lift and arches point towards the Infinite ; that magnificence should tell of supernal glory ; that hugeness and comprehensiveness should relate the All-Father ; that the gables and vaults should be peopled by the noble army of martyrs ascended, and the goodly fellowship of prophets and apostles foretelling and foregoing ; or that on pinnacle and spire angelical shapes should halt, with folded wing. It was duty, religious as well as artistic duty, that the hidden parts of crocket and finial should be carved as finely and completely as the parts which are fully seen.

And thus the great house of God grew up from the soil like a tree—like a banyan, like a copse, like a forest of foliage ; see how it flames at sunset, see how it flowers at dawn. Let us stand within it, where the shafts of sunshine fall, where the breadths of shadow lie ; the light and the dusk alike are rarefied, diffused, made supernatural ; the light is the radiance of aurora and rainbow, the dusk is the shadow of archangelic wings. Look up, and feel " the vertigo of the Gothic." Silence, immensity, splendour, mute worship by the soul. Within the thousand gleams of gules and sapphire and orange-tawny at York let us kneel, and hear the young cherubic voices go soaring through the mist of light in the vault : " It doth not yet appear what we *shall* be ! " Or within the amber gloom at Bourges let us bow the head, as we hear the deep chant, " *Te, lucis ante terminum*—To Thee, before the last light fades, Creator of all things, we pray ! " Selah, and Amen.

From " The Wander Years "

144

ON A MAP OF THE OBERLAND

"ALPHA OF THE PLOUGH"

I WAS rummaging among my books this morning when I came across Frey's map of the Bernese Oberland, and forthwith forgot the object of my search in the presence of this exhilarating discovery. Mr Chesterton, I think, once described how he evoked the emotions of a holiday by calling a cab, piling it up with luggage, and driving to the station. Then, having had his sensation, he drove home again. It seemed to me rather a poor way of taking an imaginative holiday. One might as well heat an empty oven in order to imagine a feast. The true medium of the spiritual holiday is the map. That is the magic carpet that whisks you away from this sodden earth and unhappy present to sunny lands and serener days.

There are times when books offer no escape from the burden of things, when, as Mr Biglow says—

> I'm as unsoshul as a stone,
> And kind o' suffercate to be alone ;

but there are no circumstances in which a map will not do the trick. I do not care whether it is a map of the known or the unknown, the visited or the unvisited, the real or the fanciful. It was the jolly map which Stevenson invented in an idle hour which became the seed of *Treasure Island*. That is how a map stimulated his fancy and sent it out on a career of immortal adventure. And though you have not Stevenson's genius for describing the adventure, that is what a map will do for you if you have a spark of

K   145 the boy's love of romance left in your soul. It is the "magic casement" of the poet. I have never crossed the Atlantic in the flesh, but, lord, what spiritual adventures I have had with maps in the enchanted world on the other side ! I have sailed with Drake in Nombre Dios Bay, and navigated the grim straits with Magellan, and lived with the Incas of Peru and the bloody Pizarro, and gone up the broad bosom of the Amazon into fathomless forests, and sailed through the Golden Gates on golden afternoons, and stood with Cortes " silent, upon a peak in Darien." I know the Shenandoah Valley far better than I know Wimbledon Common, and have fought over every inch of it by the side of Stonewall Jackson, just as I have lived in the mazes of the Wilderness with Grant and Lee.

Do not tell me I have never been to these places and a thousand others like them. I swear that I have. I have traversed them all in the kingdom of the mind, and if you will give me a map and a rainy day (like this) I will go on a holiday more entrancing than any that Mr Cook ever planned. It is not taking tickets that makes the traveller. I have known people who have gone round the world without seeing anything, while Thoreau could stay in his back garden and entertain the universe.

But if maps of the unvisited earth have the magic of romance in them, maps of the places you have known have a fascination no less rich and deep. They, too, take you out on a holiday, but it is a holiday of memory and not of the imagination. You are back with yourself in other days and in other places and with other friends. You may tell me that this was a dreary, rainy morning, sir, and that I spent it looking out over the dismal valley and the sad cornfields with their stricken crops. Nothing of the sort. I spent it in the Bernese Oberland with an incomparable companion. Three weeks I put in, sir, three weeks on the glaciers. See, there, on this glorious map of Frey's, is Mürren, from whence we started. In front is the mighty snow mass of the Jungfrau, the Mönch and the Eiger, shutting out the glacier solitudes whither we are bound.

There goes our track up the ravine to Obersteinberg and there is the Mütthorn hut, standing on the bit of barren rock that sticks out from the great ice-billows of the Tschingelhorn glacier. Do you remember, companion of mine, the mighty bowls of steaming tea we drank when we reached that haven of refuge ? And do you remember our start from the hut at two o'clock in the morning, roped with our guide and with our lanterns lit—and the silence of our march over the snow and ice beneath the glittering stars, and the hollow boom of distant avalanches, and the breaking of the wondrous dawn over the ice-fields, and the unforgettable view as we reach the ridge of the Peters-grat and saw across the Rhone Valley the great mountain masses beyond—the Weisshorn, the Matter-horn, Mont Blanc, and the rest—touched to an unearthly beauty by the flush of the new-risen sun ? And the scramble up the Tschingelhorn, and the long grind down the ice-slopes and the moraine to the seclusion of the Lötschenthal ? And then the days that followed in the great ice region behind the Jungfrau ; the long, silent marches over pathless snows and by yawning crevasses, the struggle up peaks in the dawn, and the nights in the huts, sometimes with other climbers who blew in across the snows from some remote adventure, sometimes alone as in that tiny hut on the Finsteraarhorn, where we paid three and a half francs for a bunch of wood to boil our kettle ?

There is the Oberaar hut standing on the ledge of a dizzy precipice. Do you remember the sunset we saw from thence, when out of the general gloom of the conquering night one beam from the vanished sun caught the summit of the Dom and made it gleam like a palace in the heavens or like the towers of the radiant city that Christian saw across the dark river ? And there at the end of the journey is the great glacier that leaps down, seven thousand feet, between the Schreckhorn and the Wetterhorn, to the gracious valley of Grindelwald. How innocent it looks on this map, but what a day of gathering menace was that when we got caught between the impassable crevasses, and night came on and the rain came down and . . . But let the magic carpet hasten slowly here. . . .

It was still dark when Heinrich of the Looking Glass leapt up from our bed of hay in the Dolfuss hut, lit the candle and began to prepare the breakfast. Outside, the rain fell in torrents and the clouds hung thick and low over glacier and peaks. Our early start from the Gleckstein hut was thwarted. Night turned to dawn and dawn to day, and still the rain pelted down on that vast solitude of rock and ice. Then the crest of the Finsteraarhorn appeared through a rent in the clouds, patches of blue broke up the grey menace of the sky, the rain ceased. Otmar and Heinrich hastily washed the iron cups and plates and swept the floor of the hut, and then, shouldering our rucksacks and closing the door of the empty hut, we scrambled down the rocks to the glacier.

It was 8.15 and the guide-books said it was a seven hours' journey to the Gleckstein. That seemed to leave ample margin ; but do not trust guide-books in a season of drought when the crevasses are open.

This wisdom, however, came later. All through the morning we made excellent progress. The sun shone, the clouds hung lightly about the peaks, the ice was in excellent condition. Heinrich, who brought up the rear, occasionally broke into song. Now, when Heinrich sings you know that all is well. When he whistles you are in a tight place. For the rest he is silent. Otmar, his brother, is less communicative. He goes on ahead silently under all conditions, skirting crevasses, testing snow-bridges to see if they will bear, occasionally pausing to consult his maps. Once only did he burst into song that day—but of that later. Otmar is an autocrat on the ice or the rocks. In the hut he will make your tea and oil your boots and help Heinrich to wash your cups and sweep the floor. But out in the open he is your master. If you ask him inconvenient questions he does not hear. If you suggest a second breakfast before it is due his silence as he pounds forward ahead humiliates you. If your pace slackens there is a rebuke in the taut insistence of the rope.

It was eleven when we halted for our cold tea and sardines (white wine for Otmar and Heinrich). The pause gave Heinrich an opportunity of taking out his pocket looking-glass and touching up his moustache ends and giving a flick to his eyebrows. Heinrich is as big and brawny as an ox, but he has the soul of a dandy.

It had been easy going on the furrowed face of the ice, but when we came to the snow slope that leads to the Lauteraar saddle our pace slackened. The snow was soft, and we sank at each step up to our shins. Otmar eased the passage up the slope by zigzagging, but it was one o'clock when we came face to face with the wall of snow, flanked by walls of rock, which form the 'saddle.' Otmar led my companion over the rocks; but decided that Heinrich should bring me up the snow face. Step cutting is slow work, and though Otmar, having reached the top of the saddle, threw down a second rope, which Heinrich lashed round his waist, it was two o'clock before that terrible wall was surmounted, and we could look down the great glacier that plunged seven thousand feet down into the hollow where Grindelwald lay with its red roofs and pleasant pastures, its hotels and its tourists.

We had taken nearly six hours to surmount the pass; but we seemed, nevertheless, to have the day well in hand. Four thousand feet down on a spur of the Wetterhorn we could see the slate roof of the Gleckstein hut. It seemed an easy walk over the glacier, but in these vast solitudes of ice and snow and rock, vision is deceptive. The distant seems incredibly near, for the familiar measurements of the eye are wanting.

The weather had changed again. Clouds had settled on the mighty cliffs of the Schreckhorn on our left and the Wetterhorn on our right. Mist was rolling over the pass; rain began to fall. We cut short our lunch (cold tea, cold veal, bread and jam), and began our descent, making a wide detour of the glacier to the right in the direction of the Wetterhorn. We descended a rocky precipice that cleaves the glacier, crossed an ice-slope on which Otmar had to cut steps, and came in view of Grindelwald, lying like a picture postcard far down below—so immediately below that it seemed that one might fling a stone down into its midst.

At half-past three it began to dawn on me that things were not going well. Otmar had, during the past three weeks, been the most skilful of guides over

150

most of the great glacier passes of the Oberland and up many a peak ; but so far we had seen nothing like the condition of the Grindelwaldfirn. The appalling slope of this great sea of ice makes a descent in normal times a task of difficulty. But this year the long drought had left open all the yawning crevasses with which it is seamed, and its perils were infinitely increased.

Again and again Otmar sought a way out of the maze, taking us across perilous snow-bridges and cutting steps on knife-edges of ice where one looked down the glittering slope on one side, and into the merciless green-blue depths of the crevasse on the other. But wherever he turned he was baulked. Always the path led to some vast fissure which could be neither leapt nor bridged. Once we seemed to have escaped and glissaded swiftly down. Then the slope got steeper and we walked—steeper, and Otmar began cutting steps in the ice—steeper, and Otmar paused and looked down the leap of the glacier. We stood silent for his verdict. " It will not go." We turned on the rope without a word, and began remounting our steps.

It was half-past four. The mist was thickening, the rain falling steadily. Below, the red roofs and green pastures of Grindelwald gleamed in the sunlight of the valley. Nearer, the slate roof of the Gleckstein on its spur of rock was still visible. Two hours before it had seemed but a step to either. Now they seemed to have receded to another hemisphere.

For the first time there flashed through the mind the thought that possibly we should not reach the hut after all. A night on the glacier, or rather on the dark ridges of the Wetterhorn ! A wet night, too.

The same thought was working in Otmar's mind.

No word came from him, no hint that he was concerned. But the whole bearing of the man was changed. In the long hours of the morning he had led us listlessly and silently ; now he was like a hound on the trail. The tug of the rope became more insistent. He made us face difficulties that he had skirted before ; took us on to snow-bridges that made the mind reel ; slashed steps with his ice axe with a swift haste that spoke in every stroke of the coming night. Once I failed to take a tricky snow ridge that came to a point between two crevasses, slipped back, and found myself in the crevasse, with my feet dancing upon nothing. The rope held ; Otmar hauled me out without a word, and we resumed our march.

Heinrich had been unroped earlier and sent to prospect from above for a possible way out. We followed at his call, but he led us into new mazes, down into a great cavern in the glacier, where we passed over the ruined walls and buttresses of an ice cathedral, emerging on the surface of the glacier again, only to find ourselves once more checked by impassable gulfs.

It was now half-past five. We had been three and a half hours in vainly attempting to find a way down the ice. The mist had come thick upon us. The peaks were blotted out, Grindelwald was blotted out ; the hut was no longer visible. Only an hour and a half of light remained, and the whole problem was still unsolved. The possibility of a night on the ice or the rocks began to approach the sphere of certainty. My strength was giving out, and I slipped again and again in the ice steps. A kind of dull resignation had taken possession of the mind. One went forward in a stupor, responsive to the tug of the rope, but indifferent to all else.

Otmar was now really concerned. He came from

a valley south of the Rhone, and was unfamiliar with this pass ; but he is of a great strain of Alpine guides, is proud of his achievements—he had led in the first ascent of the Zmutt ridge of the Matterhorn that year—and to be benighted on a glacier would have been a deadly blow to his pride.

He unroped himself, and dashed away in the direction of the ridge of the Wetterhorn that plunged down on our right. We watched him skimming across crevasses, pausing here and there to slash a step in the ice for foothold, balancing himself on icy ridges and vanishing into a *couloir* of the mountain—first depositing his rucksack on the rocks to await his return. Five minutes passed—ten. Heinrich startled the silence with a halloo—no answer. A quarter of an hour—then, from far below a faint cry came.

" It will go," said Heinrich, " get on." We hurried across the intervening ice, and met Otmar returning like a cat up the rocks. Down that narrow slit in the mountain we descended with headlong speed. There were drops of thirty and fifty feet, slabs of rock to cross with negligible foot and hand holds, passages of loose rock where a careless move would have sent great stones thundering on the heads of those before. Once Heinrich lowered me like a bale of goods down a smooth-faced precipice of fifty feet. Once he cried : " Quick : it is dangerous," and looking up at the crest of the Wetterhorn I saw a huge block of ice poised perilously above our downward path.

The night was now upon us. We were wet to the skin. A thunderstorm of exceptional violence added to the grimness of the setting. But we were down the ridge at last. We raced across a narrow tongue of the glacier and were safe on the spur of rocks where we knew the Gleckstein hut to be. But there was no light to guide us. We scrambled breathlessly over boulders and across torrents from the Wetterhorn, each of us hardly visible to the other in the thickening mist, save when the blaze of lightning flashed the scene into a sudden and spectral clearness. At last we struck a rough mountain pass, and five minutes later we lifted the latch of the hut.

" What is the time, Heinrich ? "

" Half-past eight."

" What would you have done, Otmar, if we had been benighted ? "

Otmar did not hear. But as he got the wood and made the fire, and emptied the rucksacks of our provisions, he began to sing in a pleasant tenor voice. And Heinrich joined in with his full bass.

And presently, stripped of our wet clothes and wrapped in blankets, we sat down to a glorious meal of steaming tea—in an iron teapot as large as a pail—tongue, soup, potted chicken, and jam.

" That was a narrow escape from a night on the mountain," I said.

" It is a very foolish glacier," said Heinrich.

Otmar said nothing.

Five hours later Otmar woke us from our bed of hay.

" It is fine," he said. " The Wetterhorn will go."

.   .   .   .   .

As I look up it is still raining and the sad sheaves still stand in the sodden fields. But I have been a journey. I have had three weeks in the Oberland—three weeks of summer days with the world at peace, the world that seems like a dream we once had, so remote has it become and so incredible. I roll up my magic carpet and bless the man who invented maps for the solace of men.

From " Leaves in the Wind "

"ON THE ACTUAL SPOT"

C. E. MONTAGUE

MERELY to walk about the ground before the pageant at York in 1909 was to come into stirring and effortless contact with plenty of history. You went in past a tower the Romans built under Severus ; from the grand stand your eye caught a church that was founded by Siward, who put down Macbeth ; the scene was shut in at the back by the wall of an abbey whence Fountains itself was an offshoot. The lawn where they played sloped down on the left to the Ouse, and your eye set your mind travelling up and down stream, along the level Vale of York, southward to where that natural pathway is carried on up the broad Vale of Trent until it debouches on flat Southern England, and northward to where it leads easily out, between the flanking Pennine and the Yorkshire Wolds, to the sill of flat coast that in roadless times opened a way, round hilly Durham and Northumberland, to Scotland. What a place for a city ! A bridge crossed the river in sight ; it, too, offered to tell about York's being one of the puissant company of ancient inland seaports—Chester, Bristol, Lincoln, Norwich, Canterbury, Rochester, London, Exeter, Gloucester—the ' bridge places ' or first-bridge towns at the head of tidal navigations in a time of small sea-craft. On such a site history is sensuous. York, you see with your eyes, must always have counted, as surely as Constantinople, unless you go back to some date when reddish waves were licking

155

all round the southern base of the Peak and laying
down the soft red sand with which the men of York
and Chester were to build.

 ' As you sat in the stand, replete with these pleasing
reflections and ravished to find the receipt of ideas
so painless, there entered the first players, a Neolithic
household and their friends, who quarrelled, made it
up, prayed and loved till the Bronze Age, embodied
in picturesque strangers, came in and, after some words,
intermarried with the natives, round-skull with long-
skull, for the eventual production of the reasonably
modelled skulls now exhibited by the citizens of York.
It was all most earnestly done ; it was done by Mr
Louis Parker, far the best pageant-maker then in
practice. And yet, strangely, what people would call
the appropriateness of the scene actually kept one's
mind from attending. There were the Neolithic
family and the adventitious Trojans, doing the right
thing with all their souls, and after them the Romans
and the Angles and everybody in his season, and
there at the bottom of the lawn was the bed of the
valley up which, in good earnest, Neolithic man had
chased Palæolithic man into the poorer soils of North
Britain, and Brythons had propelled Picts into Gallo-
way, and Angles at the proper time had pushed
Brythons up into Strathclyde, as naturally as the
Great North Road has flowed along the same course,
and the Great Northern Railway after it. And yet
the standing topographic pageant did not help out
the momentary dramatic one, but hindered it and
rivalled it. There was any amount of archæological
care and competence in the dresses, the weapons, and,
as far as might be, in the action ; there were lines
with music and force in them, written by Mr James
Rhoades. But somehow it was like acting now a

Plantagenet's coronation in Westminster Abbey. Acting is one mighty stimulant to imagination, and the presence of the scene of great and ancient events is another; but you cannot just add the one to the other and enjoy at once the sum of both, perhaps because some attributes inseparable from the acting take repose away from those other objects, and some attributes commonly found in those objects make acting look flimsy and cheap, though it is not.

It was the same with the later scenes—admirably chosen as they were, and rightly and richly equipped, and acted with spirit. Severus's own many-angled tower near the pageant-ground was too much for Severus in tinsel and wig. St Mary's Abbey's own wall took all the illusion out of St Mary's monks when they mutinied and ' ragged ' in the veritable precinct. At least one of us recalled another baulking of hope, ten years earlier, when Mr F. R. Benson and his comrades played the surrender scenes of *Richard II* in that very Flint Castle where Richard had fallen into Bolingbroke's hands five hundred years, to a day, before. The Castle, now a mere ring of stumps of towers, stands on a little promontory jutting into the estuary of the Dee. The stumps enclose a green courtyard, roughly round. As you enter this courtyard the eye leaves behind it the squat, smudgy town, blighted with chemical works; to right and left it sees only stretches of wet sand and bleached grass, with sea-birds moving over them; in front it looks across water and sand, then shimmering and blinking in August heat, to the low hills of the Wirral. Planted on this background there stood out the least wrecked of the towers, a ruin some thirty feet high, many of its stones eaten away almost to the texture of a honeycomb or a sponge, its upper edge tattered with decay and overgrown with grass and wild flowers. Stage scenery was hung or leant against this tower; a rough stage was built in front of it; once or twice it was brought into use as part of the scenery itself. as where Richard from the Castle walls parleys with Northumberland before descending to the 'base court.' Some of us had hoped to unite for a few hours the characteristic pleasures of the playhouse to the pleasure kindled by the sight of places and buildings that played great parts long ago. Might not those surroundings attune one's mind, in some new and more effectual way, to the theme and the poetry ?

It was a failure. Theatrical illusion, whatever it is, fell down dead in that open air which the voice could not fill, and amidst that circle of almost derisive realities. And the realities suffered loss too. The old eaten stones and the tinny stage armour, the rouge and the sunlight, the sound of the metre and the sounds of the sea-birds flying and crying over the sands, debased and insulted each other, until you felt that you never had known how much could be said both against acting and against keeping unburied the bones of dead buildings. The sensation revived on seeing Constantine the Great and Caracalla, Harold and Edwin and half the Plantagenets disport themselves, in a guise which really postulated footlights, among the stones of Roman and Norman York. Perhaps the right way to give a pageant, if at all, is in a clear space surrounded by an enormous paling and emptied of every 'property' tainted with the fatal attribute of non-theatricality. For as surely as anything non-theatrical intrudes it will make everything that is rightly theatrical look wrongly theatrical, or 'stagy,' and it may look, itself, like a mummy in a green-room.

There is a further difficulty, a deep incompatibility

between the two pleasures that these performances are meant to blend. At Flint the stones that Richard II may have trodden, the sands along which Bolingbroke marched from Chester " with great joy and satisfaction "—these, by themselves, set your fancy to work ; they delight you ; they earn an importance. And yet at the touch of the great play acted before them, they seemed not to gain, but lose, moment ; their interest dwindled. For, the more the play's passion takes you up into itself, the more do you find that the mere fact that Richard surrendered at Flint, and not at Pomfret or Conway, does not matter at all. By writing *Richard II* Shakespeare did in one sense render the event of 21st August, 1399, more memorable ; but in another he rendered it less so ; less memorable for that it happened where it did and when it did, more memorable for what it meant of tempest and revolution in men's spirits. In ascending from the rather simple, elementary range of interest in events, as fixed by certain dates or places, to the range of interest in their moral causes, he somehow inflicts on the former a kind of atrophy, a relative belittlement. What, you come to feel, have you to do with local ruins and chronology, when such a rushing tide of emotion is there to carry you along ? They become irrelevant, almost impertinent, with their little appeal, so pleasant and good at other times, to the amateur archæologist within us.

From " Dramatic Values "

CASTLES IN THE AIR

the mind ... ... their

CASTLES IN THE AIR

R. B. CUNNINGHAME GRAHAM

YOUR castles in the air are the best castles to
possess, and keep a quiet mind. In them no
taxes, no housemaids, no men-at-arms, no larders
bother, and no slavery of property exists. Their
architecture is always perfect, the prospect of and from
them is always delightful, and, in fact, without them
the greater part of humanity would have no house
in which to shield their souls against the storms of life.
It is prudent, therefore, to keep these aerial fortalices
in good repair, not letting them too long out of our
mind's eye, in case they vanish altogether into Spain.

Good business men, and those that think that they
are practical merely because they lack imagination,
have maintained that castles such as these are but the
creation of the brain, and that as fancy is but an
exercise of the mind, its creations can have no existence
in mere fact. To each man after his demerits ; to
some day books, ledgers, cash-boxes, and the entire
armour of the Christian business man. Let them put
it on, taking in their hands the sword of covetousness,
having on their arms the shield of counterfeit, the
helmet of double-dealing upon their heads, till they
are equipped fully at all points to encounter man's
worst enemy, his fellow-man. Let them go forth,
prevail, destroy, opening up markets, broadening their
balances and their phylacteries ; let them at last
succeed and build their stucco palace in Park Lane ;
to them the praise, to them the just reward of their

laborious lives ; to them blear eyes, loose knee joints, rounded backs, and hands become like claws with holding fast their gold.

But let your castle builders in the perspective of the mind have their life, too ; let them pursue their vacuous way, if but to serve as an example of what successful men should all avoid. Buoys in safe channels, lighthouses set up on coasts where no ships pass ; preachers who preach in city churches where no congregation ever comes except the beadle, a deaf woman, and a child or two ; Socialist orators who do " Ye Men of England " to a policeman and an organ-grinder—all have their uses, and may serve some day if coral insects build their reef, the *Flying Dutchman* should put in for rest, a shower fill the church, or men grow weary of the strife of parties, and why not those who dream ? They have their uses, too, because the castles that they build are permanent and suffer no decay. Tantallon, Hermitage, Caerlaverock, Warwick, and Kenilworth must crumble at the last, a heap of stones, grey ruined walls grown green with moss, and viper's bugloss springing from the crevices, some grassy mounds, a filled-up ditch to mark the moat, a bank or two to show the tilting ground, and a snug lodge, in which the lodge-keeper sits with gold-laced hat to take the tourists' sixpences—to that favour must they all come, even if masonry be fathoms thick, mortar as hard as adamant, and the men who built have builded not on the modern system, but like beavers or the constructors of the pyramids.

Your visionary castle, though, improves with time, youth sees its bastions rise, and each recurring year adds counterscarps, puts here a rampart or a mamelon, throws out a glacis or constructs a fosse, till middle age sees the whole fort impregnable. But as imagination commonly improves with years, old age still sees the castle untaken and entire ; and when death comes, and the constructor passes away to sleep beside the million masons of the past, young builders rise to carry on the work ; so that, considered justly, air is the best foundation on which a man can build ; so that he does not wish to see his ashlar scale, mortar return to lime, and to be bothered all his life with patching that which with so much pains in youth he built. The poor man's shelter in the frosts of life ; the rich man's summer house, to which he can retire and ease himself of the tremendous burden of his wealth ; the traveller's best tent ; the very present refuge of all those who fail—your visionary castle rears its head, defying time itself.

Often so real is the castle in the air, that a man sells his own jerry-built, stuccoed mansion in the mud, to journey towards his castle, as travellers have sold their lands to see the deserts in which other people live. Think what a consolation to the outcast in the crowded street, on the wet heath, straying along the interminable road of poverty, to bear about with him a well-conceived and well-constructed dream house, pitched like the ark, inside and out, against not only weather, but the frowns of fortune—a place in which to shelter in against the tongues of fools, refuge in which to sulk under the misery of misconception, half-comprehension, unintelligent appreciation, and the more real ills of want of bread—for well the Spaniards say that every evil on God's earth is less with bread.

How few can rear a really substantial castle in the clouds : poets, painters, dreamers, the poor of spirit, the men of no account, the easily imposed upon, those who cannot say No, the credulous, the simple-hearted, often the weak, occasionally the generous

and the enthusiastic spirits sent into the world to shed
as many tears as would float navies ; these generally
are famous architects of other people's fortunes.
They rear palaces set in the middle distance of their
minds, compared to which the Alhambra, the Alcazar,
the Ambraz, Windsor and Fontainebleau, and the
mysterious palaces in Trapalanda, which the Gauchos
used to say were situated somewhere in the recesses
of the Andes, beyond the country of the Manzaneros,
are heavy, over-charged, flat, commonplace, ignoble,
wanting in all distinction, and as inferior as is the
four-square house in Belgrave Square, just at the
corner of Lower Belgrave Street, to an Italian palace
of the *rinascimento*, or the old " Casa de Mayorazgo,"
in the *plaza* at Jaen.

I read of such a master builder once in a newspaper.
He was, I think, a mason, and whilst he worked
bedding the bricks in lime, or underneath his shed
hewing the stone with chisel and the bulbous-looking
mallet masons use, the white dust on his clothes and
powdering his hair, or on the scaffold waiting whilst
the Irish hodman brought him bricks, he used to think
of what some day he would construct for his own
pleasure in the far-off time when money should be
made, wife found, house of his own achieved, and
leisure to indulge his whims assured. Needless to say
he was not of the kind who rise ; master and mates
and foremen used to call him dreamy and unpractical.
His nickname was " The Castle Builder," for those
who had to do with him divined his mind was elsewhere, though his hands performed their task. Still,
a good workman, punctual at hours, hard working,
conscientious, and not one of those who spend the
earnings of a week in a few hours of booze at the
week's end. Tall, fair, blue-eyed, and curly-haired,

a little loose about the knees, and in the fibre of the mind ; no theologian ; though well read, not pious, and still not a *revolté*, thinking the world a pleasant place enough when work was regular, health good, hours not too long, and not inclined to rail on fortune, God, nature, or society for not making him a clerk. Things, on the whole, went pretty well with him ; during the week he worked upon the hideous cube-like structures which men love to build ; and Sunday come, he walked into the fields to smoke his pipe and muse upon his castles in the air. Then came an evil time— lockout or strike, I can't remember which—no work, plenty of time to dream, till money flew away, and the poor mason started on the tramp to look for work. Travelling, the Easterns say, is hell to those who ride, and how much more than hell for those who walk. I take it that no desert journey in the East, nor yet the awful tramp of the man who left afoot walks for his life, on pampa or on prairie, is comparable in horror to the journey of the workman out of work. On the one hand the walker fights with nature, thirst, hunger, weariness, the sun, the rain, with possible wild beasts, with dangers of wild men, with loss of road ; sleeping he lies down with his head in the direction he intends to take on rising, and rising tramps towards the point he thinks will bring him out ; and as he walks he thinks, smokes, if he has tobacco, takes his pistol out, looks at the cartridges, feels if his knife is safely in his belt, and has a consciousness that if all goes right he may at last strike houses and be saved.

But, on the other hand, the wanderer has houses all the way ; carriages pass by him in which sit comfortable folk ; children ride past on ponies, happy and smiling, bicycles flit past, cows go to pasture, horses are led to water, the shepherd tends his sheep, the very dogs have their appointed place in the economy of the world, whilst he alone, willing to work, with hands made callous by the saw, the hammer, file, the plough, axe, adze, scythe, spade, and every kind of tool, a castaway, no use, a broken cogwheel, and of less account than is the cat which sits and purrs outside the door, knowing it has its circle of admirers who would miss it if it died.

Oh, worse than solitude, to wander through a thicket of strange faces, all thorny, all repulsive, all unknown ; no terror greater, no nightmare, no creeping horror which assails you alone at night in a strange house, so awful as the unsympathetic glare of eyes which know you not, and make no sign of recognition as you pass. And so the mason tramped, lost in the everglade of men who, like trees walking, trample upon all those who have no settled root. At first, thinking a mason must of necessity be wanted, either to build or work amongst the stone, he looked for labour at his trade. Then, finding that wheresoe'er he went masons were as plentiful as blackberries upon an autumn hedge, he looked for work at any trade, conscious of strength and youth and wish to be of use in the great world which cast him out from it as a lost dog, to stray upon the roads.

Past villages and towns, along the lanes, by rivers and canals he wandered, always seeking work ; worked at odd jobs and lost them, slept under railway arches and in the fields, in barns and at the lee of haystacks, and as he went along he dreamed (though now more faintly) of his castles in the air. Then came revolt ; he cursed his God who let a workman, a stone mason, starve, with so much work to do, stone to be hewn, and houses built, churches to rear, docks to be made, and he alone, it seemed to him, of all mankind, condemned to walk for ever on the roads. At last, tired of his God's and man's injustice, faint from want of food, and with his castle scarcely visible, he sat him down just on the brink of a black, oily river outside a manufacturing town, the water thick and greasy, and at night looking like Periphlegethon, when ironworks belch out their fires, and clouds of steam creep on the surface of the flood.

And seated there, his feet just dangling in the noxious stream, the night-shift going to a factory found him, and as they asked him what he did, he murmured, "Castles, castles in the air," and rested from his tramp.

From " Success "

RAIN

EDWARD THOMAS

THE prejudice of poets against water has perhaps kept rain out of fashion in literature. It is true that rain is among the subtle anonymous *dramatis personæ* of Lear, and that Milton wove into the harmonies of melancholy " the minute-drops from off the eaves." Swift's famous " Shower " knocks somewhat grossly at the door. " There never was such a shower since Danae's," ran contemporary compliment. There is, too, an allusion to rain in *Childe Harold,* as a pianissimo accompaniment to storms. But it is characteristic of modern poetry, as a criticism of life by livers, that it has left the praise of rain to hop farmers and of mud to shoeblacks. If literature were faithful to life, there would have been a chorus of benedictions after the rain that whispered on the hansom window-panes and sent the grumbling Thames to sleep with soft hands, as we drove from the play on a Midsummer night ; the French Academy would have elected at least one member for his rendering of the meaning of sleet, during a grey and purple sunset over the coast of Brittany. Even at the fireside I am washed by rain until I seem to glimmer and rejoice like the white headstones on the hill !

It is falling now as I sit with paper-spoiling intention, and the sound brings back the rain that used to come from heaven on summer mornings at Oxford, while invisible cattle were lowing and doves cooing, and a distant bell was tolled : brings back the rain in a city

street by night, that softened the sky to a deep blue
that was the very hue of mercy thrown over the awful
darkness ; and—gaily, daintily—the drops that came
and went (like stars in a restless sky) on the fir-tree
foliage as we came to the trout river, in sudden sunlight. Now it is near sunset. The blackbirds are
singing lazily in the gardens. The traffic has ceased
as if the silence had cried : " No thoroughfare."
A Circean lady is playing Grieg. She could turn us
into swine ; that her quiet smile proclaims ; she does
for the time change into gods some of those who are
sitting in the great blue apartment, half shadowed, as
the expression fluctuates, tender, minatory, tumultuous, hypnotic, vast. Still the rain is falling, and the
horse-chestnuts in the street expand, their leaves shine.
Their size and beauty are as things newly acquired.
Two especially that rise between distant groups of
houses fill the whole space of sky—touch the stars ;
in a few minutes, the constellations hang in their
branches and swing as the trees are shaken. The rain
has gone to their very hearts. They sigh tremulously
as if the drops moved them with a tranquil joy   I
could wish I were a horse-chestnut now. . . .   In
winter I have seen them made much of by the heavens,
and, against the rainy blue, so vast as to touch the roof
of the temple, like the Zeus of Pheidias, particularly
when all day the shower has descended pensively and
without wind. Then songs were hushed ; the pools
rocked only with smooth leaden waves. Before evening
the rain had worked its spell. Thrushes' songs filled the
hawthorns among the gorse. The wan grass was
beautiful ; but for a time the young blades were
dominant, deep green with the depth of night, yet
fresh with the freshness of day ; black, dripping trees
overhung the grass, and both had a colour like that of

hues and forms seen through water. All things smiled
faintly so that I seemed to touch the pericardium of
eternity. The slight melancholy and the great solemnity of the rain that had passed away entered the
song of the robin.

Few pictures deal nobly with rain and mud. Yet
in a great city what elvish effects they prepare !
Coruscating, sadly but brilliantly, the mud gravely
relieves the white faces and gaudy raiment that pass
by night, and adds to the dreaminess of a scene, in
which the pageant of life is like a strange flora to the
eye. Of all the mud I have known, the most beautiful
is that which is often to be seen on the banks of the
Thames below Waterloo Bridge, lying like a crude
monster, while the sunset is rosy and green and purple
on its flanks, and two swans float and barges heave at
rest ; or while at dawn the city is all its own, a quiet,
grey city that has vanished when the mud has sunk
below the tide.

One shower I remember that wrought magic in a
London garden. A kind of judicious neglect by the
owner had made the garden a kindly party to any
unusual trick of the elements. On the lawn was a
sundial that made Time an alluring toy. At the
bottom of the garden, beyond the lawn, was an enclosed
space of warm rank grasses, and, rising over them a
vapour of cow-parsley flowers. A white steam from
the soil faintly misted the grass to the level of the
tallest buttercups. Rain was falling, and the grasses
and overhanging elm trees seemed to be suffering for
their quietness and loneliness, to be longing for something, as perhaps Eden also dropped " some natural
tears " when left a void. A hot, not quite soothing
perfume crept over the lawn. All night I was haunted
by those elms which appeared as grey women in cloaks

of that strange mist. For the time, that garden was the loneliest place on earth, and I loved and feared its loneliness.

Of rain seen from indoors, falling on a broad rich land of grass and trees, or seen (from heavenly altitudes) falling on the grey and blue slates of a town I dare not speak. But I have known the rain, hissing on the lawn, complete the luxury of tea at Oxford in November, when the heart is fresh from walking. There is a generous fire ; seven league slippers on the feet; hot buttered brown toast, and, as evening changes from grey to grey in quiet crescendo, still the rain.

In this London garden there was one day which I may not omit, for the rain that buried it said many things which I have copied.

The shadow of the lime trees lay soft upon the grass, wonderfully soft because of the shy early sunlight. A bird sang such blithe notes as wakened the soul, disrobing it of the dishonours and disgusts of ages, restoring it to Paradise. From a corner of the garden I could see, over many steeples and chimneys, the side of a great wave of land, fledged with a few white cloudlets ; and as yet I could not say whether these were of snow or blackthorn flowers. Fainter still, among distant trees, I saw a doubtful glimmer which might be the forward sweeping hem of vernal splendour. In such moments of doubt I have found the calendar's positive announcement of Spring a solace. A mist muffled the angles of the landscape, a mist where the whole force of spring might lie in ambush. The sun had burnt for an hour like the fire of a thrifty candle. Presently it flushed (it almost crackled like a faggot) with a good-humoured lustihead. Then I knew that in the grass the dewy charities of the south winds were beginning to tell, and that the haze had fostered that slumbrous warmth in which chaffinches love to sing. Through the grey air at first the sky was invisible, save a misted blue pane here and there appearing, and vanishing, and engrailed by the grey cloud. Some windows northward glowed. Something undefinable that was Spring's and Dawn's richly mounted everything ; it entered the new stone church and gave it centuries backward and forward of glory and repose. Even the shadows on a dusty road were mysterious as shadow on deep water, and had an azure unknown before. And still the blackbirds sang :

> " High trolollie lollie loe
> High trolollie lee.
> Tho' others think they have as much
> Yet he that says so lies.
> Then come away,
> Turn country man with me."

A wind just lifted the coltsfoot down. Such a wind it was as brings to corners where the willow-wrens never wander a song like the song of willow-wrens and all that their bland southern voices mean among English trees. It comes in March from between the South and the East, and passes into the cold and odourless meadows, with the odour of all the flowers of the orient and the sweetness of the sea.

My path lay between rows of houses that were hidden by almond flowers among black boughs. If I paused—and the wind dropped—I could just detect the reluctant savour of struggling green life. Then the " lane " became the bordering road of a common. Here the sun was the genius of a company of haggard poplars in whose branches it seemed to hang, and the paths are haunted by ghosts of divers faces—O Memory !

> *Tuis hic omnia plena*
> *Muneribus.*

One of these ghosts—the rain was beginning to hiss in the trees and patter on the dead leaves below—was of an old man who had played Edmund in his youth. Beaten by a slow mortal disease in his prime, he had lived happily in the midst of friends who never abated the services which his gracious feebleness exacted and made appear a duty. He who should have died first survived them all. His mind nodded and slept, leaving a childishness that was not happy. All the pleasant valetudinarian space disappeared from his memory ; the tumultuous early days returned, and at intervals he strayed amidst the pageant in which the figures of Lear and Richard the Second towered with minatory pomp. For his part had ever been traitorous and base. The evil acted " in his days of nature " haunted him fearfully. In a great voice (so that he used to say : " I fear my mother hears me ") he would repeat the speech of Lear : " Howl, howl, howl, howl. Oh ! ye are men of stones," as often as he had heard it when, as Edmund, he was borne off before the end : he seemed to whimper behind the stage, crying bitterly to be admitted to die before the King. Luckily, before his death all became dark. It was with surprise that I heard he was dead. For years he seemed not to have lived. . . .

Now the road went near several great houses, of a kind which rain makes eloquent. And the rain was falling then with a sound like the silence of a multitude. They were not the old, beautiful houses of London, but such as were built not more than sixty years ago for someone grown suddenly rich. The old houses can always chatter of what has fallen from them by indiscreet neglect or foolish care, and all must regret the blotting of the little unnecessary trifles that were part of their nobility, like the grassy spaces between the garden wall and the public road, where the fowls paraded, and the ivy was plaited with periwinkle to the edge of the macadam. These middle-aged houses make no such appeal. They gibber in premature senility, between tragedy and comedy. Nobody will live there now ; the gardens are feeble and disordered, and the dahlias fade one by one Passers-by laugh at their " style." Even the creepers have taken no hold of the wall and have fallen dishevelled. I do not believe the former occupants ever come a little way out of their path to see their house. Yonder were the gaudy doors, and blinds still hanging ; the romantic name on the folding gates ; and I remembered the autumn rain in which they took heart. Each was the gloomier for the one lamp glimmering near the gate ; the soiled crimson leaves were shaken out over the path ; the starlings screamed mechanically ; the bleared sunset was swallowed up in rain. And in that hour the house, once an anachronism, a mixture of parts of several incongruous styles, seemed to have grown very old, and against the wildly moving sky and stars, it gained an indubitable style, that of Stonehenge and the mountain crag—the natural style, the immortal style of things too old.

Beyond these houses lay the Little House, and behind a high exclusive fence, a holly hedge and a lawn. It was empty. Its orchards were praised almost as they deserved, its rent lowered, in advertisements ; nobody came. Yet the lawn was always green ; a gardener—or who ?—kept sharp the angles which it made with the drive. The crocuses came out and lasted till the West wind spilt their petals in the deep grass. The only sign of neglect was the temerity of the ivy, which crept through the chinks of the door, through the keyhole, into the letter-box.

The rooms could be dimly seen from without, especially the great shaded children's nursery that faced the North and has said to me as I have passed:

> "I know the secret of the unhappiness of childhood. A fate abides with me, and through her I know the laws that mingle with the roses of life the lilies of death. I have made festal days awful. Many a sad dreamer curses the shadows that he used to see falling on my walls in early firelight."

And it continued until I wished for a Blakesmoor where I could quiet my alarms. As a rule, there was no hint of mysterious inhabitants. The emptiness was far more mysterious. It was wonderful to see how wild the garden looked after a short desertion—not disordered or weedy, but wild—though the flowers were of the daintiest and most elaborate kinds. Years ago I heard someone playing the *Didone abandonnata* in the Little House, and in the garden the echoes struck something that repeats them still.

To us, as children, it used to be a famous day when a new tenant came to this house. We had a cruel standard of fitness to apply to whomsoever came. Best of all we liked the ancient who lived in one room of it, kept no servants, put up no curtains, and in fact left the house exactly as we wished. We used to hear him singing in a cheerful rasping voice under the big cedar when he thought no one was near. When he quitted it, sitting among his furniture in an open cart, we implored him to stay. For a time we were alternately sorry and pleased at the emptiness of the house. We used to save our pocket-money continuously for whole months, to buy the freehold. And so we came to have a sense of possession, if not of occupation, which (we thought) was stronger because it was not known. To the sequestered Sylvans whose

escaping footsteps were heard in very early morning,
we prayed :

> " Be present aye with favourable feet
> And all profane audience far remove."

So intimate we grew that the garden seemed to understand us. I would that I could understand it in return.

On Spring days—like this—when a grass scent came
into the streets as if the fields and woods were insurgent,
near at hand, it was to the garden we went, counted
daffodils and lime leaves, listening for the new-come
martins that sang before they were seen, in the dark.
In these early visits we found more in the garden
than was in the articles of sale. So we hated the
rhododendrons that were planted by a later tenant.
He took an interest in the garden that was horrible ;
frivolous music was played in the house. Nevertheless,
in spite of the laughter, the splendour, and the glossy
carriage, the house had a defiant air, hating the young
gods and goddesses that supplanted the Olympians it
once knew. All its peers in the neighbourhood had
given way to villas ; I thought that perchance it
was time for the Little House to go. At evening the
thought grew stronger ; the house itself cried :

> " Now mark me how I will undo myself."

It went on :

> " God pardon all oaths that are broke to me,"

as if perhaps it knew that I had been vain enough to
think that I could have lived there happily, as if it
cared for the foolish ritual of my sorrow. If it were
destroyed, no one could assail my ownership. I might
be content. *Car il en est toujours qu'on peut aimer*. . . .
Yet I am not sure that I would have possessed it
actually. One day two of us were looking over the
gate gathering honey with our eyes, when a gracious

little girl came smiling towards us ; we slunk away. A little later she surprised us on tiptoe at the same place and at her invitation we entered the garden for the first time. We were persuaded to sit down near the lilacs. But we did not look round ; left alone for a moment, we planned an escape. Even when she came out with a tray and sat beside us, we were not happy. I remember that we whispered together, and the child laughed and tried to put us at our ease. My friend said with a voice of discovery : "They have tea here." We were near disillusion ; only, we did not know !

I have said that there was a common next to the house. The garden was more ours than that. Independence commonly means a state in which we never know on whom we depend ; the term common was false, and those who walked on it knew no such liberty as we. The garden belonged to us as truly as the world to the children who in a great library, colour the globe, red, green, and blue, for Mary, Arthur, and Dick. On the common there were "strange fetters to the feet, strange manacles to the hands." If any should wonder at this let them go to the garden at evening. A half-moon is alone in the sky. Is it green or is it white ? Here and there clusters of poplars vein the horizon. At that hour the waving trees are as delicate as grasses. Some windows are lit. Here a song is ending ; there a door is violently shut ; but already London is growing silent. The sounds are so faint that if I pause to listen and unravel them, I can hear my heart, the ticking of my watch, but not the enormous city. Go to the garden and see, in the shadow of a cedar, the apple blossom glow.

From " Rosacre Papers "

AN AUTUMN STROLL

W. N. P. BARBELLION

O N a recent day in early autumn I stood leaning against a tall larch tree, on the edge of a broad plantation, in a woodland corner of the North of Devon. I had been an indoor prisoner for a long, long time, and this was a first country walk. What a blessing to breathe again the sweet, honey-scented air ! How fresh-looking those meadows below, how green the trees ! For, autumn notwithstanding, the herbage had just reached that stage when it crowds all its many-tinted greens and the whole of its remaining vitality into one last sunny day ; then very quickly follow death and decay.

Even now, a few leaves on that sturdy oak, solitary in the field yonder, have turned to golden russet ; the larches, too, overhead are growing ragged and thin, and as the leaves begin to fall a few hardy cones that have weathered one winter already peep from their summer bowers and prepare once more for the blasts. Just in front, over the hedge of thick black-thorn, a furze brake—or, as Devonshire folk would say, 'vuzz' brake—spreads its tangled meshes, and I hear the rabbits rustling and scuttling among the bushes as though out for a general romp ; up from the valley on the left comes the rushing sound of running water, and, far ahead, the plain is lost to view in a medley of converging hills. Plump on the horizon appear the heath-clad downs, their glowing purple clear and luscious as the bloom on a peach.

In the solemnity and silence of the fir-wood I find an analogy with the atmosphere of mysterious repose in some stately cathedral, in the midst of, yet apart from, the vortex of busy life without. Into the dim recesses of the fir-wood few sounds of natural life make their way—except, perhaps, the call of a crow passing over the tree-tops, or the scream of a startled jay; and these are but momentary. Presently I leave the still woods to pass through the gap in the hedge, and so enter the busy whirl of wild life in the fields. It is a long way down to the little ivy-covered bridge that spans the river, so I do not hurry.

Here the delicate eyebright grows so thickly that I cannot help but crush it as I walk. Clusters of red bartsia and musk mallows crowd out the green of a grassy bank. Near a tangle of bramble and sweet briar the knapweed rears its head of pink flowerets.

A few steps further on, with inquisitive intent, I overturn a large flat stone (flat stones always harbour something interesting). Under this one is a nest of black ants. Away they run, carrying their eggs into the heart of the nest; but—yes, I thought so, right in the centre of the principal doorway lolls the ugly, repulsive form of a devil's coach-horse, or, as he is sometimes called, the Rove beetle. The busy ants find him distinctly in the way, and so they energetically set to work to shift the obstruction. Two climb on to his head and vigorously gnaw the bases of his stout antennæ, and two others attack the front pair of legs— a leg apiece! Another pinches the soft elongated abdomen. The effect on the beetle is ludicrous. He snaps his jaws like an angry terrier. Then he frantically waves his ' yard-arms,' and eventually, being nipped in many additional places by a reinforcement, he cocks his tail over his back and very reluctantly

178

(for he has been most comfortably ensconced) beats a hasty retreat. This is a great victory for the ants, as the devil's coach-horse is a noted warrior in the insect world. With renewed energy the ants recommence their labours, and when I re-pass the spot on my way home not an ant is to be seen, for the treasures have been successfully removed ' downstairs.' I carefully put the stone back in its place.

Here is the little bridge at last. It is built for the cattle to cross upon from one meadow to the other when the stream is flooded with winter rains. During the summer they scorn the bridge and splash across the water. Always a beautiful spot, it is never more beautiful than in the early autumn ; moreover, for me it has pleasant associations. Up beyond the bridge is a waterfall, over which the water gallops from the shimmering, silvery weir-pool above into the boulder-scattered shallows beneath. Solitude adds to the charm. Indeed, a companion's voice could scarce be heard amidst the little thunder of these dancing ' falls.'

That huge holt held an otter once, but whether he is there now is doubtful. Anyway, if I would see him, I must be up betimes in the morning ; I shall not see him to-day. A green canopy of hazels and alders smiles over all, and through the interstices the sun shines, dappling the shady waters with light. It was in this very stream, I recall, that I first made acquaintance with the wild red deer. This is how it was. The staghounds had met in the morning up at the village, and, according to custom, tufters were taken to a large wood some miles distant, which, for some unexplained reason, is always a favourite one with the deer. I had never yet seen a wild red deer, so I was anxious to make the best of my opportunities,

No other horse but ' Shanks' pony ' was available, and those ' in the know ' told me that the best thing I could do, in the circumstances, was to walk to a certain bridge, as the deer, when roused, almost invariably came straight down the combe and entered an oak coppice, to the left of the high road and adjoining this very bridge. I took the advice, and saw something far prettier than the antlered stag, with the eager hounds in his wake. I had been waiting patiently for upwards of two hours on the bridge and was engrossed in watching a silent riverside tragedy—the capture of a water-vole by a greedy heron—when, treading softly round the bend of the stream, and advancing calmly and quietly and in the fearlessness of privacy and innocence, there swept across my vision the charmingest, dearest, prettiest little calf in creation. He was a tiny fellow with brown coat and shapely neck, slender legs, and hazel eyes. Upon his lordship's arrival, the heron dropped the struggling vole, and he lumbered away and pitched on a tall elm ; a startled trout swam headlong down-stream. The calf, small as he was, was making quite a commotion.

In the helter-skelter in the wood beyond, probably he and his mother had been separated, and for the first time in his life he had to think for himself, to act on his own initiative. The oft-repeated words of the hind, his mother, that the water carries no scent, seemed now very valuable to him. He heard the waters calling—

> " I carry no scent, come here, come here.
> For I am the friend of the wild red deer."

So down towards the bridge he came, where I saw him. But he did not catch sight of me for several minutes although he seemed to scent me. He grew fussy and

half-playfully, half-nervously, browsed the leaves of
a nut-tree. But he did not eat them—he disdainfully
tossed them over his head, as an old stag would a
turnip. In jerking his head aloft he suddenly saw
me! For a moment he looked spellbound. He did
not move, nor did I. We looked straight into each
other's eyes. Then he blinked twice or thrice, and
slowly came nearer! Had he passed below the bridge
I could have touched him with my hand. But I was
disappointed, for on moving my hand the slightest
bit downwards the little creature (now standing right
below me) pricked his ears, jumped lightly on to the
bank, and then trotted across the meadow into a copse,
where I earnestly hope he remained undisturbed.

From " Enjoying Life "

SHIP'S LOGS

E. TEMPLE THURSTON

THERE is a yard by the riverside in London—
opposite Lambeth or somewhere thereabouts, I
think it must be—where you may come so close
in touch with Romance as will set your fancy afire
and transport you thousands of miles away upon the
far-off seas of the Orient.

You may talk in disbelieving tones of wishing-rings,
of seven-leagued boots and magic carpets, counting
them as fairy tales, food only for the minds of children ;
but they are after all only the poetic materialization of
those same subtle things in life which give wings to
our own imagination, or bring to eyes tired with
reality the gentle sleep of a daydream.

Nearly every one must know the place I write of.
It is where they break up into logs the timber of those
ships which have had their day—the ships that have
ridden fearless and safe through a thousand storms,
that have set forth so hopefully into the dim horizon
of the unknown and evaded to the last the grim,
grasping fingers of the hungry sea.

And there, you will see their death masks, those
silent figure heads which, for so many nights and so
many days with untiring, ever-watchful eyes have
faced the mystery of the deep waters unafraid. There
is something pathetic—there is something majestic,
too, about those expressionless faces. They seem so
wooden and so foolish when first you look at them ;
but as your fancy sets its wings, as your ears become

attuned to the inwardness that can be found in all things, however material, you will catch the sound of dim faint voices that have a thousand tales of the sea to tell, a thousand yarns to spin, a thousand adventures to relate.

Nothing is silent in this world. There is only deafness.

It has always appealed to me as the most noble of human conceptions, that burial of the Viking lord. The grandeur of it is its simplicity. There is a fine spectacular element in it, too, but never a trace of bombast. The modern polished oak coffin with its gaudy brass fittings, the super-ornate hearse, the prancing black stallions, the butchery of a thousand graceful flowers—all this is bombast if you wish. It no more speaks of death than speaks the fat figure of Britannia on the top of the highest circus car of England. Funerals to-day have lost all the grandeur of simplicity. But that riding forth in a burning ship, stretched out with folded hands upon the deck his feet had paced so oft; riding forth towards that far horizon which his eyes had ever scanned, there is a generous nobility in that form of burial. You can imagine no haggling with an undertaker over the funeral about this. Here was no cutting down of the prices, saving a little on the coffin here, there a little on the hearse.

No—this was the Viking's own ship—the most priceless possession that he had. Can you not see it plainly, with sails set, speeding forth upon its last voyage—the last voyage for both of them? And then, as the lapping, leaping flames catch hold upon the bellied canvas, I can see her settling down in the swinging cradle of the waves. I can see the dense column of smoke mingling with and veiling the tongues of orange flame, until she becomes like a little Altar set out upon a vast sea, offering up its sacrifice of a human soul to the ever-implacable Gods.

Now every time you burn a ship's log, you attend a Viking's burial. In those flames of green and gold, of orange, purple and blue, there is to be found, if you will use but the eyes for it, all the romance, all the spirit and colour of that majestic human sacrifice— the burial of a Viking lord. As you sit through the long evenings, while the rain is beating in sudden, whipping gusts, upon the streaming window-pane, and the drops fall spitting and hissing down the chimney into the fire below, then the burning of a ship's log is company enough for anyone. With every spurt of flame as the tar oozes out from the sodden wood, and the water, still clinging in the tenacious timber, bubbles and boils, you can distinguish, but faintly, the stirring voice of Romance telling of thrilling enterprise and of great adventure. There are few sailors can spin a yarn so much to your liking. Never was there a pirate ship so fleet or so bold ; there were never escapes so miraculous, or battles so stern, as you can see when in those long-drawn evenings you sit alone in the unlighted parlour and watch a ship's log burning on the fire.

Pay no heed to them when they tell you the green flames come from copper, the blue from lead—the pale purple from potassium. The chemist's laboratory has its own romance, but it shares nothing in common with the high seas of imagination upon which you are riding now. Let the green flames come from copper ! They are the emeralds, the treasure of the Orient to you. Let the blue flames come from lead, the pale purple from potassium ! In your eyes as you sit there in that darkened room, with the flame-light flickering upon the ceiling and the shadows creeping near to listen to it all, they are the blue sash around the waist, the purple kerchief about the head of the bravest and the most bloodthirsty pirate that ever stepped.

At all times a fire is a companion. Yet set but a ship's log upon the flames and I warrant you will lose yourself and all about you; lose yourself until the last light flickers, the last red ember falls, and the good ship that has borne you so safely over a thousand seas sinks down into the grey ashes of majestic burial.

From " The Patchwork Papers "

OF LIFE AND LETTERS

CHARMIAN

ALICE MEYNELL

"SHE is not Cleopatra, but she is at least Charmian," wrote Keats, conscious that his damsel was not in the vanward of the pageant of ladies. One may divine that he counted the ways wherein she was not Cleopatra, the touches whereby she fell short of and differed from, nay, in which she mimicked the Queen.

In like manner many of us have for some years past boasted of our appreciation of the interior beauty, the substitute, the waiting gentlewoman of corrupt or corruptible heart; Keats confessed, but did not boast. It is a vaunt now, an emulation, who shall discover her beauty, who shall discern her.

She is most conspicuous in the atmosphere in smoke effects, in the 'hush,' the 'mystery'; such are the preferred words. But let us take the natural and authentic light as our symbol of Cleopatra, her sprightly port, her infinite jest, her bluest vein, her variety, her laugh, "O Eastern star!"

Men in cities look upward not much more than animals, and these—except the dog when he bays the moon—look skyward not at all. The events of the sky do not come and go for the citizens, do not visibly approach and withdraw, threaten and pardon; they merely happen. And even when the sun so condescends as to face them at the level of their own horizon (say from the western end of the Bayswater Road), when he searches out the eyes that have

CHARMIAN

⸼ ALICE MEYNELL

"SHE is not Cleopatra, but she is at least Charmian," wrote Keats, conscious that his damsel was not in the vanward of the pageant of ladies. One may divine that he counted the ways wherein she was not Cleopatra, the touches whereby she fell short of and differed from, nay, in which she mimicked the Queen.

In like manner many of us have for some years past boasted of our appreciation of the inferior beauty, the substitute, the waiting gentlewoman of corrupt or corruptible heart ; Keats confessed, but did not boast. It is a vaunt now, an emulation, who shall discover her beauty, who shall discern her.

She is most conspicuous in the atmosphere in smoke ' effects,' in the ' lurid,' the ' mystery '; such are the perfervid words. But let us take the natural and authentic light as our symbol of Cleopatra, her sprightly port, her infinite jest, her bluest vein, her variety, her laugh. " O Eastern star ! "

Men in cities look upward not much more than animals, and these—except the dog when he bays the moon—look skyward not at all. The events of the sky do not come and go for the citizens, do not visibly approach and withdraw, threaten and pardon ; they merely happen. And even when the sun so condescends as to face them at the level of their own horizon (say from the western end of the Bayswater Road), when he searches out the eyes that have neglected him all day, finds a way between their narrowing lids, looks straight into their unwelcoming pupils, explores the careful wrinkles, singles and numbers the dull hairs, even, I say, to sudden sunset in our dim climate, the Londoner makes no reply ; he would rather look into puddles than into the pools of light among clouds.

Yet the light is as characteristic of a country as is its landscape. So that I would travel for the sake of a character of early morning, for a quality of noonday, or a tone of afternoon, or an accident of moonrise, or a colour of dusk, at least as far as for a mountain, a cathedral, rivers, or men. The light is more important than what it illuminates. When Mr Tomkins— a person of Dickens's earliest invention—calls his fellow-boarders from the breakfast-table to the window, and with emotion shows them the effect of sunshine upon the left side of a neighbouring chimney-pot, he is far from cutting the grotesque figure that the humourist intended to point out to banter. I am not sure that the chimney-pot with the pure light upon it was not more beautiful than a whole black Greek or a whole black Gothic building in the adulterated light of a customary London day. Nor is the pleasure that many writers, and a certain number of painters, tell us they owe to such adulteration anything other than a sign of derogation—in a word, a pleasure in the secondary thing.

Are we the better artists for our preference of the waiting-woman ? It is a strange claim. The search for the beauty of the less-beautiful is a modern enterprise, ingenious in its minor pranks, insolent in its greater. And its chief ignobility is the love of marred, defiled, disordered, dulled, and imperfect skies, the skies of cities.

Some will tell us that the unveiled light is too clear or sharp for art. So much the worse for art ; but even on that plea the limitations of art are better respected by natural mist, cloudy gloom of natural rain, natural twilight before night, or natural twilight—Corot's—before day, than by the artificial dimness of our unlovely towns. Those, too, who praise the ' mystery ' of smoke are praising rather a mystification than a mystery ; and must be unaware of the profounder mysteries of light. Light is all mystery when you face the sun, and every particle of the innumerable atmosphere carries its infinitesimal shadow.

Moreover, it is only in some parts of the world that we should ask for even natural veils. In California we may, not because the light is too luminous, but because it is not tender. Clear and not tender in California, tender and not clear in England ; light in Italy and in Greece is both tender and clear.

When one complains of the ill-luck of modern utilities, the sympathetic listener is apt to agree, but to agree wrongly by denouncing the electric light as something modern to be deplored. But the electric light is the one success of the last century. It is never out of harmony with natural things—villages, ancient streets of cities, where it makes the most beautiful of all street-lighting, swung from house to opposite house in Genoa or Rome. With no shock, except a shock of pleasure, does the judicious traveller, entering some small sub-alpine hamlet, find the electric light, fairly, sparingly spaced, slung from tree to tree over the little road, and note it again in the frugal wine-shop, and solitary and clear over the church portal.

Yet forsooth, if, yielding to the suggestions of your restless hobby, you denounce, in any company, the spoiling of your Italy, the hearer, calling up a ' mumping visnomy,' thinks he echoes your complaint by his sigh, " Ah, yes—the electric light ; you meet it everywhere now ; so modern, so disenchanting." It is, on the contrary, enchanting. It is as natural as lightning. By all means let all the waterfalls in all the Alps be ' harnessed,' as the lamentation runs, if their servitude gives us electric light. For thus the power of the waterfall kindles a lovely lamp. All this to be done by the simple force of gravitation—the powerful fall of water. " Wonderful, all that water coming down ! " cried the tourist at Niagara, and the Irishman said, " Why wouldn't it ? " He recognized the simplicity of that power. It is a second-rate passion—that for the waterfall, and often exacting in regard to visitors from town. " I trudged unwillingly," says Dr Johnson, " and was not sorry to find it dry." It was very, very second-rate of an American admirer of scenery to name a waterfall in the Yosemite Valley (and it bears the name to-day) the " Bridal Veil." His Indian predecessor had called it, because it was most audible in menacing weather, " The Voice of the Evil Wind." In fact, your cascade is dearer to every sentimentalist than the sky. Standing near the folding-over place of Niagara, at the top of the fall, I looked across the perpetual rainbow of the foam, and saw the whole further sky deflowered by the formless, edgeless, languid, abhorrent murk of smoke from the nearest town. Much rather would I see that water put to use than the sky so outraged. As it is, only by picking one's way between cities can one walk under, or as it were in, a pure sky. The horizon in Venice is thick and ochreous, and no one cares ; the sky of Milan is defiled all round. In England I must choose a path alertly ; and so does now and then a wary, fortunate, fastidious wind that has so found his exact, uncharted way, between this smoke and that, as to clear me a clean moonrise, and heavenly heavens.

There was an ominous prophecy to Charmian. "You shall outlive the lady whom you serve." She has outlived her in every city in Europe; but only for the time of setting straight her crown—the last servility. She could not live but by comparison with the Queen.

From "Hearts of Controversy"

experiments. His performance has lately caused a

THE PLEASURES OF WORK

A. C. BENSON

I DESIRE to do a very sacred thing to-day : to
enunciate a couple of platitudes and attest them.
It is always a solemn moment in life when one
can sincerely subscribe to a platitude. Platitudes are
the things which people of plain minds shout from the
steps of the staircase of life as they ascend ; and to
discover the truth of a platitude by experience means
that you have climbed a step higher.

The first enunciation is, that in this world we most
of us do what we like. And the corollary to that is,
that we most of us like what we do.

Of course, we must begin by taking for granted that
we most of us are obliged to do something. But that
granted, it seems to me that it is very rare to find
people who do not take a certain pleasure in their
work, and even secretly congratulate themselves on
doing it with a certain style and efficiency. To find
a person who has not some species of pride of this
nature is very rare. Other people may not share our
opinion of our own work. But even in the case of
those whose work is most open to criticism, it is almost
invariable to find that they resent criticism, and are
very ready to appropriate praise. I had a curiously
complete instance of this the other day. In a parish
which I often visit, the organ in the church is what
is called presided over by the most infamous executant
I ever heard—an elderly man, who seldom plays a
single chord correctly, and whose attempt to use the

194

pedals are of the nature of tentative and unsuccessful experiments. His performance has lately caused a considerable amount of indignation in the parish, for a new organ has been placed in the church, of far louder tone than the old instrument, and my friend the organist is hopelessly adrift upon it. The residents in the place have almost made up their minds to send a round-robin to the Vicar to ask that the *pulsator organorum*, the beater of the organ, as old Cathedral statutes term him, may be deposed. The last time I attended service, one of those strangely appropriate verses came up in the course of the Psalms, which make troubled spirits feel that the Psalter does indeed utter a message to faithful individual hearts. " *I have desired that they, even my enemies,*" ran the verse, " *should not triumph over me ; for when my foot slipped, they rejoiced greatly against me.*" In the course of the verse the unhappy performer executed a perfect fandango on the pedals. I looked guiltily at the senior churchwarden, and saw his mouth twitch.

In the same afternoon I fell in with the organist, in the course of a stroll, and discoursed to him in a tone of gentle condolence about the difficulties of a new instrument. He looked blankly at me, and then said that he supposed that some people might find a change of instrument bewildering, but that for himself he felt equally at home on any instrument. He went on to relate a series of compliments that well-known musicians had paid him, which I felt must either have been imperfectly recollected, or else must have been of a consolatory or even ironical nature. In five minutes, I discovered that my friend was the victim of an abundant vanity, and that he believed that his vocation in life was organ-playing.

Again, I remember that, when I was a schoolmaster,

one of my colleagues was a perfect byword for the disorder and noise that prevailed in his form. I happened once to hold a conversation with him on disciplinary difficulties, thinking that he might have the relief of confiding his troubles to a sympathetic friend. What was my amazement when I discovered that his view of the situation was, that every one was confronted with the same difficulties as himself, and that he obviously believed that he was rather more successful than most of us in dealing with them tactfully and strictly.

I believe my principle to be of almost universal application ; and that if one could see into the heart of the people who are accounted, and rightly accounted, to be gross and conspicuous failures, we should find that they were not free from a certain pleasant vanity about their own qualifications and efficiency. The few people whom I have met who are apt to despond over their work are generally people who do it remarkably well, and whose ideal of efficiency is so high that they criticize severely in themselves any deviation from their standard. Moreover, if one goes a little deeper— if, for instance, one cordially re-echoes their own criticisms upon their work—such criticisms are apt to be deeply resented.

I will go further, and say that only once in the course of my life have I found a man who did his work really well, without any particular pride and pleasure in it. To do that implies an extraordinary degree of will-power and self-command.

I do not mean to say that, if any professional person found himself suddenly placed in the possession of an independent income, greater than he had ever derived from his professional work, his pleasure in his work would be sufficient to retain him in the exercise of it. We have most of us an unhappy belief in our power of living the pleasurable and virtuous life of leisure ; and the desire to live what is called the life of a gentleman, which character has lately been defined as a person who has no professional occupation, is very strong in the hearts of most of us.

But, for all that, we most of us enjoy our work ; the mere fact that one gains facility and improves from day to day, is a source of sincere pleasure, however far short of perfection our attempts may fall ; and, generally speaking, our choice of a profession is mainly dictated by a certain feeling of aptitude for and interest in what we propose to undertake.

It is, then, a happy and merciful delusion by which we are bound. We grow, I think, to love our work, and we grow, too, to believe in our method of doing it. We cannot, a great preacher once said, all delude ourselves into believing that we are richer, handsomer, braver, more distinguished than others ; but there are few of us who do not cherish a secret belief that, if only the truth were known, we should prove to be more interesting than others.

To leave our work for a moment, and to turn to ordinary social intercourse. I am convinced that the only thing that can account for the large number of bad talkers in the world is the widespread belief that prevails among individuals as to their power of contributing interest and amusement to a circle. One ought to keep this in mind, and bear faithfully and patiently the stream of tiresome talk that pours, as from a hose, from the lips of diffuse and lengthy conversationalists. I once made a terrible mistake. I complimented, from the mere desire of saying something agreeable, and finding my choice of praiseworthy qualities limited, an elderly, garrulous acquaintance on his geniality, on an evening when I had writhed uneasily under a steady downpour of talk. I have bitterly rued my insincerity. Not only have I received innumerable invitations from the man whom the Americans would call my complimentee, but when I am in his company I see him making heroic attempts to make his conversation practically continuous. How often since that day have I sympathized with St James in his eloquent description of the deadly and poisonous power of the tongue ! A bore is not, as is often believed, a merely selfish and uninteresting person. He is often a man who labours conscientiously and faithfully at an accomplishment, the exercise of which has become pleasurable to him. And thus a bore is the hardest of all people to convert, because he is, as a rule, conscious of virtue and beneficence.

On the whole, it is better not to disturb the amiable delusions of our fellow-men, unless we are certain that we can improve them. To break the spring of happiness in a virtuous bore is a serious responsibility. It is better, perhaps, both in matters of work and in matters of social life, to encourage our friends to believe in themselves. We must not, of course, encourage them in vicious and hurtful enjoyment, and there are, of course, bores whose tediousness is not harmless, but a positively noxious and injurious quality. There are bores who have but to lay a finger upon a subject of universal or special interest, to make one feel that under no circumstances will one ever be able to allow one's thoughts to dwell on the subject again ; and such a person should be, as far as possible, isolated from human intercourse, like a sufferer from a contagious malady. But this extremity of noxiousness is rare. And it may be said that, as a rule, one does more to increase happiness by a due amount of recognition and praise, even when one is recognizing rather the spirit of a performance than the actual result ; and such a course of action has the additional advantage of making one into a person who is eagerly welcomed and sought after in all kinds of society.

From " The Thread of Gold "

AUDIENCES

A. B. WALKLEY

AUDIENCES may be divided into first-nighters, second-nighters, and general playgoers. All audiences are important, but first-nighters most of all. Without them the acted drama would not begin to exist. For obvious reasons, I have nothing but good to say of them. I wish to live at peace with my neighbours. And I do not believe the malicious story told about a manager, now dead, that he liked to fill the second row of his stalls on first-nights with his superannuated sweethearts. Nobody is fat or old in Ba-ath, and there are no superannuitants among first-nighters.

I find, from Mr Max Beerbohm's entirely delightful book *Seven Men*, that it is possible to get tired of first-nighters. I should never have guessed it myself. But this is what he says: " I was dramatic critic for the *Saturday Review*, and, weary of meeting the same lot of people over and over again at first nights, had recently sent a circular to the managers, asking that I might have seats for second nights instead." But mark what follows: " I found that there existed as distinct and invariable a lot of second-nighters as of first-nighters. The second-nighters were less ' showy '; but then, they came more to see than to be seen, and there was an air that I liked of earnestness and hopefulness about them. I used to write a good deal about the future of the British drama, and they, for their part, used to think and talk a great deal about it.

Though second-nighters do come to see, they remain
rather to hope and pray." Because I have quoted I
must not be understood as accepting Mr Beerbohm's
implied aspersion on first-nighters. It is all very well
for him. He has retired (the more's the pity) from
dramatic criticism. But I take his account of second-
nighters on trust, because the exigencies of a daily
newspaper prevent me from observing them for myself.
Evidently they, no more than first-nighters, are
average playgoers.

Not that I would disparage the general playgoer.
Indeed, I am not sure that he is not, in another sense
than Labiche's, *le plus heureux des trois*. I can speak
for myself. Mind, I am saying nothing against first-
nighters. They are entirely admirable persons—I
could never bring myself, like Mr Beerbohm, to call
them a lot. But oh! the joy of being, on holiday
occasions, a general playgoer, of throwing one's considering cap over the mills, of garnering no impressions
for future 'copy,' of blithely ignoring one's better
judgment, of going comfortably home after the play,
like everybody else, instead of dashing madly into a
taxi for the newspaper office! The play will be well
on its run, the comedian will have polished up his
jokes, the superfluities will have been cut out, the
programme girls will long since have given up leading
the applause, you won't know a soul, and you won't
even bother to look at the author's name. You
surrender your individuality and drift with the crowd,
or, in more pretentious language, merge yourself in
the collective consciousness.

Which reminds me. The general playgoer, just
because he is general, is what Henry James called
George Sand: remarkably accessible. Everybody
knows him. He is a public theme. Theorists won't

leave him alone. In particular, the collective psychologists have marked him for their prey. For them he typifies the theatrical ' crowd,' with the peculiar crowd characteristics these theorists profess to have scientifically classified. Sarcey began it. Lemaître followed. And comparatively obscure scribes have devoted attention to the general playgoer. They have said that he is no philosopher ; he cannot adopt a detached, impersonal, disinterested view of life ; he must take sides. Hence the convention of the ' sympathetic personage.' He has not the judicial faculty, is not accustomed to sift evidence or to estimate probabilities. Hence the convention of the ' long arm of coincidence ' and the convention that the wildest improbability may be taken as the starting-point of a play. The general playgoer, as such, is virtuous and generous ; for we are all on our best behaviour in public. And he insists upon a strict separation of virtue and vice. He wants his personages all of a piece. The composite characters, blends of good and evil, he refuses to recognize. Hence the conventions of ' hero ' and ' villain,' of ' poetic justice ' and of ' living happy ever afterwards.' Further, it has been suggested that a crowd of general playgoers, having an individuality of its own, cannot but be interested in that individuality, apart from all reference to the cause which brought it together. Once assembled, it becomes self-conscious, self-assertive. It finds itself an interesting spectacle. And the general playgoer is not of the cloistered but of the gregarious type of mankind ; he must have bustle, the sense of human kinship brought home to him by sitting elbow by elbow with his neighbours. The faculty of intellectual attention is seldom high in such a temperament as this. Hence the playwright has to *force* the attention of a temperamentally inattentive audience. Mark, once more, that I am not speaking of first-nighters. Their individuality is too strong to be crowd-immersed. I would not for worlds speak of them as a crowd at all. They are an assemblage, a constellation, a galaxy. Admirable persons!

But there is one thing for which I envy the general playgoer above all. I mean his freedom and pungency of criticism. Anonymity gives him irresponsibility, and his resentment at being bored not being subject to the cooling process of literary composition, his language is apt to be really terrible. Talk of printed criticism! Actors and authors do talk of it often enough, and on the whole don't seem to like it ; but let them mingle with the general playgoer and keep their ears open! Who was the man in Balzac who said that it was absurd to speak of the danger of certain books when we all had the corrupt book of the world open before us, and beyond that another book a thousand times more dangerous—all that is whispered by one man to another or discussed behind ladies' fans at balls? So the general playgoer is the great purveyor of secret criticism. Disraeli, or another, said that the secret history of the world, which never got into the history books, was the only true history. Let us hope that secret criticism is not the only true sort, but it is certainly the most live. It is free from literary bias, the cant of criticism, the smell of the lamp. And it is the most potent of persuasives. Published criticism is powerless against it. The fate of a play is not decided by newspaper criticisms (thank goodness! I should be miserable if it were), but by what the general playgoers say to one another and pass on to their friends. How many plays with ' record ' runs have been dismissed by the newspapers on the morrow of the first night with faint praise or positive dispraise ? The general playgoer has said his say, and what he says ' goes.' I know he is giving many worthy people just now much uneasiness. They form little theatrical societies *à côté* to keep him out. They deplore his taste and organize leagues for his education and improvement. I rather fancy he is like the young lady in the play who " didn't want to have her mind improved." But that is another story. What I have been envying him for is not his taste but the heartiness with which he " abounds in his own sense " and his freedom in expressing it. After all, perhaps criticism that is so free and so pervasive and so potent is not exactly to be called " secret." I seek the *mot juste*. Or I would if that were not a back-number. Has not Mr Beerbohm finally put it in its place as the Holy Grail of the nineties ?

From " Pastiche and Prejudice "

WAR

GEORGE SANTAYANA

TO fight is a radical instinct ; if men have nothing
else to fight over they will fight over words,
fancies, or women, or they will fight because they
dislike each other's looks, or because they have met
walking in opposite directions. To knock a thing
down, especially if it is cocked at an arrogant angle, is
a deep delight to the blood. To fight for a reason and
in a calculating spirit is something your true warrior
despises ; even a coward might screw his courage up
to such a reasonable conflict. The joy and glory of
fighting lie in its pure spontaneity and consequent
generosity ; you are not fighting for gain, but for
sport and for victory. Victory, no doubt, has its
fruits for the victor. If fighting were not a possible
means of livelihood the bellicose instinct could never
have established itself in any long-lived race. A few
men can live on plunder, just as there is room in the
world for some beasts of prey ; other men are reduced
to living on industry, just as there are diligent bees,
ants, and herbivorous kine. But victory need have no
good fruits for the people whose army is victorious.
That it sometimes does so is an ulterior and blessed
circumstance hardly to be reckoned upon.

Since barbarism has its pleasures it naturally has
its apologists. There are panegyrists of war who say
that without a periodical bleeding a race decays and
loses its manhood. Experience is directly opposed to
this shameless assertion. It is war that wastes a

nation's wealth, chokes its industries, kills its flower, narrows its sympathies, condemns it to be governed by adventurers, and leaves the puny, deformed, and unmanly to breed the next generation. Internecine war, foreign and civil, brought about the greatest set-back which the life of reason has ever suffered ; it exterminated the Greek and Italian aristocracies. Instead of being descended from heroes, modern nations are descended from slaves ; and it is not their bodies only that show it. After a long peace, if the conditions of life are propitious, we observe a people's energies bursting their barriers ; they become aggressive on the strength they have stored up in their remote and unchecked development. It is the unmutilated race, fresh from the struggle with nature (in which the best survive, while in war it is often the best that perish), that descends victoriously into the arena of nations and conquers disciplined armies at the first blow, becomes the military aristocracy of the next epoch and is itself ultimately sapped and decimated by luxury and battle, and merged at last into the ignoble conglomerate beneath. Then, perhaps, in some other virgin country a genuine humanity is again found, capable of victory because unbled by war. To call war the soil of courage and virtue is like calling debauchery the soil of love.

Blind courage is an animal virtue indispensable in a world full of dangers and evils where a certain insensibility and dash are requisite to skirt the precipice without vertigo. Such animal courage seems therefore beautiful rather than desperate or cruel, and being the lowest and most instinctive of virtues it is the one most widely and sincerely admired. In the form of steadiness under risks rationally taken, and perseverance so long as there is a chance of success, courage is a true virtue ; but it ceases to be one when the love of danger, a useful passion when danger is unavoidable, begins to lead men into evils which it was unnecessary to face. Bravado, provocativeness, and a gambler's instinct, with a love of hitting hard for the sake of exercise, is a temper which ought already to be counted among the vices rather than the virtues of man. To delight in war is a merit in the soldier, a dangerous quality in the captain, and a positive crime in the statesman.

The panegyrist of war places himself on the lowest level on which a moralist or a patriot can stand and shows as great a want of refined feeling as of right reason. For the glories of war are all blood-stained, delirious, and infected with crime ; the combative instinct is a savage prompting by which one man's good is found in another's evil. The existence of such a contradiction in the moral world is the original sin of nature whence flows every other wrong. He is a willing accomplice of that perversity in things who delights in another's discomfiture or in his own, and craves the blind tension of plunging into danger without reason, or the idiot's pleasure in facing a pure chance. To find joy in another's trouble is, as man is constituted, not unnatural, though it is wicked ; and to find joy in one's own trouble, though it be madness, is not yet impossible for man. These are the chaotic depths of that dreaming nature out of which humanity has to grow.

From " Little Essays "

CONFIRMED READERS

AUGUSTINE BIRRELL

DR JOHNSON is perhaps our best example of a confirmed reader. Malone once found him sitting in his room roasting apples and reading a history of Birmingham. This staggered even Malone, who was himself a somewhat far-gone reader.

" Don't you find it rather dull ? " he ventured to enquire.

" Yes," replied the Sage, " it is dull."

Malone's eyes then rested on the apples, and he remarked he supposed they were for medicine.

" Why, no," said Johnson ; " I believe they are only there because I wanted something to do. I have been confined to the house for a week, and so you find me roasting apples and reading the history of Birmingham."

This anecdote pleasingly illustrates the habits of the confirmed reader. Nor let the worldling sneer. Happy is the man who, in the hours of solitude and depression, can read a history of Birmingham. How terrible is the story Welbore Ellis told of Robert Walpole in his magnificent library, trying book after book, and at last, with tears in his eyes, exclaiming, " It is all in vain : I cannot read ! "

Edmund Malone, the Shakespearian commentator, and first editor of *Boswell's Johnson*, was as confirmed a reader as it is possible for a book-collector to be. His own life, by Sir James Prior, is full of good things, and is not so well known as it should be. It smacks of books and bookishness.

Malone, who was an Irishman, was once, so he would have us believe, deeply engaged in politics; but he then fell in love, and the affair, for some unknown reason, ending unhappily, his interest ceased in everything, and he was driven as a last resource to books and writings. Thus are commentators made. They learn in suffering what they observe in the margin. Malone may have been driven to his pursuits, but he took to them kindly, and became a vigorous and skilful book-buyer, operating in the market both on his own behalf and on that of his Irish friends with great success.

His good fortune was enormous, and this although he had a severely restricted notion as to price. He was no reckless bidder, like Mr Harris, late of Covent Garden, who, just because David Garrick had a fine library of old plays, was determined to have one himself at whatever cost. In Malone's opinion half a guinea was a big price for a book. As he grew older he became less careful, and in 1805, which was seven years before his death, he gave Ford, a Manchester bookseller, £25 for the Editio Princeps of *Venus and Adonis*. He already had the edition of 1596—a friend had given it him—bound up with Constable's and Daniel's Sonnets and other rarities, but he very naturally yearned after the edition of 1593. He fondly imagined Ford's copy to be unique: there he was wrong, but as he died in that belief, and only gave £25 for his treasure, who dare pity him? His copy now reposes in the Bodleian. He secured Shakespeare's Sonnets (1609) and the first edition of *The Rape of Lucrece* for two guineas, and accounted half a crown a fair average price for quarto copies of Elizabethan plays.

Malone was a truly amiable man, of private fortune

o

and endearing habits. He lived on terms of intimacy with his brother book-collectors, and when they died attended the sale of their libraries and bid for his favourite lots, grumbling greatly if they were not knocked down to him. At Topham Beauclerk's sale in 1781, which lasted nine days, Malone bought for Lord Charlemont " the pleasauntest workes of George Gascoigne, Esquire, with the princely pleasures at Kenilworth Castle, 1587." He got it cheap (£1 7s.), as it wanted a few leaves, which Malone thought he had ; but to his horror, when it came to be examined, it was found to want eleven more leaves than he had supposed. " Poor Mr Beauclerk," he writes, " seems never to have had his books examined or collated, otherwise he would have found out the imperfections." Malone was far too good a book-collector to suggest a third method of discovering a book's imperfections—namely, reading it. Beauclerk's library only realized £5011, and as the Duke of Marlborough had a mortgage upon it of £5000, there must have been after payment of the auctioneer's charges a considerable deficit.

But Malone was more than a book-buyer, more even than a commentator : he was a member of the Literary Club, and the friend of Johnson, Reynolds, and Burke. On July 28, 1789, he went to Burke's place, the Gregories, near Beaconsfield, with Sir Joshua, Wyndham, and Mr Courtenay, and spent three very agreeable days. The following extract from the recently published Charlemont papers has interest :

" As I walked out before breakfast with Mr Burke, I proposed to him to revise and enlarge his admirable book on the *Sublime and Beautiful*, which the experience, reading, and observation of thirty years could not but enable him to improve considerably. But he said the train of his thoughts had gone another way, and the whole bent of his mind turned from such subjects, and that he was much fitter for such speculations at the time he published that book than now."

Between the Burke of 1758 and the Burke of 1789 there was a difference indeed, but the forcible expressions, " the train of my thoughts " and " the whole bent of my mind," serve to create a new impression of the tremendous energy and fertile vigour of this amazing man. The next day the party went over to Amersham and admired Mr Drake's trees, and listened to Sir Joshua's criticism of Mr Drake's pictures. This was a fortnight after the taking of the Bastille. Burke's hopes were still high. The revolution had not yet spoilt his temper.

Amongst the Charlemont papers is an amusing tale I do not remember having seen before of young Philip Stanhope, the recipient of Lord Chesterfield's famous letters :

" When at Berne, where he passed some of his boyhood in company with Harte and the excellent Mr, now Lord, Eliott (Heathfield of Gibraltar), he was one evening invited to a party where, together with some ladies, there happened to be a considerable number of Bernese senators, a dignified set of elderly gentlemen, aristocratically proud, and perfect strangers to fun. These most potent, grave, and reverend signors were set down to whist, and were so studiously attentive to the game, that the unlucky brat found little difficulty in fastening to the backs of their chairs the flowing tails of their ample periwigs, and in cutting, unobserved by them, the tyes of their breeches. This done, he left the room, and presently re-entered crying out, ' Fire ! Fire ! ' The affrighted burgomasters suddenly bounced up, and exhibited to the amazed spectators their senatorial heads and backs totally deprived of ornament or covering."

Young Stanhope was no ordinary child. There is a completeness about this jest which proclaims it a masterpiece. One or other of its points might have occurred to anyone, but to accomplish both at once was to show real distinction.

Sir William Stanhope, Lord Chesterfield's brother, felt no surprise at his nephew's failure to acquire the graces. " What," said he, " could Chesterfield expect ? His mother was Dutch, he was educated at Leipsic, and his tutor was a pedant from Oxford."

Papers which contain anecdotes of this kind carry with them their own recommendation. We hear on all sides complaints—and I hold them to be just complaints—of the abominable high prices of English books. Thirty shillings, thirty-six shillings, are common prices. The thing is too barefaced. His Majesty's Stationery Office set an excellent example. They sell an octavo volume of 460 closely but well-printed pages, provided with an excellent index, for one shilling and elevenpence. There is not much editing, but the quality of it is good.

If anyone is confined to his room, even as Johnson was when Malone found him roasting apples and reading a history of Birmingham, he cannot do better than surround himself with the publications of the Historical Manuscripts Commission ; they will cost him next to nothing, tell him something new on every page, revive a host of old memories and scores of half-forgotten names, and perhaps tempt him to become a confirmed reader.

From " In the Name of the Bodleian "

MASTERS OF NONSENSE

HOLBROOK JACKSON

I DO not think it is good for anyone to be always
sensible. Not that anyone is always sensible—
on the contrary ; but most of us think we are.
It is from this illusion that we require a holiday, in
fact, several holidays, and, were I autocrat, I should
make such holidays periodical, like the festivals of
the Church ; for, as Sir Thomas Browne says, " Many
things are true in Divinity, which are neither inducible
by reason, nor confirmable by sense." Doubtless I
shall be almost alone in this amiable wish, since we
live in a practical and businesslike age, and have
little time to cut capers. Material success is our aim,
and nonsense has nothing whatever to do with that
aim. Nonsense is shy of success, even of its own ;
and I believe this shyness is due to certain delicate
and even fairylike qualities which are apt to become
soiled in the market-place—as what thing does not ?
One of the inevitable results of a strenuously material
era is the brushing away of the more subtle and illusive
qualities of life ; these suffer at the hands of popular
success as butterflies' wings suffer at the hands of him
who is vandal enough to touch them. There is also
an arrogance of material success—a swagger of certainty
born of pride in accumulated substance—which spoils
the taste for finer things. Those afflicted thus, for it
is an affliction, surrounded though they are by what
the world calls great possessions, possess naught. This
is true not only of a man but of an age, for a man,

whatever he may be, is, finally, the epitome of his age. The possession of a great many things, even the best of things, tends to blind one to the real value of anything. And the humour, and the pathos as well, of such an age as ours, which values a man according to the number of more or less troublesome things he possesses, is that it places what is called good sense above what is called nonsense. " Be sensible " is the advice we are all giving one another. And I think we are agreed that to be sensible is to be rational, shrewd, useful, proper, respectable, and even honest— when there is no great risk in our being otherwise. " Honesty," we say, " is the *best* policy." You see there is no nonsense about honesty being good in itself—it is simply *the best policy*, that is all.

This good sense would be called an English characteristic ; it has made us what we are, it has made us rich (at least some of us)—the kind of richness typified so frankly in the popular pictures of John Bull ; the kind of richness that made Napoleon sneer at us for a nation of shopkeepers. And we have little doubt that this sense is good sense, since it has given us those fine things, factories and ironclads, locomotives and guns, and banking accounts. But still, it would seem, and in spite of all these sensible things, that there are some things, in every sense their direct opposites, which bear a more convincing mark of immortality than the ingenious material achievements so much admired to-day. My modern and successful reader will, of course, say, " Nonsense ! " And I shall not contradict him. It is nonsense, deliberate, unadulterated nonsense, but I am disposed to believe it is all the better for that. And, as if the Fates were on my side, is it not a little strange that this most sensible of all ages, this age of practical rationalism, should have invented, in the pauses of its pursuit of fleeting things, an art of nonsense? Maybe it is a reaction, but reaction is only bad when it throws back towards what is monstrous and unnecessary; but even if, say, the invention of the nonsense verse is reactionary, it is wisely so, for it reacts somewhat after the manner of a boomerang. It is our age laughing at itself, pulling wry faces at itself, if you will, realizing perhaps shyly and without courage that this civilization of ours is rather a joke, and perhaps a little top-heavy with seriousness.

There is undoubtedly some deeper relationship between what is called good sense and nonsense, something deeper than the popular conception of these things as the obverse and reverse of the same medal. If, for instance, we took longevity as the test of worthiness, nonsense would be found to rank higher than sense. And I, at least, should be forced to a similar conclusion were I to judge nonsense as a creator of disinterested happiness. But there are so many things in favour of nonsense that I should not be in the least surprised if, one of these days, that much-abused faculty were judged to be the final and consummate expression of sense, a kind of Nirvana of the intelligence. We even get a hint of this in our own sensible civilization; for, just as we have seen our national symbol is a rather gross and tubby person called John Bull, distinguished only by reason of his uncomfortable girth, so the most characteristic human product of our age is the millionaire. Surely these Falstaffs of finance are the climax of the sensible line of evolution, and, like all extremes, have met their opposites, though they have not yet admitted it! But to avoid the charge of trifling with modern ideals, I shall not pursue this line of thought any further. Besides, are there not happier phases of my theme?

One of these is the significant way in which those most exalted and nonsensical of creatures, our poets and dreamers, have often been evolved out of such sensible persons as mathematicians or even more laboriously learned people. Take the case of Edgar Allan Poe, who was a mathematical genius, and something of a conchologist. He might have remained a sensible devotee of science, only his genius was too much for him. It forced him to consider less rational things, and before it was too late he turned from the temple of mathematics and knocked at the door of the Muses, with results that have placed him in the forefront of the world's imaginative workers. There are many such instances in the annals of literary history. And there are other instances of men, like Rabelais and Dean Swift, who, possessing the intuition of artists, have used the language of nonsense to express the idea of sense, who have bedecked rational satire in irrational clothing ; but Time, after his manner, stripping away the causes of the irony with the passing of the years, has treated with tender care the nonsensical form in which that irony was enshrined ; thus dropping a kindly veil of forgetfulness over the crabbed words of ages that are gone. Time has touched to immortality the conceptions of Gargantua, Pantagruel, and Gulliver, leaving us to-day unmoved by any other quality but their fantastic charm.

But stranger still, and here history plays into my hands with something approaching magnanimity, the deliberate creators of nonsense for the sake of nonsense have turned to that noble work from what was acknowledged by their contemporaries to have been sound and sensible work ; but in spite of all offers of financial reward, and other temptations, they became masters of nonsense, and their whimsical ideas and images have given delight not only to past generations but to the present, and there is every sign that they will continue to give delight to many, and perhaps all, generations to come ; for nonsense rarely dies. Let me take but three examples of this type of genius : Lewis Carroll, Hans Andersen, and Edward Lear. The first of these was the creator of that classic of nonsense, *Alice in Wonderland,* and yet how strange it is to think that Alice was a mere incident—an accident really— in a life which might easily have lost itself in a morass of theology and mathematics. Doubtless he took himself more seriously as the Rev. C. L. Dodgson, mathematician and theologian, than as Lewis Carroll, creator of Alice ; but who shall say that he did not touch infinity in the latter capacity ? His mathematics, upon which he prided himself, will be forgotten (even Euclid is becoming *passé*) ; his theology, which, doubtless, was much to him, will be dead ; but Jabberwocky, the Mad Hatter, the Duchess, the Mock Turtle, and the Gryphon, and all their jolly fellows, will prance merrily down the ages, cutting happy capers for happy children and happier adults, until the crack o' doom.

Just as Lewis Carroll took himself seriously as a mathematician, so Hans Andersen took himself seriously as a novelist. But the spirit of Eternity judges neither one nor the other by such standards ; Eternity has touched neither their mathematics nor their novels with his magic wand. That wand has waved and descended gently upon Alice ; and it has waved with like immortal results over " The Ugly Duckling," " The Tinder Box," and " The Wild Swans."

But the most remarkable of all nonsense-artists is Edward Lear ; if the rest are masters of nonsense, he is surely our Prince of Nonsense. He has raised nonsense, nonsense pure and simple, nonsense free of

all sense, morals, and prettiness, to the heights of great
art. His work is the very apotheosis of nonsense ; he
is " the prophet of the utterly absurd, of the patently
impossible and vain."

His world was peopled with men and animals that
never were on sea or land ; strange lights flared in
his dreams, showing us a realm of prank here in the
very heart of our rational day. He has given us the
keys of the heaven of nonsense, and as we turn them
in the doors and enter therein we breathe lightly and
without care of the morrow, as though we were one with
a rout of children dancing and shouting :

> " Sally go round the moon !
> Sally go round the sun !
> Sally go round the chimney-pot
> On a Sunday afternoon."

And, characteristically, again, he raised himself to
that eminence in the spare moments of a busy career
devoted to the most obviously sensible things.

He permitted many years of a life, which might
have been entirely devoted to nonsense, to be dissipated
in ornithological studies and in the drawing and painting of birds and landscapes. Probably, like Lewis
Carroll, he was prouder of his learned work on " The
Family of the Psittacidæ " than of " The Pobble who
has no Toes." But, as it was in the cases of Lewis
Carroll and Hans Andersen, the judgment of Time
is against him.

Still, in spite of other endeavour, Edward Lear is
the first to have made a fine art of nonsense. His
work in that direction is irresponsibly defiant of all
the scaffolding by which the intellect is supported,
and though one is carried away on the wings of a
chuckling fascination as one reads through his verses
or looks at their illustrations, one is filled with a

disturbing, mystical, yet exhilarating feeling that something unusual is happening, that a new sort of wisdom is being enunciated, a new order of life being revealed in this scamper of the wits. It is as though a dignified ritual, long become exanimate by repetition, had suddenly been reversed by an unseen but jocular power, and creating, instead of shallow laughter, fathomless joy.

Take his autobiographical verses, for example, and, sheer nonsense as they are, how much clearer a conception of the personality of Lear do they give us than any more sensible account could have done ?—

> How pleasant to know Mr Lear !
>   Who has written such volumes of stuff !
> Some think him ill-tempered and queer,
>   But a few think him pleasant enough.
>
> His mind is concrete and fastidious,
>   His nose is remarkably big ;
> His visage is more or less hideous,
>   His beard it resembles a wig.
>
> He has ears, and two eyes, and ten fingers,
>   Leastways if you reckon two thumbs ;
> Long ago he was one of the singers,
>   But now he is one of the dumbs.
>
> He sits in a beautiful parlour,
>   With hundreds of books on the wall ;
> He drinks a good deal of Marsala,
>   But never gets tipsy at all.
>
> He has many friends, laymen and clerical ;
>   Old Foss is the name of his cat ;
> His body is perfectly spherical,
>   He weareth a runcible hat.
>
> He reads but he cannot speak Spanish,
>   He cannot abide ginger-beer :
> Ere the days of his pilgrimage vanish,
>   How pleasant to know Mr Lear !

Much of Edward Lear's work in the realm of non-sense is in the verse which has become the established medium of nonsensical utterance:

> There was an old man who supposed
> The street door was partially closed,
> But some very large rats
> Ate his coat and his hats
> While the futile old gentleman dozed.

But Edward Lear's most masterly work does not lie in the classical nonsense verse, nor yet in those delightfully futile sketches by means of which he illustrated his books of nonsense. Rather is it to be found in that series of ballads which, for whimsical fancy and deliberate abandonment of all reasonableness, stands matchless and supreme, the very negation of the rationale of things.

The finest of these ballads is certainly " The Pelican Chorus," although its excellence does not lie so entirely in the domain of nonsense as in the setting of the quality of nonsense in picturesque surroundings. The chorus itself, whimsical though it is, translates what ought to be Pelicanese into a kind of pidgin-English, which one can easily imagine to be the nearest approximation in human language of the thoughts and emotions of the pelican. There is, in fact, as the reader will readily comprehend, a strong resemblance between the personal appearance of the pelican and the quaint words of the chorus, and if it is the expression of the unseen self, then the natural historical truth of the chorus is obvious:

> Ploffskin, Pluffskin, Pelican jee !
> We think no birds so happy as we !
> Plumpskin, Ploshkin, Pelican jill !
> We think so then, and we thought so still !

Yes, when Lear tells me of the assembling of these

impossible birds on their " long bare islands of yellow sand," I am convinced that, whether they sing this pleasant verse or not, it is quite obvious that they ought to do so ; and it is an oversight on the part of nature if they do not. But I am somewhat at a disadvantage in the matter. I cannot speak with authority, because my experience of pelicans is confined to those at the Zoo. They certainly did not quote Lear. But what would you expect of creatures that live in a paddock ? And now I come to think of it, I noticed that each of those curious guests of the Royal Zoological Society did wear the absorbed expression peculiar to people who want to catch some thought which has just slipped the memory. Captivity had evidently afflicted them with aphasia, just as it afflicts many other creatures of our civilization. The pelicans at the Zoo are sad birds, and now I know why—they are trying to recollect " The Pelican Chorus," which dangles in their memories just beyond grasping-point.

For the highest nonsense, however, we must turn to the immortal " Pobble who has no Toes " :

> The Pobble who has no toes
> Had once as many as we ;
> When they said, " Some day you may lose them all ";—
> He replied, " Fish fiddle de-dee ! "—
> And his aunt Jobiska made him drink
> Lavender water tinged with pink,
> For she said, " The World in general knows,
> There's nothing so good for a Pobble's toes ! "

and to the equally great " Mr and Mrs Discobbolos " :

> Mr and Mrs Discobbolos
> Climbed to the top of a wall,
> And they sat to watch the sunset sky,
> And to hear the Nupiter Piffkin cry,
>   And the Biscuit Buffalo call.

They took up a roll and some camomile tea,
And both were as happy as happy could be—
    Till Mrs Discobbolos said—
    "Oh! W! X! Y! Z!
It has just come into my head—
Suppose we should happen to fall!!!!!
        Darling Mr Discobbolos!"

and to "The Quangle Wangle's Hat":

On the top of the Crumpetty Tree
    The Quangle Wangle sat,
But his face you could not see,
    On account of his bever Hat!
For his hat was a hundred and two feet wide,
With ribbons and bibbons on every side,
And bells, and buttons, and loops, and lace,
So that nobody ever could see the face
    Of the Quangle Wangle Quee.

In these three poems Edward Lear is seen at his best. In these poems one meets all those strange creations of his which meet their peers only in the Jabberwock and the Mock Turtle of Lewis Carroll. You are introduced to them all at once, for all of them meet at a grand reunion on the amazing hat of the still more amazing and mysterious Quangle Wangle. The Fimble Fowl, with the corkscrew leg—

And the Golden Grouse came there,
And the Pobble who has no toes—
And the small Olympian Bear—
And the Dong, with the luminous nose :
And the Blue Baboon, who played the flute,
And the Orient Calf from the Land of Tute,
And the Attery Squash and the Bisky Bat,
All came and built on the lovely hat
    Of the Quangle Wangle Quee.

There is an exalted futility about these poems suggestive of things as final and as certain as any imaginable. One cannot explain them, they baffle and elude and convince like

> 'Twas brillig, and the slithy toves
>   Did gyre and gimble in the wabe;
> All mimsy were the borogoves,
>   And the mome raths outgrabe.

Who are all these strange creatures, and why do they enter into our consciousness against all reason? Why do we sympathize as deeply with the absurd whimsies of Mr and Mrs Discobbolos as we do with the adventures of Mr Pickwick or the love of Lucy Desborough for Richard Feverel? Why should the incomprehensible Pobble creep into our lives on such a wave of sympathy? Or why, to take another expression of nonsense, should we have a deeper if more furtive regard for Jabberwocky than we have for the language of Shakespeare? Such questions are as difficult as Pilate's " What is Truth? "

These things are nonsense, unquestionably, but, as the lady in *Patience* says : " Oh, what precious nonsense ! " But nonsense does not always find expression in the same way. We even see hints of it in certain of the phenomena of wild life. Nature was certainly working in the same vein, though expressing it through a different medium, when she created the Gecko, the Duckbill Platypus, and the Tortoise ; but it is a moot point whether even she improves upon the Quangle Wangle Quee.

But in spite of it all, nonsense is one of the few things modern learning does not attempt to explain. Nonsense exists ; it is delightful : that is all. Furthermore, it is not sense, and perhaps therefore we should rejoice in the fact that it has escaped learned analysis ; not even Nonsense could withstand that.

In the hands of Edward Lear and his followers it is

becoming not only proud of its isolation, but self-assertive, articulate, and, like the mind of Mr Lear, "concrete and fastidious."

We are all, in fact, beginning to find, as Alice did, that what sounds like nonsense is no ground for objection. You will remember how she was making up her mind to run to meet the Red Queen in the reasonable way of going forward, for the Red Queen was ahead of her. "You can't possibly do that," said the Rose. "I should advise you to walk the other way." Alice refused to follow this advice, and speedily lost herself, and it was not until she acted upon the nonsensical that she eventually met the Red Queen.

This adventure in Wonderland might well serve as a parable, a hint of that higher thing than sense lying hidden in the heart of the absurd. We know the legend of Punch is a laughing tragedy truer than our truth, and on the same lines there may be long vistas of intelligence, whole realms of consciousness, whose nature mere sense cannot penetrate. Nonsense may be the striving of consciousness towards newer ways of expressing life ; it may indicate the final breakdown of intellect and reason, and the beginning of a fresh idea, the childhood of a new world ; the proof, in fact, of man's unwritten belief that what can be proved is not worth proving.

Man is an irrational creature, and the essence of the human comedy is concerned with his attempts to be otherwise. Doubtless the comedy will continue—there will be no last act. So I do not look to nonsense as one looks to some reforming or revolutionary power. It is not that. Indeed, I am not so sure that I would alter the human comedy ; I might wish it more varied —but on the whole it is good enough until we are more conscious of its purpose. Nonsense has nothing to do with progress; it is as unchanging as it is uncertain, as young as it is old. Its value lies in its futility. But by showing us the absurdity of things, nonsense may help to keep us usefully sane; by checking ultimate consistency it may help to keep us alive.

From "Southward Ho! and other Essays"

A DEFENCE OF DETECTIVE STORIES

G. K. CHESTERTON

IN attempting to reach the genuine psychological reason for the popularity of detective stories, it is necessary to rid ourselves of many mere phrases. It is not true, for example, that the populace prefer bad literature to good, and accept detective stories because they are bad literature. The mere absence of artistic subtlety does not make a book popular. Bradshaw's *Railway Guide* contains few gleams of psychological comedy, yet it is not read aloud uproariously on winter evenings. If detective stories are read with more exuberance than railway guides, it is certainly because they are more artistic. Many good books have fortunately been popular ; many bad books, still more fortunately, have been unpopular. A good detective story would probably be even more popular than a bad one. The trouble in this matter is that many people do not realize that there is such a thing as a good detective story ; it is to them like speaking of a good devil. To write a story about a burglary is, in their eyes, a sort of spiritual manner of committing it. To persons of somewhat weak sensibility this is natural enough ; it must be confessed that many detective stories are as full of sensational crime as one of Shakespeare's plays.

There is, however, between a good detective story and a bad detective story as much, or rather more, difference than there is between a good epic and a bad one. Not only is a detective story a perfectly legitimate form of art, but it has certain definite and real advantages as an agent of the public weal.

The first essential value of the detective story lies in this, that it is the earliest and only form of popular literature in which is expressed some sense of the poetry of modern life. Men lived among mighty mountains and eternal forests for ages before they realized that they were poetical; it may reasonably be inferred that some of our descendants may see the chimney-pots as rich a purple as the mountain-peaks, and find the lamp-posts as old and natural as the trees. Of this realization of a great city itself as something wild and obvious the detective story is certainly the *Iliad*. No one can have failed to notice that in these stories the hero or the investigator crosses London with something of the loneliness and liberty of a prince in a tale of elfland, that in the course of that incalculable journey the casual omnibus assumes the primal colours of a fairy ship. The lights of the city begin to glow like innumerable goblin eyes, since they are the guardians of some secret, however crude, which the writer knows and the reader does not. Every twist of the road is like a finger pointing to it; every fantastic skyline of chimney-pots seems wildly and derisively signalling the meaning of the mystery.

This realization of the poetry of London is not a small thing. A city is, properly speaking, more poetic even than a countryside, for while nature is a chaos of unconscious forces, a city is a chaos of conscious ones. The crest of the flower or the pattern of the lichen may or may not be significant symbols. But there is no stone in the street and no brick in the wall that is not actually a deliberate symbol—a message from some man, as much as if it were a telegram or a post card. The narrowest street possesses, in every crook and twist of its intention, the soul of the man who built it, perhaps long in his grave. Every brick has as human a hieroglyph as if it were a graven brick of Babylon ; every slate on the roof is as educational a document as if it were a slate covered with addition and subtraction sums. Anything which tends, even under the fantastic form of the minutiæ of Sherlock Holmes, to assert this romance of detail in civilization, to emphasize this unfathomably human character in flints and tiles is a good thing. It is good that the average man should fall into the habit of looking imaginatively at ten men in the street even if it is only on the chance that the eleventh might be a notorious thief. We may dream, perhaps, that it might be possible to have another and higher romance of London, that men's souls have stranger adventures than their bodies, and that it would be harder and more exciting to hunt their virtues than to hunt their crimes. But since our great authors (with the admirable exception of Stevenson) decline to write of that thrilling mood and moment when the eyes of the great city, like the eyes of a cat, begin to flame in the dark, we must give fair credit to the popular literature which, amid a babble of pedantry and preciosity, declines to regard the present as prosaic or the common as commonplace. Popular art in all ages has been interested in contemporary manners and costume ; it dressed the groups around the Crucifixion in the garb of Florentine gentlefolk or Flemish burghers. In the last century it was the custom for distinguished actors to present Macbeth in a powdered wig and ruffles. How far we are ourselves in this age from such conviction of the poetry of our own life and manners may easily be conceived by anyone who chooses to imagine a picture of Alfred the Great toasting the cakes dressed in tourist's knickerbockers, or a performance of *Hamlet* in which the prince appeared in a frock-coat, with a crape band round his hat. But this instinct of the age to look back, like Lot's wife, could not go on for ever. A rude, popular literature of the romantic possibilities of the modern city was bound to arise. It has arisen in the popular detective stories, as rough and refreshing as the ballads of Robin Hood.

There is, however, another good work that is done by detective stories. While it is the constant tendency of the Old Adam to rebel against so universal and automatic a thing as civilization, to preach departure and rebellion, the romance of police activity keeps in some sense before the mind the fact that civilization itself is the most sensational of departures and the most romantic of rebellions. By dealing with the unsleeping sentinels who guard the outposts of society, it tends to remind us that we live in an armed camp, making war with a chaotic world, and that the criminals, the children of chaos, are nothing but the traitors within our gates. When the detective in a police romance stands alone, and somewhat fatuously fearless amid the knives and fists of a thieves' kitchen, it does certainly serve to make us remember that it is the agent of social justice who is the original and poetic figure, while the burglars and footpads are merely placid old cosmic conservatives, happy in the immemorial respectability of apes and wolves. The romance of the police force is thus the whole romance of man. It is based on the fact that morality is the most dark and daring of conspiracies. It reminds us that the whole noiseless and unnoticeable police management by which we are ruled and protected is only a successful knight-errantry.

From " The Defendant "

MY BOOKS

GEORGE GISSING

AS often as I survey my bookshelves I am reminded of Lamb's " ragged veterans." Not that all my volumes came from the second-hand stall ; many of them were neat enough in new covers, some were even stately in fragrant bindings, when they passed into my hands. But so often have I removed, so rough has been the treatment of my little library at each change of place, and, to tell the truth, so little care have I given to its well-being at normal times (for in all practical matters I am idle and inept), that even the comeliest of my books show the results of unfair usage. More than one has been foully injured by a great nail driven into a packing-case—this but the extreme instance of the wrongs they have undergone. Now that I have leisure and peace of mind, I find myself growing more careful—an illustration of the great truth that virtue is made easy by circumstance. But I confess that, so long as a volume hold together, I am not much troubled as to its outer appearance.

I know men who say they had as lief read any book in a library copy as in one from their own shelf. To me that is unintelligible. For one thing, I know every book of mine by its *scent*, and I have but to put my nose between the pages to be reminded of all sorts of things. My Gibbon, for example, my well-bound eight-volume Milman edition, which I have read and read and read again for more than thirty years—never do I open it but the scent of the noble page restores to me all the exultant happiness of that moment when I received it as a prize. Or my Shakespeare, the great Cambridge Shakespeare—it has an odour which carries me yet further back in life; for these volumes belonged to my father, and before I was old enough to read them with understanding, it was often permitted me, as a treat, to take down one of them from the bookcase, and reverently to turn the leaves. The volumes smell exactly as they did in that old time, and what a strange tenderness comes upon me when I hold one of them in hand. For that reason I do not often read Shakespeare in this edition. My eyes being good as ever, I take the Globe volume, which I bought in days when such a purchase was something more than an extravagance; wherefore I regard the book with that peculiar affection which results from sacrifice.

Sacrifice—in no drawing-room sense of the word. Dozens of my books were purchased with money which ought to have been spent upon what are called the necessaries of life. Many a time I have stood before a stall, or a bookseller's window, torn by conflict of intellectual desire and bodily need. At the very hour of dinner, when my stomach clamoured for food, I have been stopped by sight of a volume so long coveted, and marked at so advantageous a price, that I *could* not let it go; yet to buy it meant pangs of famine. My Heyne's *Tibullus* was grasped at such a moment. It lay on the stall of the old book-shop in Goodge Street—a stall where now and then one found an excellent thing among quantities of rubbish. Sixpence was the price—sixpence! At that time I used to eat my mid-day meal (of course, my dinner) at a coffee-shop in Oxford Street, one of the real old coffee-shops, such as now, I suppose, can hardly be found. Sixpence was all I had—yes, all I had in the world;

it would purchase a plate of meat and vegetables. But I did not dare to hope that the *Tibullus* would wait until the morrow, when a certain small sum fell due to me. I paced the pavement, fingering the coppers in my pocket, eyeing the stall, two appetites at combat within me. The book was bought and I went home with it, and as I made a dinner of bread and butter I gloated over the pages.

In this *Tibullus* I found pencilled on the last page : " Perlegi, Oct. 4, 1792." Who was that possessor of the book, nearly a hundred years ago ? There was no other inscription. I like to imagine some poor scholar, poor and eager as I myself, who bought the volume with drops of his blood, and enjoyed the reading of it even as I did. How much *that* was I could not easily say. Gentle-hearted Tibullus !—of whom there remains to us a poet's portrait more delightful, I think, than anything of the kind in Roman literature.

> *An tacitum silvas inter reptare salubres,*
> *Curantem quidquid dignum sapiente bonoque est ?*

So with many another book on the thronged shelves. To take them down is to recall, how vividly, a struggle and a triumph. In those days money represented nothing to me, nothing I cared to think about, but the acquisition of books. There were books of which I had passionate need, books more necessary to me than bodily nourishment. I could see them, of course, at the British Museum, but that was not at all the same thing as having and holding them, my own property, on my own shelf. Now and then I have bought a volume of the raggedest and wretchedest aspect, dishonoured with foolish scribbling, torn, blotted—no matter, I liked better to read out of that than out of a copy that was not mine. But I was guilty at times of mere self-indulgence; a book tempted me, a book which was not one of those for which I really craved, a luxury which prudence might bid me forego. As, for instance, my *Jung-Stilling*. It caught my eye in Holywell Street; the name was familiar to me in *Wahrheit und Dichtung*, and curiosity grew as I glanced over the pages. But that day I resisted; in truth, I could not afford the eighteenpence, which means that just then I was poor indeed. Twice again did I pass, each time assuring myself that *Jung-Stilling* had found no purchaser. There came a day when I was in funds. I see myself hastening to Holywell Street (in those days my habitual pace was five miles an hour), I see the little grey old man with whom I transacted my business—what was his name?—the bookseller who had been, I believe, a Catholic priest, and still had a certain priestly dignity about him. He took the volume, opened it, mused for a moment, then, with a glance at me, said, as if thinking aloud: " Yes, I wish I had time to read it."

Sometimes I added the labour of a porter to my fasting endured for the sake of books. At the little shop near Portland Road Station I came upon a first edition of Gibbon, the price an absurdity—I think it was a shilling a volume. To possess those clean-paged quartos I would have sold my coat. As it happened, I had not money enough with me, but sufficient at home. I was living at Islington. Having spoken with the bookseller, I walked home, took the cash, walked back again, and—carried the tomes from the west end of Euston Road to a street in Islington far beyond the *Angel*. I did it in two journeys—this being the only time of my life when I thought of Gibbon in avoirdupois. Twice—three times, reckoning the walk for the money—did I descend Euston Road and climb

Pentonville on that occasion. Of the season and the weather I have no recollection ; my joy in the purchase I had made drove out every other thought. Except, indeed, of the weight. I had infinite energy, but not much muscular strength, and the end of the last journey saw me upon a chair, perspiring, flaccid, aching—exultant !

The well-to-do person would hear this story with astonishment. Why did I not get the bookseller to send me the volumes ? Or, if I could not wait, was there no omnibus along that London highway ? How could I make the well-to-do person understand that I did not feel able to afford, that day, one penny more than I had spent on the book ? No, no, such labour-saving expenditure did not come within my scope ; whatever I enjoyed I earned it, literally, by the sweat of my brow. In those days I hardly knew what it was to travel by omnibus. I have walked London streets for twelve and fifteen hours together without ever a thought of saving my legs, or my time, by paying for waftage. Being poor as poor can be, there were certain things I had to renounce, and this was one of them.

Years after, I sold my first edition of Gibbon for even less than it cost me ; it went with a great many other fine books in folio and quarto, which I could not drag about with me in my constant removals ; the man who bought them spoke of them as ' tomb-stones.' Why has Gibbon no market value ? Often has my heart ached with regret for those quartos. The joy of reading the *Decline and Fall* in that fine type ! The page was appropriate to the dignity of the subject ; the mere sight of it tuned one's mind. I suppose I could easily get another copy now ; but it would not be to me what that other was, with its memory of dust and toil.

From " The Private Papers of Henry Ryecroft "

STYLE

G. W. E. RUSSELL

" *L*E *Steel Say Lum*—the Style is the Man, that's
why it's so important for us to attend to
Style," said Mr Edward Ponderevo, when
considering the value of a French advertisement for
Tono-Bungay, and added, with great truth, " As for
accent, no Englishman has an accent. No Englishman
pronounces French properly. It's all a bluff."

The Style is the Man. I linger lovingly over the
words, because they have just received a pointed and
flattering application to my own case. An unknown
friend invites me to write on Style, " with illustrations
from the works of Literary Men." Unfolding his
theme, my friend enumerates several styles—" the
distinguished style, the strong, racy, graceful styles,
the commonplace and ponderous styles," and others.
And then, after referring to an article of mine published
some years ago, he says, reflectively, " I am inclined
to think that that article reached the ' Distinguished '
level." Yes—The Style is the Man ; and a writer
who even once, in a long life of literary composition,
has reached " the Distinguished level," must himself
be a Distinguished Man. It was all very well for Mr
Ponderevo to pride himself on his skill in penning
advertisements, but I, too, am an author, and " *Le
Steel Say Lum.*" Thus encouraged, I proceed with
the task assigned to me, but I fear that the limits of
space will not allow me to indulge my friend with
many " illustrations from the works of Literary Men."

He must kindly take my opinions for what they are worth, and confirm or refute them by reference to books.

Matthew Arnold once said to me—" People think I can teach them style. What stuff it all is ! Have something to say, and say it as clearly as you can. That is the only secret of style." *Have something to say*—excellent counsel. A man who sits down to write, having nothing to say, soon finds himself playing with words for their own sake. He is not using them to express his meaning, for he has no meaning to express; but is choosing them because they are rare, or melodious, or emphatic, and is arranging them in the combinations and sequences in which they will sound prettiest or most forcibly attract attention. Hence come preciousness, and artificiality, and a thousand evils. " Have something to say "; and then, " say it as clearly as you can." This canon at once dismisses the ' ponderous ' style to which my correspondent justly objects. A man who wished to say as clearly as he could that he was going to bed would not say, " Ere yet I consign my limbs to repose." For the perfection of the ponderous style, the reader is referred to Miss Jenkyns' letters in *Cranford*; and Dr Johnson at his worst runs her close.

What, on the other hand, are ' clear ' styles ? Pre-eminently, Arnold's own. He realized (with Mr Ponderevo) that " French is a very useful language—puts a point on things "; and, though critics have censured his style as too French, it makes amends by being the perfection of lucidity. In my humble judgment, the greatest master of English prose in the Victorian age was Cardinal Newman, and, in his style, light and colour and music and all the best treasures of our English tongue are joined with a crystalline clearness. Newman's closest disciple in the realm of letters was R. W. Church, Dean of St Paul's, by Lord Morley pronounced to be the finest flower of Oxford culture; and his style has exactly the same clearness as his master's, though the general texture of his prose is less rich and more austere. Every boy who uses his pen has to go through a period of Macaulay. The History and the Essays are imposed upon him, as Shakespeare and Milton are imposed upon men. And for a few years we think nothing so beautiful as Macaulay's trick of cutting up a paragraph into short, sharp sentences, and then rounding it off with a rhetorical thunder-roll. After three or four years of this apprenticeship, we pass on to masters at once subtler and simpler; but from Macaulay we have learnt clearness. His judgments are often mistaken, and always prejudiced, but his mind was perfectly expressed in his writing. No human being could ever misunderstand a sentence that Macaulay wrote: that was "the Style," and "the Man" was like unto it. "I wish," said one of his friends, "that I could be as cocksure about anything as Tom Macaulay is about everything."

Perhaps we do not fully appreciate the full value of lucidity in style until we are confronted with its opposite. Let anyone who wishes to know the obscurity of which the English language is capable study the writings of the late Bishop Westcott, and then he will return with a fresh zest to the *Apologia*, or *St Paul and Protestantism*. For the 'strong' style, I could not refer my friend to a more perfect instance than William Cobbett, worthily echoed in our own day in the Public Correspondence of John Bright, who wrote thus concerning a slanderous opponent—
"He may not know that he is ignorant, but he cannot

be ignorant that he lies. I think the speaker was named Smith. He is a discredit to the numerous family of that name." Of the ' racy ' style—the style bubbling with fun and sarcasm, yet using each joke to clinch an argument—the supreme example is Sydney Smith. To have absorbed his Essays and the *Letters of Peter Plymley* is to have acquired an entirely new sense of the function of Humour in serious controversy.

' Graceful ' is a rather more elastic word. Thackeray's was, methinks, a graceful style, drawing part of its grace from Latin and some from French. Froude's writing, on other accounts to be detested, is admirable for grace. Dean Stanley, describing a landscape or a pageant, was graceful exactly where the hack-writer is clumsiest and most ponderous ; and Mr Frederic Harrison, depicting an historical scene or building, disposes of the ridiculous superstition that learning and grace are incompatible.

Of the ' commonplace ' style—the style which is grammatically correct, but contains not a spark of distinction, interest, or character—we have indeed abundant examples all round us. It has been culti-vated with great success by historical writers. It is seen to perfection in the historical works of the late Sir Spencer Walpole, while J. R. Green's pictures and patches, and Mr Herbert Paul's epigrams and antitheses, are the vehement efforts of historians to shake themselves free from commonplace.

The ' distinguished ' style must be approached with reverence, especially by a writer who has only once attained to it, and in discussing it some cross-division is inevitable. Distinction is not incompatible with other virtues. Newman, Arnold, Froude, and Stanley all wrote ' distinguished ' styles, though their special distinction may have lain in some particular quality, such as lucidity, or picturesqueness, or grace. Distinction may mean distinctiveness—the quality in a style which makes one say, " This must be Sydney Smith," or " That certainly is Macaulay " ; or else it may mean what Matthew Arnold meant by ' the Grand Style,' and may therefore be common to several writers of the highest rank. If this is what we mean by distinction, Gibbon's style was distinguished, and still more so Burke's—" the greatest man since Milton." Ruskin's style was in both senses distinguished. He handled the English language as it had never been handled before, eliciting undreamed-of harmonies, and visions of loveliness which, till he interpreted them, had escaped the ken of man. And, though his writings bear on every page the traces of the laborious file, they often attain the very height of rhetorical beauty.

From the days of Jeremy Taylor and Isaac Barrow the English pulpit has had a literature of its own. I doubt if anyone could nowadays read Henry Melvill, esteemed by Mr Gladstone the greatest preacher he had ever heard ; but there are sermons of Liddon's, more especially those preached before the University of Oxford, in which the ' Grand Manner ' of sacred eloquence is maintained in its perfection. If by a ' distinguished ' style we mean a style which at once proclaims its authorship, which makes us say, " So-and-so and no one else wrote that," we find a striking instance in the style of the Rev. H. Scott Holland, Regius Professor of Divinity at Oxford. I forbear to describe it except negatively—it is not ' commonplace.'

But all this time I have been, as it were, only skirmishing round my subject. Now I must grapple it. Who of writers now living is the greatest exponent of the ' distinguished ' style ? I answer, without hesitation, Lord Morley. Indeed he seems to me to stand alone. His style is natural, easy, fluent, lucid. Here and there it takes a turn which suggests foreign influence; but English prose, even in its greatest days, never was too proud to borrow additional adornment from a wider world. It is full of life and fire and colour; it moves to no ordered march, but just as it is swayed by the inspiration of the moment. It seems to me to be the one utterance now left to us which is a worthy vehicle of the highest and most solemn thinking. "The doubtful doom of human kind" may be a melancholy, but it is an ennobling, subject of contemplation, and he who has long gazed on it with clear eyes and a steady soul will have learnt to think nobly, and to find words which match his thought.

Experience has shown me that to utter the word ' Style ' to a circle of cultivated readers is as rash as to whistle when an avalanche is on the move. Heedless of risk, one pursues one's path with one's mind full of pleasant thoughts, till they incautiously express themselves in sound, and then down comes the accumulated mass. To anyone contemplating a discourse on Style, I would say, as the Alpine peasant said to the young man who cried "Excelsior" (when, by the way, he meant something else)—

> "Beware the pine-tree's withered branch !
> Beware the awful avalanche ! "

Ever since I first wrote of Style these allied terrors have been rattling round my head, and even now I am by no means sure that I have done with the pelting of this pitiless storm. "The pine-tree's withered branch " may be taken to typify the older sort of scholar—Carp of Brasenose, and his rival Mr Casaubon

—who resent my neglect of the ancients. "You affect," they say, "to write on Style, and you do not mention Plato. Had Cicero no style? Did you ever hear of an obscure pamphleteer called John Milton, and do you know the sources from which his style was drawn?" To these ungenerous reproaches I can only reply that, when a friend asked me to write about style, I understood him to be thinking of modern English. But this is no sufficient defence against the overhanging peril. "The pine-tree's withered branch" may be successfully evaded, but who shall shield me from the "awful avalanche" of younger criticism? Every post brings a letter protesting against the omission of some favourite name. Froude evidently has a strong following, and his admirers complain that I gave him grudging praise. But the description of the execution of Mary Queen of Scots can never be forgotten or forgiven. An Oxford don, with a fellow-feeling for other dons, says, "You ought to have treated Pater"; but Pater was self-conscious, and his style is full of the preciousness and artificiality which I began by proscribing. A dignitary, who is also a Cambridge man, is grieved because I cited Westcott as a type of obscurity, and says that Westcott was a Mystic. But, as F. D. Maurice used to say, "I wish people would believe that Mysticism is not another name for Mistiness." The world, we know, is full of Stevensonians, but, though they are all devoted to the master, they do not seem to be agreed about his merits. "Surely a magician," writes one. "Conscious, elaborate, and distinguished," says another—a curious combination of attributes.

Mr Herbert Paul once observed, in his pungent way, that he almost wished that Matthew Arnold had not translated "Gorgo and Praxinoe"; for most people

Q

fancied that Theocritus had never written anything else. This thought recurs to my mind when I answer a critic who says, " Surely dear old Charles Lamb deserves a place among English stylists." Assuredly Yes, and among the highest : only let his admirers bind themselves by solemn oaths never again to mention Roast Pig or Mrs Sarah Battle. One of my critics cites De Quincey : a similar caution applies to *Murder Considered as One of the Fine Arts*. When we are trying to infect others with our own enthusiasm in literature, we must be careful not to insist too heavily on our favourite bits ; and no one needs the caution oftener than the present writer.

Has George Eliot come to the end of her reign ? I hope not ; but it is significant that only one of my critics has remonstrated against the omission of her name, and even he condemns her later style as " loaded and artificial." Twenty years ago I should have been snowed-under by similar reproaches, and the protesters would have admired equally the style of *Silas Marner* and the style of *Theophrastus Such*. For my own part I am a staunch believer in George Eliot's genius, though I should not call her " a second Shakespeare," nor affirm that she could have written the Bible if it had not been written already. Those eulogies are rather too boisterous ; but I reckon her as one of the greatest of English novelists. She had the indispensable power of constructing a plot ; never more subtly than in the despised *Felix Holt*. She had humour, pathos, lifelike dialogue, knowledge of nature, and a keen insight into the hidden springs of human action. But somehow I should never have considered her style remarkable. No doubt it is very good ; correct, clear, and resonant ; but it is not, I think, plainly marked out from other good English of its time. It is not individual, and I should not call it particularly distinguished.

Another critic reminds me of J. H. Shorthouse. Why did I not include the author of *John Inglesant*? (The rest of his books may be disregarded.) Well, I think because he is 'precious,' over-elaborated, and self-conscious; and when he tries to write archaic English—the English of the time that he is describing—he constantly slips into modernism and journalese. But as I said in the last chapter, there are passages in *John Inglesant*—the Communion at Little Gidding, the apparition of Strafford to Charles, and the midnight ride through the Italian forest—which one will remember as long as one remembers anything.

The literature of the pulpit requires a paragraph to itself. Newman's Anglican Sermons would, I suppose, be unanimously pronounced supreme, not only for their spiritual discernment, but for their incomparable felicity of phrase. We do not forget Matthew Arnold's tribute to the " words which were a religious music, subtle, sweet, mournful," flowing in his undergraduate days from the pulpit of St Mary's Church. Newman's closest disciple was Dean Church, of whom I have already spoken, and whose style is seen to perfection in his sermons. Those who are not afraid of a little difficulty in their religion are recommended to study the sermons of J. B. Mozley, and I will not be laughed out of my conviction that F. W. Farrar in his early days was the master of a very splendid eloquence. If the gainsayer should murmur that it was tinged with Ruskinese it is not for me to say that it was the worse on that account.

" Hang your preachers," cries an angry physicist " Barrow be blowed. Who the deuce was Melvill? If clericalism had not absolutely warped your intellect, you would say that Huxley was the greatest master of style who ever addressed a popular audience." I bow my head before this reproach, in patient, deep disdain. It was no clerical pen that drew the picture of " Professor Huxley, in a white sheet, brought up at the Surrey Tabernacle between two deacons, whom that great physicist, in his own clear and nervous language, would no doubt describe as ' of weak mental organization and strong muscular frame,' and penitently confessing that science contradicts herself." There is Arnold's tribute to Huxley's style.

When I am asked why I say so little about living writers, I suppose the answer is that I know a good many of them, and wish to keep friends with them all. But one risk I will venture to take, and will record my opinion that Mr George Trevelyan writes an almost perfect style, as clear and easy and natural as running water, and as full of lights and shades and deeps and shallows.

As I bring this chapter to a close, there comes into my hand an Examination Paper, recently propounded by a famous College to candidates for its scholarships. From it I extract this admirable exercise in the study of Style—

" Indicate the authors parodied in the following quotations, stating the grounds of your opinion :

(*a*) ' Professions lavishly effused and parsimoniously verified are alike inconsistent with the precepts of inner rectitude and the practice of external policy : let it not then be conjectured that because we are unassuming we are imbecile ; that forbearance is any indication of despondency, or humility of demerit.'

(*b*) ' I'd scarce done asking myself whether I'd formulated my inquiry into the identity of this Sansjambes with an air of sufficient detachment, or, in default of this, had so clearly underlined the suggestion of indifference by my manner of manipulating my cigarette as to assure myself against the possible suspicion, easily avoidable, I had hoped, of a too immediately concerned curiosity, when " Ah! the fellow without legs!" replied Mallaby, with, as it, perhaps unwarrantably, seemed to me a levity so flippant that it might have appalled a controversialist less seasoned by practice than I'd the permissible satisfaction of crediting myself with the reputation of being.'

(c) 'Jocasta is known as a woman of learning and fashion, and as one of the most amiable persons of this court and country. She is at home two mornings of the week and all the wits and a few of the beauties of London flock to her assemblies. When she goes abroad to Tunbridge or the Bath, a retinue of adorers rides the journey with her; and besides the London beaux, she has a crowd of admirers at the Wells, the polite among the natives of Sussex and Somersetshire pressing round her tea-tables, and being anxious for a nod from her chair.'"

From " Selected Essays on Literary Subjects "

THE ESSAYS OF MR LUCAS

EDMUND GOSSE

UNLESS my judgment is much at fault, there has written in English, since the death of R. L. Stevenson, no one so proficient in the pure art of the essayist as Mr E. V. Lucas. In saying so, I do not forget how much excellent prose is constantly being produced among us, nor what a variety of stimulating merit labours for our entertainment. But the particular thing which Montaigne invented in the second story of the Tower of his Castle in the month of March 1571, is delicate and rare. It has not been cultivated with great success anywhere but in England —except, of course, by its immortal French inventor— nor in England save occasionally and by a few select pens. I confess to the heresy of not being able to consider Bacon's highly ornamented chains of didactic wisdom ' essays ' in the true sense, there being so little in them that is personal or even coherent. On the other hand, Cowley, who first understood what Montaigne was bent on introducing, is a pure essayist, and leads on directly to Steele and Addison, and to Charles Lamb. If we read Cowley's chapter " On Myself," we find contained in it, as in a nutshell, the complete model and type of what an essay should be—elegant, fresh, confidential, and constructed with as much care as a sonnet. There have not been many true essayists, even in English, but Mr Lucas is one of them.

That Mr Lucas has learned much from his long and

intimate communion with the text of Charles Lamb
is manifest, but he is a disciple, not an imitator, of
that admirable man. He early felt that it was an
error to copy the tricks and the archaisms of even so
exquisite a master, and that there is a danger in
producing a mere pastiche of the quaintnesses of Lamb,
or of such an earlier model as Addison. How cleverly
this can be achieved, when it is done of set purpose,
may be seen in Sir James Frazer's marvellous *Sir
Roger de Coverley* (Macmillan and Co.), but this has
not been Mr Lucas's aim. He has perceived that
much of the ' colour ' of Steele and Addison was actual
colloquialism in their own age, and that the charm of
the Tatlers and Spectators lay, not in their oddity,
but in the unaffected grace with which they said perfectly simple things in the straightforward language
of well-bred people.

Lamb made a perilous experiment when he determined to secure a whimsical effect by imitating the
speech of a century and a half before his time. His
genius enabled him to carry the adventure off with
complete success, but none the less it was dangerous.
Less adroit writers simply fall into affectation in their
effort to be fantastic, especially if they happen also
to have adopted the fashionable contortions of George
Meredith. The essay does not achieve genuine success
unless it is written in the language spoken to-day by
those who employ it with the maximum of purity and
grace. It should be a model of current cultivated
ease of expression and a mirror of the best conversation.
The essays of Mr Lucas fulfil this requirement.

Possibly the fecundity of Mr Lucas, which is aston-
ishing, has stood in the way of his reputation. Readers
become restive, or tend to turn ungrateful, when a
favourite writer makes his bow to them with a book

too often. The abundance of Mr Lucas is certainly surprising. His present publishers announce twenty-nine volumes issued by themselves alone, and I know not how many more are in other hands. The fluency is more apparent than real, for most of these are slender books, and some are scarcely more than brochures. A rigid calculation would probably show that, while Mr Lucas's bindings are very numerous, the bulk of his printed matter does not exceed that of rarer visitants. His earliest ' book of wayfarers,' that delightful collection happily named *The Open Road*, is now more than twenty years old, and is still, no doubt, the volume of his which has penetrated the greatest number of households. But of works entirely his own, *Listener's Lure* is probably that which has been most universally appreciated. His essays, pure and simple, have, I conjecture, enjoyed a very uniform welcome, modified only by the more or less popular or amusing nature of the subjects he treats. Some day I hope he will find time to rearrange his writings in that ' collected ' form which is the Mecca to which every pilgrim-author looks pathetically forward.

The little volume (*The Phantom Journal and Other Essays*) which gives me a thread on which to hang these wandering remarks, is wholly miscellaneous in character. It strings together specimens of Mr Lucas in each of his moods, and offers therefore a good opportunity for the comparative study of his mind. We see that, with all his versatility, he avoids (as Lamb contrived to avoid) the purely didactic. This successful resistance to the instinct for teaching amounts to a positive, not a mere negative, quality. The desire to instruct, to occupy a pulpit, has been one of the greatest snares in the path of British essay-ists, and they have fallen the more inevitably into it because of the curious fact that, at the start, nothing is more eagerly—and even greedily—welcomed than the didactic. Moral reflections, especially if introduced with a certain polite air of solemnity, are to the British public what carrots are to a donkey; they cannot be resisted, the audience runs to read. But the appetite is satiated as quickly as it was aroused, and no form of literature fades out of sight more suddenly or more completely than do volumes inculcating Magnanimity in Humble Life or the Combating of Error by Argument.

A curious example is the fate of *Lacon*, a book first published over one hundred years ago—that is, early in 1820. It was a series of essays by a clergyman, the Rev. Caleb Colton, the success of which was sudden and overwhelming. The printing presses could not turn out copies of *Lacon* fast enough to satisfy the demand. Mr Colton was so uplifted by his popularity that he took to gambling on a large scale and had to fly his incumbency and the country. He made a fortune by cards, and lost it, and blew out his brains in the Forest of Fontainebleau. Meanwhile, thousands of infatuated readers were drinking in moral truth from the pages of *Lacon*, which suddenly lost its attraction for everybody, and is now deader than the deadest of the dead books that "Solomon Eagle" has been bewailing. Such is the fate of the didactic essay.

The two sections of the present volume which have entertained me most are those which deal, very irregularly, with the little town of Monmouth. Mr Lucas visited that borough, as I gather, during the war, and made inquiries regarding two objects—the Man of Ross's armchair and a comely work entitled *The Elegant Girl*. Each of these is a subject which suits the genius of Mr Lucas to perfection, and the consequence is that we have here two of the most typical essays which his entire writings are able to present to us. The first is informing—for Mr Lucas, though never didactic, is willing, and even anxious, to share his information with the reader—the second is simply entertaining. Mr Lucas went to Ross itself, which, indeed, rewards a visitor. Unhappily, he entered it at a moment when Ross could not have been looking its best, for " intensity and density of rain " are no embellishments to landscape.

I have a happier memory of my first sight of the little embattled town much more than fifty years ago, for we approached it, as I suppose visitors infrequently do, by boat, sailing and rowing up " pleased Vaga," as Pope called the Wye. I still recall the dark and velvet woods that ran down to the lustrous river, and then, at a turn, the sudden apparition of the sunlit spire of the famous church of Ross. How much depends on the hour of view, as well as on the point of view ! Later, on a second visit, I felt as much as Mr Lucas does the squalor and the commercialism of Ross, which, for all its teashops and its post cards, has no honest appreciation of John Kyrle. As an easy and yet careful and deliberate investigation of a point of literary and historical psychology nothing could be more adroit than this delightful study.

Our essayist is always happy when some by-way of literature invites him to saunter down it. He loves to dwell on the oddities of Borrow, as all good souls do, and will, until the old man of Oulton has been over-praised and over-analysed into a commonplace. In *An East Anglian Bookman* Mr Lucas expatiates on Green's *Diary of a Lover of Literature*, which he introduces as a new discovery. Of this interesting diary

(1796–1800) I was the first person to analyse the merit, in a causerie first published thirty years ago. I grieve that Mr Lucas has forgotten that fact, and I administer to myself this little advertisement, as a lozenge, to take away the taste of my disappointment. An enchantingly whimsical essay " On Epitaphs " was manifestly started by a perusal of that very strange miscellany *Spoon River Anthology*. The inscription on the tomb of Mrs Jones is singularly pleasing—

Here lies
MARY JONES,
the Wife of William Jones.

Honour her memory, for she
was lenient when her husband
was in liquor.

The churchyards of our country villages would be far more inviting than they are now, and would even be more instructive, if they contained more sincere and more vivid epitaphs than local habit now thinks decorous. It is impossible to believe that the entire population of a village has lived and died resigned to unbroken tribulation and unsullied by a single fault. Our cemeteries are like the pastorals of M. de Florian, of which M. de Thiard said that they were charming, but that a wolf would improve them.

From " Books on the Table "

A CRITICAL CREDO

J. MIDDLETON MURRY

IT is a waste and weary labour to open up again the old question of reviewing and criticism. On the one hand, there should be no distinction between them; the reviewer's business is to criticise the book before him. But too often in practice the reviewer is expected to compile a library list for the average unintelligent reader. On the other hand, economic necessity nowadays compels the critic to become a reviewer. So that the valuable modern distinction is not so much the distinction between the critic and the reviewer, which the impossibilists frequently urge, as that between the critic-reviewer and the puff-reviewer. We must leave out the puff-reviewer. God will reward him as surely as his employer does.

Speaking of criticism, Remy de Gourmont said that " the whole effort of a sincere man is to erect his personal impressions into laws." That is the motto of a true criticism, conscious of its limitations and its strength. The emphasis falls even more decidedly upon the law-making than upon the personal basis of the impressions, for that is inevitable. The man who is content to record his own impressions, without making an effort to stabilise them in the form of laws, whatever he is, is not a critic. A law or rule, or rather a system of laws or rules, is necessary to the critic; it is a record of all his past impressions and reactions; but it must be his own law, his own system, refined by his own effort out of his own experience. Otherwise he is a pedant and not a critic.

The function of criticism is, therefore, primarily the function of literature itself, to provide a means of self-expression for the critic. He begins like any other writer, with the conviction (which may, of course, be an illusion) that his views and conclusions on the subject-matter, which is literature, are of importance in themselves and to others; and he proceeds to promulgate and propagate them. Like any other writer, he stands or falls in the long run, by the closer or more remote approximation of his views to the common experience of that comparatively small fraction of the human race which itself comes to conclusions about life and literature, which is the concentrated record of life. As Dr Johnson said—

" Nothing can please many and please long, but just representations of human nature. Particular manners can be known to few, and therefore few only can judge how nearly they are copied. The irregular combinations of fanciful invention may delight awhile, by that novelty of which the common satiety of life sends us all in quest; but the pleasures of sudden wonder are soon exhausted, and the mind can repose only on the stability of truth."

The critic stands or falls by the stability of his truth, and necessarily by his skill in communicating his truth.

That the critic has to interest his readers is true, but in exactly the same sense as it is true that every writer has to interest his readers. He does not have to aim at being more interesting than other writers. This is one of the prime heresies of modern criticism. Its adherents appear to hold that a critical article is a kind of knockabout turn. Unless the critic is turning a somersault in every paragraph and making a grimace in every sentence, he is dull. Another, and more persuasive, heresy is that it is the critic's business to make the best of a bad book by picking out the one or two plums that have wandered into the wilderness of dough. A critic, argue its adherents, has to communicate ' gusto ' to his readers, no matter what the quality of the book he is writing about. These seem to me to be pure heresies, and the critics who embrace them will surely be forgotten.

Criticism is a particular art of literature. It is possible not to like the art, and possible for the critic to regret that his art is not liked. But it is not, or ought not to be, possible for a critic to play the traitor to his art in order to get a bigger audience for his raree-show. Because a sculptor knows that sculpture is not popular, he does not paint moustaches on his figures or plant billycock hats on the top of their heads. The critic's business is to express himself by expressing his opinion on the work of literature before him. He has therefore to make sure that his opinion is his true opinion ; he has to safeguard himself against accidental and temporary disturbances of his sensibility. Hence the need for a system of principles, refined out of his more constant reactions, to control momentary enthusiasms and passing disgusts.

Moreover, he is concerned to elucidate the significance of the work before him, for his verdict is a verdict as to significance. A work of literature may possess significance of various kinds ; it may have historical, ethical, or æsthetic significance ; that is, it may have importance at a particular phase of the human consciousness, or it may be valuable as expressing a particular attitude towards human life, or it may have more or less of a certain kind of artistic perfection which compels a peculiar artistic emotion in the reader. A work may have significance of one of these kinds, or all of them, or any combination of them. A critic is bound to have a predisposition towards one of these kinds of significance ; he will be predominantly a historian, like Sainte-Beuve, a moralist like Matthew Arnold, or a technician like Dr Bridges. He ought to be aware of his predisposition and alert to prevent it from running away with him. A perfect critic would combine all these predispositions in equal parts, but perfect critics are at least as rare as perfect writers. It is as much as one can ask that a critic should try to correct his predisposition by training his appreciation of other kinds.

Once criticism is accepted as an independent literary art, there need be no heart-searching among critics because they have so little practical influence on the sale of books. That is the fact in England at any rate. It is a hundred times more profitable to an author for the *Daily Mail* to declare " This book will be a success," than for the best critic on the *Times Literary Supplement* to give exact and convincing reasons why the book ought to be a success. Critical articles and essays are read for themselves ; at their best they are perfectly self-contained ; they do not demand that the reader should dash out and purchase the books which they discuss, and as often as not they are read with the greatest interest by those who are themselves profoundly familiar with the subject already.

Putting a valuation upon new books is perhaps the least valuable, as it is certainly the most dangerous, part of criticism. It is almost impossible for a literary critic to be really sincere in dealing with contemporary production. It is as difficult for him to tell the truth about the bad work of men who have done good work, as to tell the truth about the good work of men who have done bad. In the first case his hand is checked by fear of doing harm, in the second by the fear of doing good. Again, it is intolerable to be severe to a well-meaning beginner, although a critic knows that the road to hell is paved with good intentions. There are too many thorns in the path of criticism of contemporaries. For we have not even mentioned the personal resentment too often cherished by our victims. The dangers of log-rolling are at least equalled by the dangers of revenge. A successful author, however much he may be dubious of the genuineness of his own powers, cannot help believing that his success is somehow due to his merits ; he is bound to persuade himself that a slating is the expression of some personal hostility.

Unfortunately, few critics are in the happy position of being able to write about contemporaries only when they can sincerely praise them. For the most part they have to conform to the exigencies of reviewing, to write on texts they could not choose, to consider susceptibilities that are an obstacle to their free expression. No doubt the English tradition of anonymity is a defence against some of these evils. But it leaves the door open to other worse ones. A critic does not care to hide behind the editorial ' we ' when he attacks a writer ; nor, on the other hand, is it good for him to be compelled always to hide his light under a bushel. A good criticism is as much a work of art as a good poem ; its author deserves his reward in reputation as well as money. Besides, if his readers are not permitted to distinguish his work they cannot follow the sequence and evolution of his ideas. A critic cannot be always enunciating his principles. What looks like the veriest dogmatism in an isolated review may, if put into relation to other utterances, be seen to have a convincing scheme of values behind it.

Criticism is an art. It has its own technique. Ideally, at least, this technique would have its different perfection for each several critic. But we may outline so much of the method as seems to be essential to the most important kind of criticism, appreciation.

First, the critic should endeavour to convey the whole effect of the work he is criticising, its peculiar uniqueness. Second, to work back and define the unique quality of the sensibility which necessitated this expression. Third, to establish the determining causes of this sensibility. (Here the relevant circumstances of the writer's life have their proper place.) Fourth, to analyse the means by which this sensibility was given expression, in other words, to conduct a technical examination into the style. Fifth, a still closer examination of a perfectly characteristic passage, that is, a passage in which the author's sensibility is completely expressed. This fifth and final movement is really a return to the first, but with the important difference that the relevant material has been ordered and placed before the reader.

The various phases in this symphonic movement of an ideal criticism may, of course, be ordered quite differently. The historical or the ethical critic will enlarge more on the nature of the sensibility, its value in itself and its relation to other types of sensibility; he will pay little or no attention to the means by which this sensibility is expressed. He will not be a whit the worse critic for that, but he will be a less *literary* critic. On the other hand, the critic who is unable to adjudicate between the values of the various kinds of sensibility has no means of distinguishing between great art and perfect art. That judgment is essential to a true criticism, in spite of (or rather in virtue of) the fact that it is in the last resort an ethical judgment.

We need not worry ourselves about the function of criticism any more than we worry about the function of poetry. Both are arts ; both have to give delight ; both have to give the delights which are proper to themselves as arts. If it gives this delight criticism is creative, for it enables the reader to discover beauties and significances which he had not seen, or to see those which he had himself glimpsed in a new and revealing light. What, I think, we may reasonably ask is that criticism should be less timid ; that it should openly accept the fact that its final judgments are moral. A critic should be conscious of his moral assumptions and take pains to put into them the highest morality of which he is capable. That is only another way of saying that the critic should be conscious of himself as an artist. He should be aware of the responsibilities imposed by his art ; he should respect the technique of his craft. He should not be cheap, he should not be shallow, he should not be insincere, either in praise or blame, but above all in these modern times, he should not be insincere in praise.

From " Countries of the Mind "

EXERCISES

EXERCISES

ON PIRATES: Richard Middleton

1. Make a list of all the pirate stories you remember having read. Arrange them in order of preference.

2. What do you suppose Stevenson meant when he said that Marryat's *Pirate* was " written in sand with a salt-spoon " ?

3. Write a letter of advice to a friend who has announced his intention of writing a story for boys.

4. Discuss the statement that the revolutionary spirit is " that which youth should cherish most."

5. Write a story in which doubloons, the yardarm, the " Jolly Roger," and an island in the Pacific all figure prominently.

6. Quote what you consider to be the most telling sentence in this essay.

7. Write an essay on either (i) " Fond Parients," (ii) " Of walking the plank," or (iii) a homily on the text, " Things are not what they were when I was young."

THE SECRET DRAWER: Kenneth Grahame

1. Notice the detailed description which the author gives of the snake that George bought at the fair. Give a similarly exact account of any toy which you remember having had in your possession.

2. Name half a dozen stories in which hidden treasure figures prominently, and give a critical account of one of them.

3. " To him who is destined to arrive, the fates never fail to afford on the way their small encouragements." Expand and illustrate this dictum.

4. Observe the part which personification plays in the development of this essay. Quote two good instances.

5. When the search is nearly at an end, we are taken to the window to notice the sunset and made to listen to the faint notes of the horn. So we get the right background or setting. Quote other examples of setting that you have noticed.

6. Observe the skilful way in which sights, sounds, and scents are related, so that one is made to provide an apt commentary on the other. Cite an example.

7. Write an essay on one of the following subjects:

    (i) Of Uncles and Aunts.

    (ii) Hoards and Hiding-places.

    (iii) In Olden Times.

    (iv) Blind Alleys.

LANDFALL AND DEPARTURE: Joseph Conrad

1. Either from your own personal knowledge or from your reading give other examples of Landfall and Departure. (You might notice, for example, how Captain Ahab, in Herman Melville's *Moby Dick*, took his Departure. Consider which one of Mr Conrad's captains he most resembles.)

2. Quote two of Mr Conrad's similes and comment on their appropriateness.

3. Observe the skilful use which the author makes of details in this essay. He speaks, for instance, of the "maple-wood veneered cabin-door with a white china handle," and so gives the reader at once an exact picture. Quote other notable examples.

4. Compose a character-sketch answering to one of the following titles:

    A Grumpy Recluse.

    A Man in whom the Sense of Duty is Strong (or perhaps only the Sense of Self-importance).

5. Notice the touches of quiet humour in this essay, and cite one or two instances.

6. Write a paragraph enlarging on one of the following passages from the essay:

    From land to land is the most concise definition of a ship's earthly fate.

EXERCISES

The captain's state-room is surely the august place in every
vessel.

No sailor is really good-tempered during the first few days
of a voyage.

7. Write an essay on one of the following subjects :

    (i) Temper and Temperament.

    (ii) Irritating Trifles.

    (iii) The Benefits of Routine.

    (iv) Rhythm and Life.

GOING AWAY AND ARRIVING : FILSON YOUNG

1. Write down what impressions remain to you of the first
holiday of which you have any recollection.

2. Suggest a suitable alternative title for this essay.

3. Write a critical paragraph commenting on the writer's
use of simile and metaphor.

4. After reading the essay carefully so as to note all the
necessary evidence, try to complete the rhymes on page 44.

5. Make a conjectural pen-portrait of Jimmy Leary.

6. You will notice how certain impressions formed in childhood remain for no discoverable reason whatsoever, while
others apparently much more important vanish. In this
essay, for instance, the child " shook hands with servants, and
was strangely aware of the texture of their skin." And there
was " the *almost intolerable tremor of being* " with which he
read the notice To THE STEAMER, while on the steamer itself
the smell " made *one clench one's teeth.*" Give other instances
of queer associations, either from literature or from your own
recollections.

7. Write an essay on one of the following subjects :

    (i) Night and Morning.

    (ii) August.

    (iii) On being Seasick.

    (iv) The Joys of Packing.

ESSAYS OF TO-DAY

A HERMITAGE IN SIGHT: Maurice Hewlett

1. Note the qualities which Mr Hewlett attributes to the Iberian stock, and say what you can of the characteristics of any other race that has come under your observation.

2. Comment on : Oreads, Glaucus, Diomede, Iberian, Venus de Milo, *Gunnera manicata*, Helikon, Lucca.

3. You have read Mr Hewlett's idea of the ideal place for retirement. This has always been a favourite topic with writers of all kinds. You will remember, for example, Samuel Rogers's "Mine be a cot" and Mr Yeats's "Lake Isle of Innisfree," among many others. Give your own ideas of the sort of place where you would like to end your days, emphasizing particularly those points where you differ from Mr Hewlett.

4. Discuss the statement : "Fig-trees are like poets; if you want them to sing you must torture their roots."

5. Criticize this writer's notions of domestic architecture.

6. Write an account of any interesting facts concerning the distribution of seeds that may have come under your notice.

7. Write an essay on one of the following subjects :
   (i) "God Almighty first planted a garden."
   (ii) In Praise of Silence.
   (iii) The End.
   (iv) "Nature is the prodigal's foster-mother."

A BROTHER OF ST FRANCIS: Grace Rhys

1. Explain the significance of the title given to this essay.

2. Enlarge upon the effectiveness of the *tu quoque* form of the argument, mentioning other occasions you know where it has been, or could be, employed.

3. The writer evidently considers the hippopotamus the most loathsome of all the creatures. Her friend had that opinion of the pig. Give your own opinion.

4. Write on "Shoving as a Rule of Existence."

264

EXERCISES

5. Mr G. K. Chesterton says: "I myself have a poetical enthusiasm for pigs, and the paradise of my fancy is one where the pigs have wings." Comment on this statement.

6. Charles Lamb also praised the pig, but from a slightly different point of view. Write a few paragraphs comparing his "Dissertation upon Roast Pig" with the present essay.

7. Write an essay on one of the following subjects:
   (i) "Pigs might fly."
   (ii) "You're another!"
   (iii) A Chicago Stockyard.
   (iv) "Things are not what they seem."

GOLDEN FRUIT: A. A. Milne

1. Notice the unexpected conclusion of this essay. Compare it in this respect with others in this book, and say which seems to you to be the most effective.

2. Write a paragraph of not more than twelve lines on "The virtues of the —— and the vices of the ——," inserting the name of a fruit in each of the blanks according to preference.

3. Much of the charm of this essay is due to the author's easy and intimate style. He seems to take you at once thoroughly into his confidence. Make a note of the informal repetitions and playful touches that contribute particularly to this end.

4. Compile your own list of fruits in order of preference, and then write a defence of your list wherever it differs from that suggested by Mr Milne.

5. "The cherry is a companionable fruit." Sum up the outstanding qualities of each of the following in a similar sentence: pine-apple, nectarine, hip, haw, sloe, pomegranate.

6. Write comments on this essay supposed to have been made by a retail fruit-merchant.

7. Write an essay on one of the following subjects:
   (i) Wild Fruits.
   (ii) Gardeners and Gardening.
   (iii) The Deceitful Apple.
   (iv) Cherry-stones.

ESSAYS OF TO-DAY

THE DOODLE DOO : Dixon Scott

1. Observe the solemnity and weight of the long introductory sentence, preparing the reader for the serious discussion of a great problem. The very brief second sentence has the effect of cutting the string and letting the cat out of the bag. Take the topic " Going to Bed Early," and, after the same fashion, frame a long opening sentence that shall have for its object the mystification of the reader, and a short one following it which shall disclose the real nature of the subject.

2. Mention the finest example of mock-heroic treatment which you have met in the course of your reading.

3. Quote any examples of antithesis that you observe in this essay.

4. Comment upon Dixon Scott's whimsical use of the word ' civilian ' in this essay, and give any other examples of the unexpected use of words that you notice.

5. Of what other essay in this collection does " The Doodle Doo " remind you ? Compare the respective styles of the two writers.

6. Write a letter of thanks or otherwise to the man who invented alarm clocks.

7. Write an essay on one of the following subjects :
    (i) Beauty-sleep.
    (ii) Day-dreams.
    (iii) Of Virtues that are really Vices.
    (iv) On Missing the Morning Train.

THE TOWN WEEK : E. V. Lucas

1. Say what you can about the sentence-length in this essay in relation to the whole mode of treatment. Compare with one or two other essays in this book.

2. Comment upon the saying that " anticipation is better than realization."

3. Add illustrations from your own experience for or against the statement that " nothing ever happened on a Tuesday."

266

EXERCISES

4. Write an essay entitled " The Months," endeavouring to do for the months of the year what Mr Lucas has here done for the days of the week.

5. Notice the use which the author makes of personification, and make a concise list of the seven days of the week together with the personal attributes with which he has endowed them.

6. Write some notes upon the light touch in essay-writing, giving illustrative quotations drawn from this essay.

7. Write an essay on one of the following subjects :
    (i) On Beginning.
    (ii) Week-ends.
    (iii) On Living like the Lilies.
    (iv) Luck.

ON CHRISTMAS : ROBERT LYND

1. Write a letter to a very enthusiastic young friend, advising him how to spend an enjoyable Christmas without uncomfortable after-effects.

2. Devise four original mottoes for Christmas crackers.

3. " Dickens was pugnaciously benevolent in all his work— except when he was writing about Dissenters and Americans." Expand and illustrate this statement.

4. Say what you can about the tendencies in popular feeling with regard to Christmas since this essay was published (1915).

5. Write a sketch entitled " Scrooge Up to Date."

6. Comment on Mr Lynd's idea of Utopia, and compare with any others you may have met.

7. Write an essay on one of the following subjects :
    (i) Carol-singers.
    (ii) Crackers.
    (iii) Compulsory Happiness.
    (iv) The Spirit of Brotherhood.

LOSING ONE'S TRAIN: VERNON LEE

1. Read again the beautiful little vignette of the woodland scene which Vernon Lee gives you. See if you can make a word-picture of your own of one of the following scenes :

    (i) High cliffs, a waste of waters, and gulls screaming.

    (ii) Moonlight on still water.

    (iii) Rock-strewn moorlands with stunted oaks in the foreground.

2. Comment upon the fitness of these metaphors, and quote any others that impressed you when reading the essay :

> The throwing out of so much moral ballast does not help one to overtake that train.
>
> A chasm suddenly gapes between present and future.
>
> The walls and towers of Serravalle, which have beckoned to my fancy almost ever since my childhood.

3. Write a short story with a definite plot, ending with the words, " and how thankful he was that he had missed that train ! "

4. Some of us obey the beckoning finger, visit our Serravalle, and return sadly disillusioned. If you have had any such experience, describe it ; or, on the other hand, pay tribute to Serravalle if you found it all that or more than you had anticipated.

5.   Change as such is often fruitful of improvement.
> VERNON LEE

> Change jest for change is like the big hotels
> Where they shift plates an' let ye live on smells.
> J. R. LOWELL

Note these different ways of regarding the subject, and add your own comments.

6. You will notice instances here of those unexpected turns that add so much to the charm of an essay, *e.g.*, " When I got to the farm where the key of that church was kept, *the key had gone to town* in the pocket of the peasant." Quote other instances from the essay.

7. Write an essay on one of the following subjects :

    (i) On Losing One's Temper.

    (ii) Blessings in Disguise.

EXERCISES

(iii) " For there was never yet philosopher
That could endure the toothache patiently."

(iv) Impressions.

AUTUMN : ROGER WRAY

1. Find six appropriate figurative expressions for summer and winter respectively.

2. Study carefully the use made of personification in this essay. Mention the three most striking instances.

3. Make a companion study of winter, personifying the season in way similar to that in which autumn is personified here.

4. After you have read this essay and compared it with the conventional view of autumn, give your own conclusion.

5. Search for references to autumn in the poets other than those given here. Mention at least four.

6. Note the use made of colour in this essay. Write a paragraph of not more than fifteen lines on " A Day in Early Spring," concentrating on colour effects.

7. Write an essay on one of the following subjects :
   (i) October.
   (ii) Of Getting Wet Through.
   (iii) Harlequin and Columbine.
   (iv) Wind-music.

SOME LONDON MEMORIES : A. ST JOHN ADCOCK

1. Describe the place where you happen to be now as you imagine it must have appeared about three hundred years ago.

2. Notice the choice of words in the following examples :

The *sobbing* of a harp, the *wailing* of a cornet, the *shrilling* of a flute.

Shadowy, book-crammed streets *brooding* to right and left.

A musty, *pinched* side door.

Collect other examples that seem to you to be characteristic of the writer.

3. The faithfulness of the portrait-studies cannot fail to

strike the reader. The solicitor and his Testament, the man with the water-buckets, the man with the snuff-box, and the three musicians—all these deserve careful attention.

Make a portrait-study of a postman, a policeman, or a parson, taking care to describe an actual person whom you remember.

4. Read again the description of the lawyer's office in Bell Yard. Then write a description of an interior with which you are acquainted, selecting one which by reason of its quaintness and singularity will provide salient features upon which you may fasten.

5. Write brief notes on Jack Sheppard, Temple Bar, and Chatterton.

6. Read the fine description of night in a great city in the third chapter of Carlyle's *Sartor Resartus*, and then write a prose-study of your own entitled "A Night Scene."

7. Write an essay on one of the following subjects :

    (i) Some Changes I have Seen.
    (ii) The Glamour of the Past.
    (iii) Ghosts.
    (iv) Romance in Bricks and Mortar.

THE LAST GLEEMAN : W. B. YEATS

1. Discuss the statement that woman, "perhaps because she is wholly conventional herself, loves the unexpected, the crooked, the bewildering."

2. Note that the conclusion of this essay owes not a little of its effectiveness to its contrasting touch and to its unexpectedness. Quote three or four of the best endings that you can find in this book.

3. Compose a suitable funeral oration for Michael Moran, the Last Gleeman.

4. What sidelights does this essay cast upon life in Dublin ? Do you think that the incidents recorded would be possible in London, for instance ?

5. Try to compose suitable verses so as to complete the parody beginning, " In Egypt's land, contagious to the Nile."

EXERCISES

6. Read Charles Lamb's essay, "A Complaint of the Decay of Beggars in the Metropolis," and discuss his dictum that "Much good might be sucked from these Beggars. They were the oldest and the honourablest form of pauperism."

7. Write an essay on one of the following subjects :
   (i) The Biter Bit.
   (ii) Mountebanks and Mummers.
   (iii) " All the world's a stage."
   (iv) The Silver Lining.

DELFT : Hilaire Belloc

1. Give a description of any beautiful building that is familiar to you. Aim at bringing out all the poetry and charm that is in it rather than giving an inventory of its architectural features.

2. "That *untragic* sadness which you may find also in the drooping and wide eyes of extreme old age." Comment upon the fitness and unexpectedness of the word italicized. Search for other examples in this essay.

3. Notice the effect of the repetition of the word " bells." Mention any notable examples of this device in the work of other writers that may have come under your observation.

4. Observe the wealth of vocabulary that is characteristic of Mr Belloc's writing. Make a list of all the words he uses to describe bells. See if you can add any appropriate words to the list.

5. Mr Belloc calls Delft a " neat " city. Mention any town familiar to you which you think deserves that epithet ; then think of another which presents a marked contrast with it in this respect.

6. Criticize " peace, labour, and content," as " three very good words . . . summing up . . . the goal of all mankind."

7. Write an essay on one of the following subjects :
   (i) The Most Charming Town in England.
   (ii) Sights and Sounds.
   (iii) The Beauty of Middle Age.

NIAGARA FALLS: Rupert Brooke

1. Note the prominence given to colour in this description of the falls. Write a descriptive passage of your own dealing with mountain scenery or a seascape similarly concentrating upon the colour effects.

2. What touches in this essay would lead you to suppose, even if you had no other evidence, that it was written by a poet ?

3. Comment on the statement that " The Victorian lies close below the surface in every man." What light does this shed on the position of Rupert Brooke himself ?

4. Read the first part of the essay again, noticing particularly the author's description of the side-shows and the touts. It consists of skilfully constructed catalogues. If you read the same author's " The Great Lover," you will see that there you have a poetic inventory on a more extended scale. Endeavour to describe the Zoo or a village circus in a similar way, either in prose or verse.

5. Read Byron's description of the Falls of Terni (*Childe Harold*, IV, lxix), Ruskin's of the Falls of Schaffhausen (*Modern Painters*, vol. i, ch. ii), and any other good descriptions of waterfalls that you can find. Then make a comparative study of them all and embody the results in a short essay.

6. Note the very effective contrast at the end of the essay. Mention three or four other striking examples of the use of contrast that you have met with in the course of your reading.

7. Write an essay on either (i) " Of Platitudes," (ii) " The Wonders of the World," or (iii) " Beauty and Utility," or (iv) a homily on the text " Human nature is the same all the world over."

THE SOUL OF A CATHEDRAL: Sir James Yoxall

1. " In every man there are many more personalities and entities than Stevenson or Oliver Wendell Holmes counted up." If you have not already done so, read *Dr Jekyll and Mr Hyde* and *The Autocrat of the Breakfast Table*, and explain the references in this statement.

EXERCISES

2. In the preface to the volume from which this essay is taken the author defends his choice of out-of-the-way words to express his meaning. " If an exotic word best conveys one's allusion or shade of meaning, why not adopt it frankly ? May not a roamer be cosmopolitan in his diction somewhat ? " Give half a dozen examples of exotic words taken from this essay, and, bearing in mind the author's plea, consider whether their use is justified. Name any other author who was fond of extending his vocabulary in this way.

3. You will notice here and there a curious turn given to the sentence by inversion. Give one or two examples and comment on their effect.

4. Enlarge upon the following statement : " The Gothic church plainly originated in a rude adaptation of the forest trees with all their boughs to a festal or solemn arcade, as the bands about the cleft pillars still indicate the green withes that tied them." EMERSON.

5. Explain the following terms : crocket, finial, narthex, triforium, apse, flying buttress, transept, gargoyle.

6. The writer prefers Gothic to Romanesque. Westminster Abbey pleases him better than St Paul's. State your own preference in this matter.

7. Write an essay on one of the following subjects :

    (i) Symbolism.
    (ii) " I never weary of great churches. It is my favourite kind of mountain scenery."—R. L. STEVENSON.
    (iii) Tourists.
    (iv) Description of the interior of a great building.

ON A MAP OF THE OBERLAND
" ALPHA OF THE PLOUGH "

1. This essay is, as you will have observed, noteworthy for its vivid descriptive passage. Notice the long sentences in which the writer gradually unfolds the panorama of the glaciers so as to produce the effect of grandeur and of isolation. Then, as admiration is lost in an overmastering feeling of discomfort and a sense of danger, so the rolling periods give place to short, snapping sentences that speak eloquently of

numbing weariness. Write a short description of a sea-voyage, following a somewhat similar plan.

2. Make character-sketches of Heinrich and Otmar.

3. Can you judge from internal evidence the approximate date when this essay was written?

4. Make an inventory of the similes used in the essay, and mention that one which strikes you as being most effective.

5. Write a short paragraph on each of the following: Mr Biglow, Magellan, Pizarro, Cortes, Stonewall Jackson, Thoreau, and the author of the phrase "Silent, upon a peak in Darien."

6. Give an account of the most thrilling moment you have ever experienced ; or, if your life has been singularly free from thrills, describe an experience that would have answered to that description if it had happened.

7. Write an essay on one of the following subjects :
   (i) Imagination.
   (ii) A Recipe for a Good Holiday.
   (iii) The Land of Make-believe.
   (iv) Benighted !

"ON THE ACTUAL SPOT" : C. E. MONTAGUE

1. Comment on the sentence-length in this essay and show that it is appropriate.

2. The writer gives you some exquisite vignettes of scenery. Quote one of these and observe how apt are the descriptive words. Then try to compose a similar vignette of your own of a place that is familiar to you.

3. Sum up the main teaching of this essay in a single paragraph.

4. Observe the skilful use of contrast, all the more effective because the contrasted things are commonly supposed to resemble each other, and, indeed, do so well enough as long as they are not brought into juxtaposition. "The old eaten stones and the tinny stage armour, *the rouge and the sunlight, the sound of the metre and the sounds of the sea-birds flying and*

crying over the sands, debased and insulted each other."
Compose a similar sentence giving instances of your own.

5. Note how clearly the situation of York is described in a
few words. Take any town that you know and endeavour
to do the same for it.

6. Give an account of your impressions on first going to
the play.

7. Write an essay on one of the following subjects :
  (i) Incompatibles.
  (ii) Of Pageants.
  (iii) Disenchantment.
  (iv) The Sternness of Reality.

CASTLES IN THE AIR : R. B. CUNNINGHAME GRAHAM

1. Observe the effect of dignity and majesty which proper
names as they are here used give to the page. Mention two
or three other instances of the successful use of this device in
literature.

2. Read carefully the character-sketch of the castle-builder,
and see how this gives point to the general remarks that
precede it. Quote the most vivid bit of portraiture that you
remember having met in the course of your reading.

3.
>   Happy the man, whose wish and care
>   A few paternal acres bound,
>   Content to breathe his native air
>   In his own ground.   POPE

> With this piece of land I had purchased a thousand cares.
> If the wind roared in its fury, formerly it merely blew down
> *a* tree, and thus provided me with a spectacle ; now it
> destroyed one of *my* trees,—a fear in prospect, and both a
> regret and a loss in retrospect.—ALPHONSE KARR

Consider these two quotations in conjunction with Mr
Cunninghame Graham's essay, and then write on " The
Futility and Joy of Possessing."

4. Write a review of this essay as from the pen of Mr
Gradgrind.

5. " The generous and the enthusiastic spirits sent into the
world to shed as many tears as would float navies." Cite an

instance giving such details as are necessary to show that the words are really applicable.

6. Write a few lines of illustrative comment on the Spanish proverb which the author quotes.

7. Write an essay on one of the following subjects :

    (i) " To each man after his demerits."

    (ii) The House of Dreams.

    (iii) The Practical Man.

    (iv) On Making the Best of a Bad Job.

RAIN : EDWARD THOMAS

1. Mention any allusions to rain in literature other than those given in this essay.

2. " Description is like painting ; for it chooses to reject some irrelevant or unimportant parts, and to intensify and brighten the others. Photography takes all, big and little alike, without always making the chief details significant." Comment on the present essay from this point of view.

3. How far does Edward Thomas make use of contrast, personification, and colour in making his pen-pictures ?

4. There is a certain wistfulness characteristic of the work of Edward Thomas. As Austin Dobson said of *London Lyrics*, " it wavers 'twixt a smile and tear," but it is never wholly either of these. Give illustrations from the present essay and add your own comments where you consider them necessary.

5. What single word in the essay seems to you to be the most striking and effective ?

6. Give a description of a road that you know well.

7. Write an essay on one of the following subjects :

    (i) The Glory of Mud.

    (ii) Snow.

    (iii) " The old order changeth."

    (iv) A Landscape.

    (v) Literature and Life.

    (vi) An Old House Speaks.

EXERCISES

AN AUTUMN STROLL: W. N. P. Barbellion

1. Read Thoreau's account of the desperate struggle between the red and black ants in the chapter of *Walden* entitled "Brute Neighbours," and compare with the battle described here.

2. What evidences of keen and sympathetic observation do you note in this essay? Compare this writer's methods with those of any other open-air writers that you know.

3. "*Plump* on the horizon appear the heath-clad downs." Comment on the choice of the word italicized, and make any general remarks that you think necessary on the diction of the whole essay.

4. Compose two brief animal or plant studies embodying, if possible, the results of your own observations.

5. Give a discussion between a humanitarian naturalist and an old-fashioned sportsman who both have read this essay.

6. Give a page from a nature diary applicable to the time and place of your writing.

7. Write an essay on one of the following subjects:
    (i) A Winter Landscape.
    (ii) Hidden Life.
    (iii) Intruders.
    (iv) The First Day of Spring.
    (v) "It was a famous victory.'

SHIP'S LOGS: E. Temple Thurston

1. "Nothing is silent in this world. There is only deafness." Enlarge on this statement, adding illustrations of your own.

2. Write a short story entitled "The Wishing Ring."

3. Notice carefully how the device of personification is used in this essay. Quote one or two examples. Mention another essay in this book where the same device figures prominently.

4. Study the paragraph-form. There is one very short paragraph. What is it? Can you give a reason for the isolation of the statement in this manner?

5. Notice the varying length of the sentences. Quote one of the longest and one of the shortest, and then try to justify each.

6. In connexion with the subject-matter of this essay take down *The Old Curiosity Shop* and read again the account of that " small, rat-infested, dreary yard called ' Quilp's Wharf ' " that was " on the Surrey side of the river." Then write a brief sketch entitled " Quilp as a Prince of Romance."

7. Write an essay on one of the following subjects :
   (i) A Wood Fire.
   (ii) Fairy Tales.
   (iii) The Old Vikings.
   (iv) Funerals, Ancient and Modern.

CHARMIAN : ALICE MEYNELL

1. " It was very, very second-rate of an American admirer of scenery to name a waterfall in the Yosemite Valley the ' Bridal Veil.' His Indian predecessor had called it ' The Voice of the Evil Wind.' " Write a paragraph on " Names," citing examples of your own of both kinds.

2. " Keats confessed, but did not boast." Note the terse and reticent character of this expression. Read the whole essay again, and see how this economy and justness of expression is characteristic of Mrs Meynell's writing, giving it at once both strength and delicacy. Quote the sentence that, as it seems to you, best represents her in these respects.

3. Refer to Shakespeare's *Antony and Cleopatra*, and give a detailed character-study of the original Charmian.

4. " Men in cities look upward not much more than animals, and they—except the dog when he bays the moon—look skyward not at all." Discuss this assertion.

5. The very deformities of London, which give distaste to others, from habit do not displease me. . . . Nursed amid her noise, her crowds, her beloved smoke, what have I been doing all my life, if I have not lent out my heart with usury to such scenes !—CHARLES LAMB.

Comment on this attitude in the light of what you have read in this essay.

EXERCISES

6. Comment upon the personification in " a wary, fortunate, fastidious wind that has so found his exact, uncharted way between this smoke and that, as to clear me a clean moonrise and heavenly heavens." Quote any other notable instance of the use of this device in literature.

7. Write an essay on one of the following subjects :

    (i) The Second Best.

    (ii) Londoners.

    (iii) Travel.

    (iv) A Town Prospect.

THE PLEASURES OF WORK: A. C. BENSON

1. Write a descriptive sketch entitled " The Amateur."

2. Discuss the statement that " on the whole, it is better not to disturb the amiable delusions of our fellow-men, unless we are certain that we can improve them."

3. Write down half a dozen platitudes that you remember as having often been inflicted on yourself, and comment on them in the light of the essayist's dictum given in the first paragraph of this essay. What is your own conclusion on the matter ?

4. Judging from this essay, what do you take to be the outstanding qualities of Mr Benson's writing ?

5. Draw up some rules that should be observed by any one who aspires to be considered a good conversationalist.

6. Write down the funniest anecdote you can recollect in connexion with any one of the following subjects : (i) Village Organists ; (ii) Schoolmasters ; (iii) Conversational Bores.

7. Write an essay on one of the following subjects :

    (i) Talk and Talkers.

    (ii) The Secret of Popularity.

    (iii) Of the Man who makes his Work his Hobby.

    (iv) Of Suffering Fools Gladly.

AUDIENCES: A. B. WALKLEY

1. Comment on the statement that " the secret history of the world, which never got into the history books, was the only true history."

2. Write an account of the most uninteresting hero or the most engaging villain you have ever met either in a novel or on the stage.

3. " I hate false words, and seek with care, difficulty, and moroseness those that fit the thing."—LANDOR. Note in this connexion Mr Walkley's reference to the *mot juste*, and give what you imagine might be Mr Beerbohm's comment on the statement quoted above.

4. Write a disquisition on " Readers," as if by a book-reviewer.

5. Give an imaginary conversation on the present state of the theatre in the course of which an actor, a first-nighter, a dramatist, a general playgoer, and Mr Walkley take part.

6. Note Mr Walkley's classification of audiences. Think of other possible ways of dividing them, and give the one which strikes you most forcibly.

7. Write an essay on one of the following subjects :

    (i) Of the Young Lady who " didn't want to have her mind improved."

    (ii) Crowds.

    (iii) On " living happy ever afterward."

    (iv) Critics and Criticism.

WAR: GEORGE SANTAYANA

1. When a Mammonite mother kills her babe for a burial fee,
And Timour-Mammon grins on a pile of children's bones.
Is it peace or war ? better, war ! loud war by land and by sea,
War with a thousand battles, and shaking a hundred thrones.
                    TENNYSON

The main cause of war is Fear acting upon Fear.
                    DEAN INGE

Discuss these two pronouncements in the light of the present essay.

EXERCISES

2. Adduce examples of the rise and fall of races in support of Mr Santayana's argument.

3. This essay was first published in 1905. Comment on the soundness of its main conclusions in the light of happenings since that date.

4. " Instead of being descended from heroes, modern nations are descended from slaves." Discuss this statement fully.

5. Make a summary of the essay, setting forth clearly the author's chain of reasoning, and giving due prominence to his main conclusions.

6. Comment on the sentence-construction of the essay, comparing with other examples in this book.

7. Write an essay on one of the following subjects :
   (i) On Playing Skittles.
   (ii) Of Cowardice, and Blind Courage.
   (iii) Of Soldiers, Captains, and Statesmen.
   (iv) Schoolboy Fights.

CONFIRMED READERS : Augustine Birrell

1. Search the essay for whimsical turns of expression such as " This staggered even Malone, who was himself a *somewhat far-gone* reader." Quote three or four that strike you.

2. Note the use that Mr Birrell makes of the short sentence. It comes every now and then with a conclusive, snapping finality that leaves the reader breathless. Find one or two good examples.

3. " They learn in suffering what they observe in the margin." Amplify this statement, and add any examples that have come under your own notice.

4. Note the sly humour of the following passage : " Malone was far too good a book-collector to suggest a third method of discovering a book's imperfections—namely, reading it." Find another good example of humour in the essay.

5. Write a conjectural account of the unhappy love-affair that drove Malone to books as some men are driven to drink.

6. Observe the skilful way in which anecdotes are woven into the texture of this essay. Take any story you know and endeavour to frame it in a similar fashion.

7. Write an essay on one of the following subjects:

    (i) Books and Bookishness.
    (ii) Practical Jokes.
    (iii) First Editions.
    (iv) What to Read on a Rainy Day.

MASTERS OF NONSENSE: HOLBROOK JACKSON

1. Read Mr G. K. Chesterton's " Defence of Nonsense " in the volume of essays entitled *The Defendant*, and compare his views with those advanced here.

2. Make a list of six nonsense-books in the order of your preference.

3.   For nothing worthy proving can be proven,
       Nor yet disproven.

                            TENNYSON

Quote the parallel statement in this essay, and discuss the whole question.

4. What is the verse which " has become the established medium of nonsensical utterance " ?   Endeavour to write one of your own after the model given.

5. " The use of nonsense is to give the reader a holiday from himself."   Discuss this statement.

6. If you were given the choice of being the author of an erudite treatise on, say, wireless telegraphy, or a book like *Alice in Wonderland*, which would you choose, and why ?

7. Write an essay on one of the following subjects:

    (i) On being Sensible.
    (ii) " Nonsense is shy of success."
    (iii) What might have been.
    (iv) The comments of a typical self-made man upon this essay.

EXERCISES

A DEFENCE OF DETECTIVE STORIES
G. K. CHESTERTON

1. Give any notable examples of paradox that you notice in this essay. Note the value of this device in startling the reader into attention and forcing him to think by upsetting all his preconceived ideas.

2. In a certain provincial guildhall there is a stained-glass window representing King Edward VII (then Prince of Wales) in the conventional frock-coat and top-hat. What comments do you suppose Mr Chesterton would pass upon this ? What is your own opinion ?

3. Summarize what you can gather from this essay of Mr Chesterton's views on crime, and then give your own views.

4. Draw up a list of twelve books that, as far as your own observation goes, are popular at the present moment. Give what reasons you can for this popularity.

5. Mention half a dozen detective stories, and give a few rules that are to be observed in the telling of a good story of this kind.

6. "Every fantastic skyline of chimney-pots seems wildly and derisively signalling the meaning of the mystery." What other great writer do you know who had this habit of puckish personification ?

7. Write an essay on one of the following subjects :
    (i) The Romance of the Policeman.
    (ii) Symbols.
    (iii) The Poetry of Lamp-posts.
    (iv) Of the Necessity of being Shocked.

MY BOOKS : GEORGE GISSING

1. Discuss the statement that "virtue is made easy by circumstance."

2. Most people have certain idiosyncrasies about the format of books. Some prefer a small pocket edition ; others a spacious library edition. Some have not the patience to read even the wisest words when they are in small print and double

columns ; others are quite indifferent to the niceties of typo-
graphical arrangement so long as the subject-matter pleases
them. State any preferences that you may have in this
matter.

3. Should books be classed as necessities or as luxuries ?

4. Write down the names of four writers of books who have
also been notable book-lovers, and give evidence in each
case.

5. Reply suitably to the sceptic who, when confronted with
this essay, merely remarked, " Nothing like leather."

6.
> Books ! tis a dull and endless strife :
> Come, hear the woodland linnet,
> How sweet his music ! on my life,
> There's more of wisdom in it.
>
> WORDSWORTH

Discuss this in connexion with the dictum that " there are
times when books offer no escape from the burden of things."

7. Write an essay on one of the following subjects :

 (i) A Good Pull-up for Carmen.
 (ii) Second-hand Bookstalls.
 (iii) My Last Sixpence.

STYLE : G. W. E. RUSSELL

1. Write a critical essay embodying your own opinions on
style, taking your examples from this anthology.

2. Name the author whose prose-style pleases you most.
As far as you are able, diagnose the pleasure that his work
gives you, and give examples.

3. Ruskin's " writings bear on every page the traces of the
laborious file." Comment on this.

4. Notice how effectively Mr Russell quotes from what is
perhaps the most hackneyed poem in the language in such
a way that we forget that it is hackneyed. Study this, and
write a few lines on the use of quotations.

5. You will have noticed the various points raised by

objectors in the earlier part of this essay. Consider whether
there are not a few mild objections that you would like to
make on your own account, and then frame a short letter
on the subject.

6. Try your own hand at answering the examination paper
given at the end of this essay.

7. Write an essay on one of the following subjects :

    (i) On being Distinguished.
    (ii) Critics, and Criticisms.
    (iii) Bluff.

THE ESSAYS OF MR LUCAS : Edmund Gosse

1. Read again the essay by Mr Lucas that is printed in this
volume, and say how far you find yourself in agreement with
Mr Gosse's estimate.

2. Write a discursive review of any interesting book that
you have read recently.

3. Note carefully what Mr Gosse has to say about the art
of the essayist, and write a short paragraph summarizing his
conclusions. Compile a list of half a dozen essays, not necessarily taken from this collection, that seem to you best to
fulfil the requirements specified.

4. Write an imaginary dialogue between Lord Macaulay
and Mr Gosse on the subject of essay-writing.

5. Make illustrative comments on each of the following
phrases : (i) " the fashionable contortions of George Meredith";
(ii) " the charm of the Tatlers and Spectators " ; (iii) " the
quaintness of Lamb " ; (iv) " Bacon's highly ornamented
chains of didactic wisdom."

6. Say how far Mr Gosse himself appears to you to be
successful, judged by the canons which he here lays down.

7. Write an essay on one of the following subjects :

    (i) First Impressions.
    (ii) Epitaphs.
    (iii) In Praise of Rain.
    (iv) Some Byways of Literature.

A CRITICAL CREDO: J. Middleton Murry

1. Make an analytical summary of this essay, giving due prominence to the main principles enunciated by the writer and showing clearly the logical sequence of the reasoning.

2. A true criticism is the elegant expression of a just judgment.
R. A. Willmott

Criticism is the adventures of a soul among books.
Anatole France

Comment on these *dicta*, and say how far they agree with the position taken up by Mr Murry.

3. Name half a dozen prominent critics of the present day, and examine the work of any one of them in the light of this essay.

4. Criticize the style of the present essay in relation both to the subject-matter and to the purpose which it is intended to serve.

5. Give in succinct form what the author terms " the various phases in this symphonic movement of an ideal criticism." Proceed to apply them to any example that you may choose.

6. What does Mr Murry mean by saying that the most important kind of criticism is appreciation ?

7. Write an essay on one of the following subjects :
    (i) Of Laws, Lawgivers, and Lawbreakers.
    (ii) Anonymity.
    (iii) Of Praise and Blame.
    (iv) Plums.
    (v) On being Interesting.

INDEX OF AUTHORS

"The Golden Age" — Kenneth Grahame —
"The Mirror of the Sea — Joseph Conrad.
"Rosacre Papers" — Edward Thomas